THE POETRY OF DADA
AND SURREALISM

THE POETRY OF DADA AND SUR-REALISM:

Aragon
Breton
Tzara
Eluard &
Desnos

by Mary Ann Caws

PRINCETON UNIVERSITY PRESS
PRINCETON, NEW JERSEY

1970

LC Card: 68-56304

SBN: 691-06164-5

This book has been composed in
Linotype Times Roman

*Publication of this book
has been aided by the Whitney Darrow
Publication Reserve Fund of
Princeton University Press*

PRINTED IN THE
UNITED STATES OF AMERICA BY
PRINCETON UNIVERSITY PRESS

La réalité est l'absence apparente de contradiction.
Le merveilleux, c'est la contradiction qui apparaît
dans le réel.

—ARAGON, *Le Paysan de Paris*

ACKNOWLEDGMENTS

I should like to thank M. Louis Aragon for permission to quote his poetry; M. Luis Espinouze for permission to consult unpublished material of Robert Desnos; Dr. Michel Fraenkel and Editions Gallimard for permission to quote from Robert Desnos, *Panorama de l'évolution du mouvement Dada jusqu'à 1927*; and M. Christophe Tzara for permission to consult the unpublished material of his father in the Fonds Doucet, and to quote it, as well as the published material.

I wish to thank *The Explicator* for permission to quote the discussions of Aragon's "Mon coeur battait comme un voile" (from Vol. XXV, No. 6, February 1967) and of Desnos' "Le Paysage" (from Vol. XXVI, No. 9, May 1968). I should also like to thank Editions Gallimard for permission to quote the poem "Ma fontaine vivante" from André Breton, *Poèmes*, copyright © 1948 by Gallimard; "Le Dernier poème" from Robert Desnos, *Domaine public*, copyright © 1953 by Gallimard; and "Le paysage" from Robert Desnos, *Contrée*, copyright © 1962 by Gallimard; passages from "Nuits partagées" and "Sans âge" from Paul Eluard, *Choix de poèmes*, copyright © 1951 by Gallimard; and Paul Eluard "Enfermé seul" from the Pléiade edition of his *Oeuvres complètes*, copyright © 1968 by Gallimard, as well as the letter from Desnos to Eluard from the *Album Eluard* published with the Pléiade edition just mentioned. In addition, I wish to thank Editions Seghers for permission to quote the poem "Tu prends la première rue à droite" from *Robert Desnos*, edition Poètes d'aujourd'hui, copyright © 1965 by Seghers; and M. Claude Courtot for permission to quote his letter on recent developments among the Paris surrealist group.

I am greatly indebted to the Bibliothèque littéraire Jacques Doucet and to M. Jacques Chapon; to the library of the Museum of Modern Art; to the French Institute and Mr. David Finch for his constant encouragement; to Hunter College and the Graduate Center of the City University of New York, the former for use of the Abbie and Nora Fund in the initial preparation of the manuscript, the latter for its generosity in awarding me a City University Faculty Summer Research Grant and then a Doctoral Faculty Research Grant; and to Mrs. Frederica Goldsmith for her help.

Finally, I am most grateful to Professor Michel Beaujour, whose critical perception was invaluable. My husband contributed, as always, his intelligence, his resourcefulness, and his patience.

Mary Ann Caws
New York, May 15, 1969

CONTENTS

THE POETRY OF DADA
AND SURREALISM

INTRODUCTION

METHOD

La connaissance est la chose au monde dont je me suis lassé le plus vite.
—DESNOS, *Cinéma*

In his autobiography, Louis Aragon says of himself: "I am an ordinary Frenchman and like all my countrymen I have a passion for painting, an *irrational* passion for painting. Nothing can so excite us in this so-called country of moderation."[1] All the writers dealt with here share his love of art, and none of them make any distinction between the theory of poetry and that of plastic art. When they speak of one they speak for the other; they are passionate about both. Since any attempt on the part of a nonsurrealist and a nonpoet to theorize about the nature of surrealist (or ex-surrealist) poetry and art is necessarily at a remove from the poet's own view of his art and of art in general,[2] and since

[1] Louis Aragon, *J'abats mon jeu* (Gallimard, 1959), p. 94. (Throughout the footnotes Paris is the place of publication unless otherwise indicated.)

[2] Which is in itself already sufficiently complicated. In his *To Criticize the Critic*, T. S. Eliot draws a sharp distinction between "a theory of poetry propounded by a student of aesthetics and the same theory held by a poet"—are the surrealist critics speaking as the former or the latter? Moreover, says Eliot, once the theory is applied by the poet to his own writing, the theory changes. His position

we are fortunate enough to have the reflections of these poets on their own work as well as on the writings and paintings
of others, their opinions make an obvious starting point. The
major themes which they discover and elaborate when they
are judging or theorizing are at the same time the focus of
their own poetic work: in other words, these particular themes
are *constants* in their criticism, their manifestos, and their poetry. In spite of the stated affiliation with surrealism, or with
a politically committed art, these preoccupations continue
unchanged.

If all surrealist poetry were the product of automatic writing, as it is frequently said to be, then any discussion of such
poetry might limit itself to the themes regarded as indications
of the unconscious desires of the poet, of past or future events,
and so on. André Breton's interpretation of his own poem
"Tournesol" is the most obvious example of this approach.
But taking into account his own eventual disillusion with
automatic writing and his statement that the mind always
exerted some control over surrealist productions, it should be
possible to discuss this poetry freely without restrictions on
the methods of discussion. In the place of any abstract disser-
tation on questions such as the definition of and even the
possibility of the "surrealist poem,"[3] the discussion here
originates in certain texts, all of which can be considered
"poetic," whether they are critical, theoretical, or "poetry"
in the literal sense. After all, even a completely "automatic"
or spontaneous poem conveys a certain feeling, and may

---

is, naturally enough, that the practice should precede the theory and
determine it, not the other way around.

[3] See the chapter entitled "Endophasie et écriture automatique," in
Jean Cazaux, *Surréalisme et psychologie* (Corti, 1938), for an analysis
of the differences between a poem (which "recreates an emotion")
and an automatic transcription. One of the most revealing anecdotes
about the Dada-surrealist experiments is the following: Breton is
said to have explained that when Theodore Fraenkel drew words
from a hat, the technique produced no interesting results ("ça ne
donne rien"), because Fraenkel was not a writer.

For a more abstract discussion of the problem of the "surrealist"
poem, see Yvon Belaval, "Poésie et psychanalyse," *Poèmes d'aujourd'hui* (Gallimard, 1964).

focus on certain themes: these can be analyzed or at least pointed out, without regard to the manner in which they were produced. In every case the stress falls on the individual poets rather than on the general attitudes of Dada, surrealism, or "social realism," and wherever possible on the texts rather than on the known attitude of the poet. This book will follow themes and images rather than chronological lines, and the texts will not be oriented as to their exterior circumstances. For instance, a poem written by Eluard to Gala may be for that reason entirely different from one he writes to Nusch or to Dominique, but they will all be considered manifestations of his poetic personality and not autobiographical illuminations, a point which will be taken up later.[4] Nor is any particular attempt made to balance the proportion of critical, theoretical, and strictly "creative" texts: the weight falls heavily on the latter, for which the other texts serve as a backdrop.

The basic position taken here is that, whatever outlook one may adopt toward other "schools" or currents of literature, Dada and surrealism, which consider themselves literature's opposite, cannot be (or should not be) theorized about, exemplified, and handled at an efficient arm's length—that they are, by their nature, present and possible only *within* their manifestations. Breton firmly believed in the principle of internal criticism, and on several occasions he brilliantly demonstrated it. To dwell on the factual circumstances of the surrealist movement, no matter how important they may have been in the formulation of the texts, is necessarily to remain outside those texts. Without forcing a point already sufficiently obvious, the approach of this book follows from the assumption that the most decidedly "Dadaist" or "surrealist" qualities in the products of Dada and surrealism must never take second place to any "realistic" considerations, and that

---

[4] For a treatment of the connections between Eluard's poems and his life, see, for instance, Raymond Jean, *Eluard par lui-même* (Seuil, 1968), or English Showalter, Jr., "Biographical Aspects of Eluard's Poetry," *PMLA*, LXXVIII, No. 3 (June 1963).

in this field the importance given to creation must always predominate over that given to information.

The question of what is Dada and what is surrealist is not an easy one. No single quality is alone sufficient to classify a text as surrealist, neither polar opposites and their dialectical resolution, nor manifestations of the unconscious in the realm of the conscious, nor the power of the analogical image, nor language as an alchemical work. Were one to examine a series of texts, it might be the case that the texts showing the highest proportions of those preoccupations had been written by people calling themselves surrealists. But that is far from being a reliable test. Breton claimed that the distinction of a surrealist work was its surrealist *motive*, that it was written *as* a surrealist text; the fact that no exterior categorization is possible leaves the text open. And openness is precisely the quality emphasized by the most striking images and descriptions of Dada and of surrealism: Dada as the place where the "yes" and the "no" meet, not in castles but on street corners, Dada as a spontaneous grouping of productive forces shouting their liberty on crystal mountains, surrealism as an "open realism" characterized by images of communicating vessels, swinging doors, and open windows.

Both Dada and surrealism lay heavy stress on the parallel notion of spontaneity (automatism, chance revelations of language and experience, refusal of the logical straitjacket, etc.) and moral commitment (revolt against bourgeois attitudes and literary modes). Both center their hope for the remaking of the world in the analogical process—the bringing-together of elements from distant spheres, as in Pierre Reverdy's celebrated definition of the startling image, and the connection of the disparate by the conduit of poetic vision—and in the magic power of language. What will be depends on what is now seen and said; to change reality we must first radicalize our timid vision and our tired verbal habits.

Finally, the structure of this study of dualistic thinking and expression is parallel in form to the attitude it examines; it finds its double center in theoretical and creative vision, and it assumes their implicit union in the surreality of the text.

Such an emphasis on the text is not meant to give weight to any nonsurrealist idea of *aesthetics*[5] or *literature*, but instead to the idea of the genuine poetic spirit and the poetic word.

HISTORY AND POETRY

Si l'appétit du nouveau vient à nous abandonner, prenons précipitamment notre retraite.
—SCHUSTER, *Archives 57/68*

The nature of the relations between Dada and surrealism and between the "heroic" period of surrealism and the later periods has caused bitter controversy. Most contemporary surrealists take the view that Dada was a purely negative phenomenon which served only to clear the ground for the construction of their movement (see the proceedings of the "Décade du surréalisme" held at Cerisy-la-Salle in July 1966), while the positive contributions of Dada are emphasized by the Dada enthusiasts; Michel Sanouillet, the most prominent of the latter, calls surrealism "the French form of Dada," and maintains that Dada and surrealism are alternating waves of the same spirit.[6] Neither the historical details of the Dada movement, nor those of the surrealist movement which is usually considered to have superseded it, are discussed here, since for the purposes of this book *history* is to be considered secondary to *presence*. Surrealism is variously said to have perished little by little in its exclusions and its losses, or from its nonrelevance to the events of the

[5] In an essay entitled "Le Surréalisme et la beauté," *Surrealismo e simbolismo* (Padova, 1965), Ferdinand Alquié explains the impossibility of a surrealist *aesthetic*, properly speaking: "What the surrealist condemns is beauty as a spectacle, beauty separated from action and from life, a beauty to be contemplated, which does not instantly transform the person perceiving it. For all aesthetic perception of the beautiful supposes precisely an attitude of onlooking, of detachment, of withdrawal." Surrealism is total presence; any attitude implying distance is foreign to it.

[6] This attitude is partly responsible for the surrealists' objections to Sanouillet's *Dada à Paris*; there are, of course, subsidiary reasons, such as his description of some of the surrealist "myths" and personalities. See the two sessions devoted to discussions of his book at the Cerisy Décade.

1940's (Tzara's point of view in *Le Surréalisme et l'après-guerre*), or from the death of André Breton in 1966; or again it is said to be fully alive and unflagging in its spirit and manifestations, to have remained on "the level of effervescence" where Breton saw it in 1963. Of course, from the point of view of the present surrealists, to concentrate on the texts of the first surrealists is to imply the decease of surrealism as a movement and to make its autopsy, just as surely as if one concentrated on the historical events or on the purely aesthetic value of surrealist writing. Aesthetic commentary is in any case threatened with "almost total failure," say the contemporary surrealists, since it falls in the realm of poetic *criticism* (i.e. statements or observations on poetry made by nonsurrealists).[7] Any discussion which points away from the present generation of surrealists or away from their intensely moral stance is considered a betrayal of surrealism's living spirit, usually in the interests of "academic profiteers," whom the surrealists call their would-be embalmers or gravediggers. Surrealism is neither to be thought of as dead, nor as merely textual, but as a living commitment.[7a]

[7] Gérard Legrand, "La poésie en nouveaux francs," *La Brèche*, No. 12 (May 1962). It is in the same spirit that J. H. Matthews says that surrealism "cannot be *used* for any purpose other than its own." (*An Anthology of French Surrealist Poetry*, Minneapolis, University of Minnesota Press, 1965, p. 37.)

[7a] In 1969 Schuster, Audoin, José Pierre, Gérard Legrand, Silberman, Courtot and some others separated from former members of the Paris surrealist group. (See Schuster's *Archives 57/68*.) Such crises are not only familiar to surrealism, they are to be expected in its highly charged atmosphere, in which extreme positions are adhered to with extreme passion. The following statement of Claude Courtot (in a letter to the author, July 23, 1969) underlines the basic significance of surrealism itself, beyond individual personalities and conceptions of it: "Volontairement, nous avons décidé de renoncer *provisoirement* et *officieusement* à l'étiquette 'surréaliste,' afin de libérer chacun d'un héritage pesant. Il est donc désormais certain que jusqu'à nouvel ordre, personne ne pourra se prévaloir autrement que de manière abusive du label 'surréaliste.' Il est non moins certain que le *surréalisme* reste un mouvement vivant qui nous dépasse tous et qui n'a nul besoin d'empreintes digitales, de cartes d'identité et autres fiches anthropométriques pour affirmer son existence délibérément hors la loi." And in Jean Schuster's "Le Quatrième chant," *Le Monde* (Oct. 4, 1969), "historical" surrealism is indeed declared dead, cut off from "eternal" surrealism.

In June 1923, Desnos predicted a time of deserted amphitheaters and streets full of passionate action; in June 1968, a special number of the surrealist periodical *Archibras* celebrated the uprisings in France as a passionate revolution against the entire past: "April 1968, is a time gone by. The cutoff is definite, absolute. . . ." But the words of Desnos are certainly among those which "secretly arm the revolution." And it is no less his spirit than Rimbaud's which pervades this statement of the present surrealists: "I surrealism is another, a free captive of a torrent which he will permit no one to control, himself or anyone else. Everything now depends on the quantity of passion—the measure of everything which nothing can measure—hurled into the street. I surrealism—dissolved in the anonymous revolution—producer of passion."[8] For surrealism, poetry is the precise equivalent of passion. It is a way of life, not a manner of expression.[9] Its violence is directed against institutions, and against those who would make of it an institution about which one can be informed, or a monument commemorating the past, to which one can make a guided tour. This book attempts to show that surrealist poetry, whatever its date, is less than any other a poetry of the past, and that the language of surrealism, always turned toward the future, does not age. The catalogues of surrealism are often descriptions of a marvelous to come: "Il y aura une fois,"[10] or a real not yet perceived. Possibly

[8] "Je surréalisme est un autre" is a reference to Rimbaud's statement: "Je est un autre" (I is another), in which the subject is separated from the verb linguistically to emphasize the emotional division. The surrealists also refer to Tristan Corbière's expression "je parle sous moi," sometimes to evoke the same separation of conscious and unconscious, sometimes in a slightly different sense. See Jean Schuster, *Archives 57/68, Batailles pour le surréalisme*, 1969, p. 193.

[9] Tzara opposes "Poetry as a means of expression" to "Poetry as an activity of the mind"; the former being the traditional (therefore, to be rejected) transcription of *thought* into literature, and the latter being the spontaneous dynamism of the working out of thought, not in two stages but in one.

[10] There are also, of course, "catalogues" in the *form* of the present, but the vision always has the feeling of the future; they seem to be not so much statements as predictions. Compare for instance the surrealist "catalogues" with the "catalogues" of Apollinaire ("il y a").

even surrealist poetry can be killed by the weight of exterior details, by discussions of events and personalities which subtract from its total presence, but that is true no less of contemporary history than of the history of the past. It is best to speak of surrealist poetry in its own terms and in the light of its own themes, which bear, beyond the intricacies of personal relationships, a brilliant and continuous witness to the revolutionary spirit.

DADA AND SURREALIST POETS

. . . nous, les chevaliers du double-moi . . .
—TZARA, *Faites vos jeux*

The following sketch of the relations between these five poets—Aragon, Breton, Tzara, Eluard and Desnos—and between these particular movements glosses over the extraordinary complications, nuances, and ambiguities which have been treated in many works written expressly in order to clarify and expound them.

Briefly, all of these poets, except Desnos, were closely associated with the Dada movement in Paris after Tzara arrived from Zurich in late 1919. (Desnos recounts his efforts to have Benjamin Péret introduce him to Breton and the others, and in his own "Panorama de l'évolution depuis le mouvement Dada (y compris) jusqu'à 1927" he does not count himself among the Dadas.) After the demise of the Dada movement in 1922, a movement which never had a president ("we are all presidents of Dada"), and Breton's assumption of the leadership of the surrealist movement, there were various quarrels between the Tzara faction and the Breton faction, various realignments of position, and so on (see accounts of the Congress of Paris, the affair of the *Coeur à gaz*, the affair of the lost wallet). In 1929, Desnos was expelled (or, according to which account one reads, resigned) from the surrealist group "for journalistic activities."[11] *La Révolu-*

---

[11] It is scarcely necessary to say that the account of the various personalities and events differs greatly with the author of the account. For Breton's version of the break with Desnos, see his *Entretiens*

tion surréaliste became *Le Surréalisme au service de la révolution* as the surrealists affiliated themselves with the Communist party; but in 1932 Aragon resigned from the group

and his *Deuxième manifeste*, where he discusses Desnos' repeated use of "fixed forms" of poetry, his "dangerous reliance on his own talent," and his "immoderate usage of his verbal gift . . . to mask his radical absence of thought"; for Desnos' version, see his *Troisième manifeste*. For Eluard's version of his break with Breton, see the notes to the Pléiade edition of his works (Gallimard, 1968), Vol. i, 1537-38. For the early history of the relations between Tzara and Breton, see their correspondence published in Michael Sanouillet, *Dada à Paris* (Pauvert, 1966).

Because Desnos seems to have been able to keep himself at a certain distance from the events, for reasons of his own nature and his own instinctive separation even from his own work (a quality related perhaps both to his success with the sleep-writing experiments as well as to his radio and journalism practice) and because in his "Panorama du mouvement Dada (y compris) jusqu'à 1927" (MS 3361-63 of the Fonds Doucet) he discusses all the poets here at some length, it may be pertinent to quote, without comment, some of his judgments there:

ON ARAGON: "Louis Aragon is in fact a sentimental person. I imagine that it is with no shame that he permits his great, his very great intelligence, to become aware of that. . . . I am, in spite of having adopted an attitude different from his, among those who have no doubt about the perfect morality of his evolution."

ON BRETON: "Rare are those who have been able to survive the pitiless interrogations that he holds, and one might say that to be the friend of Breton is one of the moral horrors of the times; many persons who have fallen into an irremediable decline give no further excuse than the fact of having been, for only one day, his friend. Breton's evolution is a road broken in appearance, in reality rectilinear."

". . . a credulity and an incredulity equally excessive, and a certain persecution complex."

ON ELUARD: ". . . some persons like Eluard who pass through the intricacies of the moral revolution of Dada, more preoccupied with adopting an attitude than with any self-examination."

ON TZARA: ". . . who wanted to divide in order to reign. He divided friends so skillfully that he was bound to find himself alone, and those he had opposed were bound to become reconciled."

". . . already preoccupied with literary success. . . ."

"In spite of appearances, all had not yet renounced literature, its pomp and its works. Tzara first of all began, probably in 1920, to put on his little Chateaubriand act, as Aragon expresses it."

"Tzara seeks more and more a compromise between violence and success."

ON DADA AND SURREALISM: "While the Dada movement had ac-

in complicated circumstances ("L'Affaire Aragon").[12] In the
meantime, Tzara had realigned himself with the surrealist
group and Desnos, not aligned with it, continued to call himself a surrealist, according to his own meaning of the term
(see his *Troisième manifeste*). By 1935 the relations between the surrealists and the Communist party had become
strained, particularly over the question of the autonomy of
art. (See Eluard and Aragon on the notion that poetry must
be useful: "Nous déracinerons notre rue inutile.")[13] Finally

---

complished the break between *littérateurs* and poets, surrealism made
the break between the people of intelligence and those of sensitivity."

Obviously, these remarks are to be balanced with those of the
other poets—it is together that they are particularly interesting. But
the same themes predominate: sensitivity, sincerity, morality and moral
evolution, renouncement of literature for something more essential,
the notion of poetry as revolution.

[12] "L'Affaire Aragon" was in one sense a test case for surrealism,
since it revolved around the extent to which the "content" of poetry
can be taken literally. Aragon's poem "Front rouge" (see excerpts in
Chapter 2 on Aragon) was interpreted by some as a call to anarchy,
and he was brought to court. Breton and other surrealists defended
him ("Misère de la poésie") on the grounds that poetry is not to be
read as an exact statement, not to be judged on its "immediate content" or in a literal sense. Aragon himself, with a number of sup-
porters, claimed that surrealism being above all a revolt, and an
intensely *moral* one, against "art for art's sake" it should not try
to claim immunity for its poetry in the "social battle" against the
bourgeois mentality. That bourgeois society should now be fright-
ened by a poem was to be interpreted as a tribute to the potentiality
of poetry and not as an attack against its freedom. The Belgian surrealists were delighted that poetry was at last taken literally, which,
according to them, proved its content efficacious. (See the letter of
Paul Nougé in the collection of 222 pieces on the subject compiled
by Breton—n.a.f. 25094 in the collection of the Bibliothèque Nationale—containing letters from Aragon, Breton, Eluard, Romain
Rolland, Giacometti, etc.) Of course, this question forms part of the
more general debate of a committed or uncommitted art; and, of
course, the complications of the exterior circumstances are omitted
here, along with the emotional and personal complications (see
Eluard's "Certificat").

[13] For them, it is not enough that poetry should be linked to circumstances; it must have as its inspiration a "bon sujet," which naturally eliminates such works as Claudel's poem on the parachutists
in Indochina: "Poetry cannot be linked to what is declining or dying" (Eluard, II, 1940).

the surrealist group broke with the Communists, declaring the surrealist conception of the revolution to be broader than the Communist conception in calling for a "liberation" in the spiritual as well as in the material realm.

The group continues to call itself Marxist, further defining its leanings as Trotskyite; and in fact, Breton and Trotsky collaborated in Mexico on a letter about the freedom of art (signed, however, by Breton and Diego Rivera). In 1934 Tzara, by his own account, separated from the surrealists again, this time for "ideological reasons," and Eluard broke off from Breton in 1938 (see his explanation of the personal reasons in the Pléiade edition of his works); by 1940 they had both realigned themselves with the French Communist party.[14] On some occasions, such as a declaration of intellectuals on the Algerian war, etc., the surrealists and the Communists have signed the same statements. Aragon denies any bitterness on his part toward the surrealists (*J'abats mon jeu*), but the surrealists' attacks on the Communist party (which they consider entirely "Stalinist") are sometimes virulent.[15] On the other hand, the surrealists vigorously approve of Aragon's criticism of the writers allied with the journal *Tel quel*, and in one of their tracts, "Beau comme," they quote his judgments on Lautréamont as representative of their own.

Aragon remains the leading intellectual of the French Communist party. Desnos died in the concentration camp at Terezina, Czechoslovakia, of typhoid fever in 1945; he spoke of surrealism just before his death, declaring that his best friends were Breton and Eluard. Eluard died in 1952, and though the City of Paris refused him a public burial, the event was marked by wide demonstrations of sympathy; he

[14] For the enthusiasts of iconography, there is a picture of Eluard's party card in the Album Eluard published together with the Pléiade edition.

[15] See Jean Schuster's *Aragon au défi*, written on the occasion of Aragon's defense of Sinayevski and Daniel. For a statement of the political positions taken by the surrealists on the questions of Vietnam, Hungary, Algeria, Cuba, black power, etc., see Schuster, *Archives 57/68.*

continues to be the most read and most loved of all French poets since Apollinaire. Tzara died in 1962 and Breton in 1966. The choice of these five poets might be objectively defended, but it is only honest to say that this choice depended primarily, as did the choice of texts, on purely subjective considerations. The other poets connected with the two movements do not appear to demonstrate the same strength in poetry and in critical thinking: for example, Péret's poetry is magnificent, as is generally agreed, but his theoretical work tends toward the simplistic.

What is indisputable is that all of these five are unmistakably poets in all senses of the word, although of unmistakably unequal talent. Their statements, their criticism, their vision, and the structure of their writing convey the real atmosphere of the surreal landscape, and the widest perspectives of the "point sublime." That these five poets were so different in personality and yet at one time so closely linked, that they should have ended by so strongly opposing each other after having written manifestos and statements together for years is undoubtedly interesting. But from the point of view of this study, it is far more significant that the concerns which mark the critical and theoretical statements of each poet and of all the poets together should be precisely those which show up in their creative work. And even the temptation to undertake such a study is a testimony to the pervasiveness (or the obsessiveness) of the main theme.

POLARITY, AMBIGUITY, DOUBLING, DIALECTIC: A Brief (Subjective) Definition of Terms

For the purposes of this book, these terms are used in the following ways. An obvious *polarity* shows two elements opposite to each other without any implications of their unity in the present or the future, if they are left to themselves. A simple example is the cliché imagery: happy X sad = sun X rain; the terms are (usually) mutually exclusive. Ambiguity is less simple, since it demands the meeting, and the holding together, of the opposite terms (AB as in the sentimental cliché "bittersweet"). The surrealist aim could be loosely defined as the intention of transforming (with all the deliberately alchemical force which attaches to the latter verb) sets of static polar contraries into potentially powerful juxtapositions, intellectually uncomfortable to contemplate, shocking to the normal perception in their intense irrationality (it is to this sort of irrationality that the adjective in *L'Amour fou* refers). Clearly irrational juxtapositions are here called ambiguous, as are implied juxtapositions: the latter are the ground of Dada and surrealist word games as well as of the deliberately unresolved and "suspended" endings in some surrealist poetry, particularly that of Desnos.

If Breton writes a poem describing the dream of a woman simultaneously combing her hair and jumping rope as a little girl, simultaneously crossing the street and lying on her bed, the poem is marvelous from the surrealist point of view for just this impossible ambiguity. No one can "in reality" be a woman and a little girl (although this is the ideal conception of surrealist woman, Mélusine or the "femme-enfant"), nor can she be in any danger from cars when she is in her room, but such "double vision" is proper to surrealism, essential in surrealist vision.

But the surrealist poem moves toward an *identification* of the opposites, refusing the contradictions it observes in the world for an intentional unity, conceived in analogical terms and unvarying across the whole space of surrealist development. The frequent image of the bridge stretched across the abyss, that is, reconciling the two banks, is a material and less extreme image than that of the sublime point. The bridge joins polarities, but it does not unify them. On the other hand, the *point sublime* is the place at once abstract and precise, where all the contraries are identified, that is, a metaphoric *double* of surrealist poetry in its most subtle, difficult, illogical state.

To the notion of the double there are, appropriately, two concurrent and opposite aspects. First, two separate things can be doubles of each other, identified by the imagination to such an extent that to act on one is to act on the other. Thus, for Artaud (once a surrealist), the theater is the double of life, in a necessary and "cruel" relationship, while for Breton, language is the double of reality and poetry the double of the alchemical work; for Tzara, language is the double of gesture, and poetry, of action. This is the more positive aspect, doubled in its turn by a negative one. For an entity may feel itself unwillingly split into two parts, sensing the division as anguish. I, the double of the other, demonstrates a total alienation from the self which Breton, referring to Rimbaud, calls "the marvelous wound" (see note 8). Suffered, it is therefore passive; the opposite of the positive action, or work, of poetry on the world, it nevertheless provides the framework for the dictation of the unconscious, and for the revelation of dream discussed in the next section.

Dialectic, which can be described as the resolution of two opposing elements into a third, which then becomes the first element of another group, so that the mobility is constant, is the infinitely complex and serious *play* of polarities and resolution, as familiar to surrealist thought as to Marxist thought. The surrealist resolution within the realm of poetry, while effective, is always to be recreated, as the polarities are always suffered or observed. The moment of repose is no more habitable than the *point sublime*: "It was never a question of my living at that point. From then on it would have ceased to be sublime, and I would have ceased to be a man," says Breton to his daughter at the end of *L'amour fou*. Surrealist poetry is never static: many of the poetic procedures are definite vehicles whereby the poet is enabled to act out the play of opposites and resolution. It is the exposition (and occasionally, the brief analysis) of these procedures which is the aim of this book.[16]

[16] Robert Champigny, in an essay on *Le Genre poétique* (Monte Carlo, Editions Regain, 1963), speaks of the aesthetic tension or complementarity essential to poetry, and the possible *convergence* of the terms of each series of complements. In surrealist poetry, however, he distinguishes only the tension between the elements and not its resolution: "The 'images' found in so-called surrealist texts frequently have a value of complementarity. But the convergence escapes me" (p. 160). This study tries to show both the complementarity and the convergence.

DADA AND SURREALISM:
A CONTINUITY OF CONTRADICTIONS

. . . l'indivisible suite de présences et de nécessités . . .
—TZARA, "A Propos de Joan Miró"

It is a matter of general knowledge that the Dada group, whose most colorful figures were Picabia, Duchamp, and Tzara, originated in Zurich in 1916 and provoked numerous scandals (effectively directed against the bourgeois mind) there and in all the places to which it spread; it finally "died" or rather disbanded itself in Paris in 1922 as a last negative act. It is also known that surrealist theories and experiments (the early ones with automatic speaking and writing as well as the later ones with dream transcriptions and hypnotic sleep) are all directed toward the liberation of the thought processes from rational control and social convention so that they can be placed in a state of total freedom and openness to the marvelous. The goal of surrealism as Breton defined it in the early days of the movement, when he had just finished his wartime service in various neuropsychiatric centers,[17] was the simple attempt to transcribe unconscious workings of the

---

[17] *Les Champs magnétiques,* an example of "automatic writing," on which Breton and Soupault collaborated starting in 1919 (republished in 1968) is usually cited as the beginning of surrealist experimentation. For the Dadaists also, spontaneous expression was valued as antiliterature and antilogic. See Tzara's statement that thought is made in the mouth (or, in the case of Picasso, with the paint brush). Breton's description of the aim of automatic writing as the direct transcription of thought in the *Premier manifeste* is well known; one can compare the remarks made by Tzara in *Faites vos jeux, Les Feuilles libres,* No. XXXI (March-April 1923):

The desire to know if I could transcribe at top speed everything that fell, rolled, opened, flew, and continued within my head overcame me. The simple technical exercise of unpacking one's heart. . . . I wrote to destroy the feeling which incited me to write. . . . I think . . . that transcendental thought does not exist outside of language, and that it occurs between the throat and the palate at the same moment that the vibrations assembled one after another take on the sound of the words. . . . And is not logic too an elegant form of imagination, apparently the cause of the intertwining of words, but in reality only the embroidery whose decorative foliage accompanies the race of the animal across the forest wilderness?

mind. But the surrealist endeavor quickly extended to the more complex aim of the complete liberation of man's spirit by whatever means available.

Surrealism insults reason for the benefit of spontaneity, logic for the benefit of the lyric sense of the marvelous, and everyday reality for the glorification of the *insolite*, in which elements of the real are transfused with the light of the "super-real" by the inexplicable and unexpected workings of objective chance ("a solution more perfect than one could have hoped to a problem one was not aware of having"). Breton, who formulates surrealist theory most clearly and at greatest length, acknowledges surrealism's obvious relations with romanticism, with the ideas of analogy, correspondences, and so on. For him, and for all the surrealists, the *point sublime* "where the yes and the no meet" and are united is visible only to those in an "état d'attente,"[18] a constant state of readiness. Poetry is at once the open landscape where the "point sublime" is located and the quality which best describes the surrealists' uncompromising attitude ("le comportement lyrique"). So that one can, in the surrealist universe, manifest poetic behavior in its fullest sense while never writing a line, or commit the most serious crimes against *poetry* while writing verses of an apparently "surrealist" nature. All of this is widely understood and accepted, and none of it in any way contradicts the usual opinion that as Dada denies, surrealism asserts, that Dada's negativism broke down the aesthetic barriers and cleared the way for surrealism which then built up a new set of theories.

It is easy to underestimate the continuities of theme in favor of a stereotyped formula; but formulas are, like facts, inimical to the spirit of poetry. Tzara's phrase "Poetry—a state of mind" holds good for the Dada movement as well as for surrealism. The briefest glance at his 1917 notes on poetry and on art or even at the famous Dada manifestos should be enough to undercut the notion of total Dada negativity.

[18] It should be noted that this readiness, a general state of mind and not a specific *expectation*, in no way detracts from the *unexpected* workings of chance.

For Dada, the role of poetry is to create and develop, against the closed and the prosaic, a permanent atmosphere of openness—similar to the surrealist notions of "attente" and "disponibilité"—of clarity, intensity, and rapidity, to which the energetic oppositions of contradictory elements is absolutely essential. "Surrealism is a dynamics," claims Breton;[19] Dada was that too.

The attitudes and images which these poets, seen individually and as a group, take with them from Dada to surrealism (and even into their political writings) is best demonstrated in the texts themselves. What needs to be reemphasized at the outset is both the dualistic form of all their thought and the continuity of the ideas and the images which haunt it. It is not surprising that having developed surrealist theory, which resembles Dada in its accent on contradictions and resolutions, these writers should all have been strongly attracted by Marxist dialectical theory.[20] The closest bond these poets have with each other is their unique attraction to opposing elements which underlies all their critical and imaginative ventures and marks all their prose and their poetry. Whether the unconscious result of a common pattern of thought, or the conscious (or semiconscious) structure appropriate to the expression of a certain kind of thinking, surrealist writing in general is characterized by its basic double center—reality and dream, presence and absence, identity and distance, intimacy and loneliness, unity and multiplicity, continuity and discontinuity, language and silence, mobility and immobility, clarity and obscurity, and so on. Even the recurring themes which do not at first glance appear to be built on contrary images or notions are essentially connected with the play of oppositions. For instance, the emphasis on

[19] "Perspective cavalière," *La Brèche* 5 (October 1963).

[20] In 1921, Aragon's essay "L'Ombre de l'inventeur" explains the dialectical relationships of the mind to the real, through the progressive steps of observation, negation, and reconciliation by an "absolute mediator," the final step including both the mind and the real.

In his *Petite anatomie de l'inconscient physique* (Le Terrain Vague, 1957), Hans Bellmer discusses the dialectics of physical duality (pain and pleasure, and so on), of dualities experienced in dream, and of the "taste of reversibility" present from the origins of language.

simplicity demands that all resolution of contraries merge into a single whole, while the parallel emphasis on freedom and on dizziness ("le vertige") demands that no resolution be permanent.

That Breton's famous image of the communicating vessels depends on a dual perception is clear enough; in fact, even the concept of the *merveilleux* implies a basic opposition. When Aragon says that the marvelous is the exact embodiment of human freedom, he explains the statement in the following terms: "The relationship which is produced from the negation of the real by the marvelous is essentially ethical, and the marvelous is always the materialization of a moral symbol in violent opposition with the morality of the world in whose center it appears."[21] Surrealism, like Dada, never ceases to consider itself a strongly ethical movement; as is obvious in the above quotation, the moral sense itself implies an equally strong emphasis on what must be overcome by the surrealist revolution.

LANGUAGE, IMAGE, AND COLLAGE

As much as anything else, Dada and surrealism are experiments with and investigations of language. From the word plays and "automatic" transcriptions to the essays on "words in liberty," "unwrinkled words," on gesture and language, there is evident a connecting thread or conducting wire (the *fil conducteur* discussed in the next section): an almost superstitious faith in language as a magic incantation, effective *out of all proportion* to its intelligible content. "Language was given to man for him to make a surrealist use of it":[22] to treat the Word as an ordinary logical or practical thing is to betray the gift entirely.

Taken as communication, language makes its own resolution of the distance between the speaker and the listener, addressed directly or by implication. There is nothing magical about this, or about the image of the communicating vessels,

[21] Quoted by Patrick Waldberg in *Le Surréalisme: sources, histoire, affinités*, a catalogue published by the Galerie Charpentier, 1964.
[22] *Premier manifeste du surréalisme* (Pauvert, 1962), p. 48.

first mentioned in *Le Surréalisme et la peinture* of 1928, in which the correspondence is natural and physical. But the connection between the hidden unconscious and the open consciousness is not so simple, is not really even of the same order as the communicating vessels. All the images of swinging doors (*Nadja*) and half-open doors (*Les Vases communicants*—although Breton seems to have slightly modified the original scientific experiment by the same name), of the relationships between the container and the contained (such as in Eluard's title *La Jarre peut-elle être plus belle que l'eau?*) imply a passing-through or a conceptual reversal of two elements of the same importance, if not of the same nature. The surreality contained within the reality, the dream passing through into everyday life, the sense of interior desire suddenly confronting exterior events and revealing the necessities in what we thought was chance, are all *merveilleux*, they are even *passionnants* (in the sense that surrealism wants to "repassionner la vie")—but they are rarely frightening.

However, the split between the *Je* and the *autre* or, more serious still, between the unconscious and the conscious, can be anguishing and even dangerous. The image container/contained represents unemotionally the concept of another within the familiar self but an image like the door ajar between the inside world and the outside world is potentially more expressive, partly because of the implicit possibilities of freeing, surprising, confronting, challenging. As in the phrase "obeying the dictates of the unconscious" it shows the differentiation within the self and the importance conferred on the unknown that speaks in us *as if it came from without*.

In *Les Vases communicants*, this double image is itself doubled by the balance between Breton's interpretations of dreams by the events in his daily life and the parallel interpretations of the latter in the light of the predictions contained in his dreams. The unconscious workings of chance affect human conscious life, and the conscious observer brings his own desires, of which he may be unaware, into the world he perceives, so that finally the subjective and objective necessities meet. But poetic images are the double of experience itself, and some of Breton's preferred images exemplify (or better, play out) the danger he always feels: the girl seated in a rocking chair on a bridge, the bridge itself with no railing (an image which conveys both the distance between the polar opposites to be bridged and the danger of attempting to cross), and the mirror showing a different reality on each side, traversable only by the poetic act. Breton's highest praise is bestowed on those like Artaud, or the Nadja of his own book, who "pass to the other side of the mirror" as payment for having listened to the voice of the unconscious within themselves.

One other preferred comparison is the electric charge resulting from the deliberate bringing into contact of highly differentiated elements to form the "marvelous" image; instead of suffering from the differentiation of the outside and the inside worlds, or from the clash of opposing forces to the point of insanity, it is possible to apply the energy produced by such a clash to the world beyond, as if this energy were magical. Over the period of development of surrealist theory, the occupations of listening to and transcribing the dictates of the marvelous or the "other," of observing the distant elements of the image, change their passive metaphors for active ones. The elements brought into confrontation from opposite poles and stuck together in a temporary and vigorous collage serve as centers of energy for the analogical work of surrealism (although those who share the Dada-surrealist affection for puns and word-games may prefer the expression "struck together," since the aim is the creation of a spark). Where the Dada-surrealist work appears most purely lyric, it is intended also as efficacious: the doubling is continuous. And yet it is also mobile—one could call it a montage, or even, as we call it here, a game. The double attributes of the work and the game are fitting.

At least in theory, and to the extent that the game of poetry can manifest the theatrical-alchemical process Breton so firmly believes in, the surrealist poem (an extension of the surrealist image, an attempt at the creation in language of a *point sublime*) is, unlike "ordinary" poetry, a form of magic.

In fact, the possible "validity" or "invalidity" of this theory may in no way affect our attitude toward the poetry itself—that is, one may find surrealist poetry convincing as poetry while considering the theory behind it impossible, illogical, untenable, and childish—but that is just the problem. We are *not* justified in "appreciating" this poetry on the same grounds as we appreciate other poetry, or in excluding from our "appreciation" its theoretical basis; they are inseparable doubles. Surrealism excludes the observer, admitting only the actor, the participant, the believer. Whatever critical judgment we may make of it, does not affect it: and from the judgment it passes on us there is no appeal.

THEMES:
ALTERNATION AND LINKING, EXALTATION AND
ENNUI, GAME

Nouez les rires aux douleurs. . . .
—ELUARD, "L'Amour la poésie"

It is of course true that external circumstances often influence the mood and the images of the poems written in them: of the poets discussed here, Eluard, Aragon, and Desnos make their later poetry a deliberate reflection of its moment. For instance, Eluard's poems can easily be, and have often been, divided in cycles of dark images and radiant ones, the former prevalent in periods of despair over Gala's infidelity, Nusch's death, or the ravages of war, and the latter prevalent in periods of peace, reciprocal love, and political commitment. But this is often a surface impression, under which there is an extraordinary and permanent balance in all the poets between the poems of simplicity and luminosity and a corresponding set of terrible and destructive poems; it is this balance which can be interpreted as typical of the Dada and surrealist poetic vision.

Many of Eluard's most famous titles, such as "La Lumière et le pain" and "Le Lit la table," describe the qualities of childlike presence and unity, of faithfulness to the moment—qualities prized by all the surrealists. His poetry is generally of a total clarity and an extreme simplicity. It is in the simplest things that he attempts to "make the moment of ecstasy supreme" (as he says of the paintings of Jacques Villon), and to render it eternal in its purity and its order. These qualities illuminate and perpetuate illumination in a *Poésie ininterrompue*:

Rien ne peut déranger l'ordre de la lumière
Où je ne suis que moi-même
Et ce que j'aime
Et sur la table
Ce pot plein d'eau et le pain du repos
. . .
De l'eau fraîche et du pain chaud
Sur les deux versants du jour

Aujourd'hui lumière unique
Aujourd'hui l'enfance entière
Changeant la vie en lumière
. . .
Aujourd'hui je suis toujours[23]

(Nothing can upset the order of light
Where I am only myself
And what I love
And on the table
This jug full of water and the bread of rest
. . .
Cool water and warm bread
On the two slopes of day

Today unique light
Today childhood complete
Changing life into light
. . .
Today I am always).

This is the atmosphere described by Desnos in his frequent references to the elemental vision of everyday life, to the

[23] Paul Eluard, *Poèmes* (Gallimard, 1951), p. 325.

dust on a sidewalk, or the sunlight on a piece of fruit and on a bottle, and by Tzara in his poems of *plénitude*, where the image of bread most often appears, and where all the fruits of the earth are represented in their pure simplicity. These poets have a particular warmth and brightness characterized by the repeated greetings: "bonjour!," "salut!":

ELUARD: Et le matin bonjour dîmes-nous à la vie

DESNOS: Salut de bon matin . . .
Salut de bon matin

—

Bonjour de bon coeur et de tout notre sang
Bonjour, bonjour, le soleil va se lever sur Paris
Bonjour, bonjour, de tout coeur bonjour

TZARA: Bonjour ma vie
Bonjour bonjour à haute voix
Bonjour à haute flamme
Bonjour le soleil dans la main

On the other hand, violent images associated with the theme of cruelty (discussed in Chapter 2 on Aragon) recur insistently in all this poetry; italicized in the following passages are references to damaging, breaking, laceration, tearing apart, rending, to the scraping out of wounds and the dissecting of nerves, to cracking, piercing, whipping, shattering, strangling, spitting, scourging, to wailing, brutality, and bleeding:

ARAGON: Ah *faire un mal* pareil aux *brisures* d'os

—

Déchirez ma chair *partagez* mon corps
Fouillez fouillez bien le fond des *blessures*
Disséquez les nerfs et *craquez* les os comme des
noix tendres
. . .

On peut mc *déchirer* de toutes les manières
M'écarteler briser percer de mille trous

BRETON: La *déchirure* unique

—

Mon oeil à la pointe du *fouet*

TZARA: *Brisée* est la transparence . . .
Le vent *étrangle* la parole dans le gosier du village . . .
. . .
Cassée est la chaîne
. . .
Et le vent nous *crache* à la figure
L'infatigable *brutalité* de tout cela

—

Qui *crachait* l'image par terre
Et *brisait* l'éclatante jeunesse—des traces de
sang trainaient quelque part

—

Déchirant déchiré

—

Au coeur des *déchirures*

DESNOS: Des cygnes *étranglés*

—

Que mes mains abusées ont *déchiré* parfois
La chair *sanglante* et chaude et vierge

ELUARD: L'enfant leva son fouet . . .
Puis *déchira* la campagne

—

Les ronces de tes yeux *déchirant* l'églantine
Déchirant ce champ de blé noir

—

Le tranquille *fléau* doublé de plaintes

"A la flamme des fouets," one of the poems from Eluard's
Capitale de la douleur (1926) indicates even in its title a
peculiarly sensual form of human cruelty which is the absolute contrast to any peaceful arrangement of clarity and
simplicity; and its "bonjour" is the sarcastic opposite of the
salutations just mentioned:

Métal qui nuit, métal de jour, étoile au nid,
Pointe à frayeur, fruit en guénilles, amour rapace,
Porte-couteau, souillure vaine, lampe inondée,
Souhaits d'amour, fruits de dégoût, glaces prostituées
. . .
Bien sûr, bonjour à vos harpons,
A vos cris, à vos bonds, à votre ventre qui se cache!
(Harmful night metal, metal of day, star in the nest,
Frightening point, fruit in tatters, rapacious love,
Knife-sheath, vain defilement, inundated lamp,
Amorous yearnings, fruits of disgust, prostituted mirrors
. . .
Of course, good morning to your shafts,
To your shouts, to your springing, to your belly hiding!)

Such alternations can be traced through almost every
family or group of images for all these poets, so that the
transfer from light to dark is or gradually appears natural
enough to contradict any conscious effort or *art*. The surrealist universe is above all a changing one, full of metamorphosis and extreme variation. As surrealist mobility includes
even a paradoxical immobility, so surrealist language, ideally
"limpid," "clear," "radiant," "fiery," sometimes avows itself
powerless before the melancholy fixations of habit: "The
plough of words is rusted." This double current is itself the
necessary element of surrealist vision and language, and determines the complex variation of the images.

The image of the bird, for instance, has an obvious appeal
for poets like Tzara and Eluard, who speak so often of the
sun; the bird is the vertical or pure parallel of the "plénitude"
of the earth. He easily soars beyond all mortal shadows, like
Eluard's description of Braque's paintings, which he compares
to a bird enclosed in the lightness and luminosity of his own
shadowless flight. He is able to preserve his own individual
"forme éclose / Et son plaisir / Parmi tant d'oiseaux à venir."
He has a *direct* right to the sky, and the motion of his wings
enlarges space itself, like the ideal force of the surrealist
poem: "croissance de l'aile/croissance d'espace." Or again,

he refuses the artificial separation of categories—"il confond d'un seul coup d'aile / Les champs nus et les récoltes." The bird exemplifies pure freedom and constant revelation of light: "Un bel oiseau nu montre la lumière." For Tzara, the bird is again the simple creature of light ("la lumière des oiseaux") and at the same time his motion is of such an intensity that it is seen as burning—Tzara's highest qualification of praise. The bird radiates the bright hardness of natural things, "l'acier unanime de leur terrible soleil"; his flight is intractable and of a difficult and supreme clarity:

le vol durci d'acier d'un oiseau oblique
d'hiver est son remous de diamant
le bec tirant son crissement acide sur le verre dépoli[24]

(the hardened steely flight of an oblique bird
his wake is winter's, his beak of diamond
drawing its acid path along the frosted glass).

And yet it shows like all the products of Dada and surrealist experience, a contrasting side: "Toute l'innocence des oiseaux durs comme le fer." It is precisely because of his innocence and luminosity that the bird is threatened. If his vertical movement can be reversed, his fall will have all the force which characterized his flight: "Les puissantes chutes des oiseaux de lumière." Or again the instruments of his power once used to emphasize the purity of his flight can be destroyed, so that he is denied in his *essence*, as in Eluard's image of the bird with his wings pulled off. Since it is the bird in motion which appeals to the surrealist poets, the denial of this motion is seen as the gravest possible threat, entailing as it does a denial of liberty. In the moments of deepest pessimism Eluard laments the spectacle of a bird paralyzed on a motionless path ("les oiseaux n'ont qu'une route toute d'immobilité"), and Tzara pictures an atmosphere of nonclarity, "les régions boueuses où les oiseaux se collent en silence," or contrasts the fragility and innocence of the bird with his probable fate:

[24] Tristan Tzara, *L'Homme approximatif* (Editions Fourcade, 1931), p. 104.

il ne pesait pas lourd l'oiseau joliment
mollement figé dans des yeux d'araignée.[25]
(He weighed little the bird prettily
gently transfixed in a spider's eyes.)

Here the notion of being "fixed" involves a future threat and
an exterior one, but at the extreme limit, the threat is trans-
ferred to the interior. The poet whose power of speech has
enabled him to be a "conqueror," lifting him beyond the
ordinary modest human realm, so that he is "plus près du
soleil et plus sûr de durer," suddenly becomes a victim of his
own power:

Tout est brisé par la parole la plus faible
Les ailes rentrent dans l'oiseau pour le fixer.[26]
(All is broken by the weakest word
The wings retract into the bird transfixing him.)

All the marvelous quality of "transparent metamorphosis" on
which the surrealist universe depends can be transfixed into
immobility.

Les oiseaux désséchés
Prenaient des poses immortelles
. . .
Chemins paralysés
Incohérents (I, 816)
(The dried-out birds
Assumed immortal poses
. . .
Paths paralyzed
Disconnected).

At one moment Eluard sees enormous birds who can find no
place to rest and at the next he is assured both of the flight
and of the necessary cessation of flight:

[25] Tristan Tzara, "Mauvais souvenir," *Terre sur terre* (Geneva,
Editions Trois Collines, 1946), p. 47.
[26] Paul Eluard, "Puisqu'il n'est plus question de force," *Les Derniers poèmes d'amour* (Seghers, 1963), p. 49.

. . . les oiseaux les hommes
vont s'envoler
ceux qui volent vont se poser. (ii, 421)

(. . . the birds the men
will fly off
those who fly will alight.)

All one can be sure of is that the apparent immobility ("rien n'est en mouvement") can be no more permanent than the apparent mobility ("tout est en mouvement") : both are indispensable parts of the general principle of variation. So the presence and the future of the birds of flight is balanced by the negation of their movement, or of our vision:

Aucun oiseau ne vole (ii, 688)
(No bird flies)

—

L'oiseau qu'efface un nuage (i, 1124)
(The bird a cloud obliterates).

The extremes of alternation are often as far removed from each other as the two poles of the perfect surrealist image, a distance which determines all the force of each poetic juxtaposition. Surrealist poetry or Dada poetry is not "art" in the usual sense; it is rather the creation of a whole universe of relationships between seemingly opposed objects and ideas, even when the juxtaposition of those objects and ideas includes the violent opposition of mood and vision within the creation itself. The theory of *linking* is of primary importance in Dada and surrealist writings, and there are numerous references to it in the poetry, the manifestos, and the critical essays. Eluard's poem beginning "J'établis des rapports entre" could be taken as the preface to a great number of the texts important in the two movements. His statement "Everything is comparable to everything" and his insistence on the notion of similarity ("frères semblants," "ressemblant") have the same theoretical basis as Breton's suggested surrealist technique of linking any noun to any other to widen the scope of language and vision. Tzara sees certain images as conduit images, carrying an electric charge from one element to the other, and in an essay on the artist Pougny he underlines the importance of the attempt to find once more the thread ("le fil") of primary spontaneity; in his *Homme approximatif*, he laments the useless motion of the men who walk about unable to find the "bout du fil." Breton maintains that the task of the eye is to establish new links by a system of "fils conducteurs," or connecting wires, and in his poem "Vigilance," after the fire has burned away all the obstacles to the final purity and unity of vision, the hero of the surrealist universe can say: "Je tiens le fil."

It is probably this theory of analogy and the desire to combine elements of vision, suppressing the distance usually separating them, which determines the repetitive ("secular litanic") form of writing so often to be found in the work of all these poets:

ARAGON: Pour quel bagne pour quel destin
Pour quelle nuit qui n'a limite
Pour quelle nuit qui n'a matin

—

Je crois en toi dans le vacarme et le silence
Je crois en toi dans la douleur
Je crois en toi comme à la preuve d'être

—

C'est l'heure où chaque chose de lumière à toi seul est
donnée
C'est l'heure où ce qu'on dit semble aussitôt occuper tout
l'espace.

BRETON: Ma femme aux yeux de savane
Ma femme aux yeux d'eau pour boire en prison
Ma femme aux yeux de bois toujours sous la hache
Aux yeux de niveau d'eau de niveau d'air de terre et de feu

—

Toi qui ne remonteras pas à la surface
Toi qui me regardes sans me voir dans les jardins de la
provocation pure

Toi qui m'envoies un baiser de la portière d'un train qui
  fuit

TZARA: Les cloches sonnent sans raison et nous aussi
  Les cloches sonnent sans raison et nous aussi
  Sonnez cloches sans raison et nous aussi

  —

  Dans la tête par le monde
  Dans la pierre dans le vent
  L'amitié et le sourire
  Comme les chiens à l'abandon
  Comme des chiens

ELUARD: Merci pour la faim et la soif
  Merci pour le désastre et pour la mort bénie
  Merci pour l'injustice

  —

  Je t'aime pour ta sagesse qui n'est pas la mienne
  Pour la santé
  Je t'aime contre tout ce qui n'est qu'illusion
  Pour ce coeur immortel que je ne détiens pas

DESNOS: Jamais d'autre que toi ne saluera la mer à l'aube. . .
  Jamais d'autre que toi ne posera sa main sur mon front et
    mes yeux
  Jamais d'autre que toi et je nie le mensonge et l'infidélité

  —

  J'appelle à moi les amours et les amoureux
  J'appelle à moi les vivants et les morts
  J'appelle les fossoyeurs j'appelle les assassins
  J'appelle les bourreaux j'appelle les pilotes les maçons et
    les architectes

The same theory also underlies repetitions of imagery and of
sound, as well as certain stylistic details. When Desnos writes:
"de la rose de marbre de la rose de verre de la rose de charbon
de la rose de papier buvard" (rather than "une rose comme
du marbre," etc.), he refuses all punctuation which would
separate the two things, or all these things, from each other.
Breton's *point sublime* is the meeting place for all these

various linkings and relationships, the culminating instant
of the movements and images linked by the *fil conducteur*.
The surrealist state of unity being also the field of the
marvelous, this is a unity new at every moment:

BRETON: Toujours pour la première fois

ELUARD: Demain je ne recommencerai pas, je commencerai

DESNOS: Le monde date de maintenant
Le matin est neuf, neuf est le soir.

But at the same time, in accordance with the essential
union of contradictions, this theme of identity is associated
not only with the exaltation of the *point sublime*, but with
the state of nonmoving anguish known as *ennui*:

BRETON: l'ennui, les belles parallèles

TZARA: . . . je vis parmi les rapports de l'ennui

ELUARD: où l'habitude et la surprise
créent l'ennui à tour de rôle

—

mais, plus bas que tout, il y avait l'ennui

—

Un navire inutile joint mon enfance à mon ennui

—

Gagner sur mon ombre au fond de l'ennui

DESNOS: C'était l'ennui, grande place ensoleillée.

Much surrealist poetry instantly brings to mind the art of
film, since both are above all concerned with the changing
moment, with the metamorphosis of the instant,[27] and the
issues of *Etudes cinématographiques* devoted to "surréalisme
et cinéma" (Nos. 40-42, 1965) are particularly interesting
on this point. Stan Brakhage speaks of trying to achieve in his
films "the virtue of immobility" which he sees in surrealist
painting and poetry, to reduce the ratio of motion to stillness.
And F. Mizrachi says of *L'Année dernière à Marienbad* that

[27] Compare, for instance, the feeling of Eluard's "Nuits partagées"
or Breton's poem beginning "Je rêve de toi" (both quoted here) with
the scene in *L'Année dernière à Marienbad* of the various transpositions of the woman in a dress of feathers seated on the bed.

it is "the poetic synthesis of an abolition of the temporal discontinuity we live," and goes on to compare this with the "point sublime." Surrealism has often been called a search for the continuous,[28] but to go so far as to associate the *point sublime* with the contrary and yet intimately connected notion of *ennui*, that is, to insist that the exaltation is always accompanied by tedium, may verge on the sacrilegious from the point of view of a narrowly interpreted conception of surrealism. But the opposites are the extreme poles of the surrealist marvelous, and the momentum and the intensity of the marvelous depend on the sudden abolition of the space between them.

At its most forceful, surrealist poetry transforms all this momentum into a revolution against things as we ordinarily see them. It is aimed at *expansion* and *extension*, and is the direct opposite of the notions of stability and classic "measure" ("Je me savais démesuré"). It has all the rules and all the freedom of play, together with the seriousness of creation, both qualities essential to surrealist games, of which Aragon

---

[28] In a persuasive essay on *Nadja* (special Breton issue of *La Nouvelle revue française*, April 1, 1967), Michel Beaujour analyzes Breton's deliberate cultivation of "les ruptures," of certain discontinuities between heterogeneous elements juxtaposed without any principle of chronological ordering. He associates this technique with Eisenstein's method of cinematic *montage* (a procedure in which the successive shots are linked by the memory of the spectator, where significance lies in the passage from one to the next), with the deck of cards (which can be reshuffled and used in an unlimited number of games), and with the notions of chance, coincidence, and ambiguity (the elements being at once separate and linked). Breton meant his work to be left *open*, so that any part could be interchanged with any other part: hence the images of swinging doors and communicating vessels.

It might be profitable, in speaking of the poetry, to compare this sort of procedure with the litanic form (and with its double, the form of successive approximations); although the goal is presence, and the guiding principle is that of the linking thread or *fil conducteur*, it may present, from the linguistic point of view, some type of hiatus between the recapitulations of its elements. Certainly it is intended to be a form of complete openness. Perhaps, according to an appropriate formal duality, it is as much the succession of *trous* or absences as the accumulation of repetitions which leads to the final presence.

says in 1921: "These are not games, they are philosophic acts of the first magnitude." From the point of view of this book, the most perfect and most subtle surrealist game and the one most closely related to the nature of surrealist poetry is the game called *l'un dans l'autre.* Here one thing is seen as potentially within the other (for instance, a lion's mane within the flame of a match), opposites are joined, and the distance between the present and the future is annihilated. The presence of one element is in some way seen as predictive of the opposite element(s) by a deliberate and yet spontaneous stretching of vision. This form of play, or collage in motion, is at once a rigid discipline and a mobile "fête," at once rite and celebration, so that it also holds within itself the opposition of poles, which it then abolishes in a supreme synthesis whose charge is operative not only on the player or poet but on all he touches. The poles are endlessly recreated, as are the annihilation of the distance and the resulting synthesis: that the Dada group places a slightly stronger emphasis on the annihilation, and the surrealists on the synthesis is less important than their equal emphasis on the generative quality of the game.[29] The momentum is passed on and multiplied

[29] That even the game should occasionally be associated with the contrary concepts of *ennui* and linking is perhaps the supreme example of the essential paradox within the Dada-surrealist point of view. Tzara's *Faites vos jeux* (the first parts of which were published in *Les Feuilles libres*) describes the endless motion of the pawns on the board as they are linked together by the *fils* of the observer's gaze, and as the movements betray, like poetry itself, the character and the unconscious of the player (or the poet):

Each game shows the fingerprints of the player's character. There are slow, inoffensive games, retiring and predictable ones, restless and capricious ones. . . . There are precipitous games. . . . I like to take risks; my strategies are poised on an edge of danger. I make all my moves by summing up the other positions and comparing the results—often the mental scale of constellations makes desperate swings. The demonstrations glance briefly at my ennui. . . . I like the measure of unconsciousness in the different sets of a game, their definite proportion of important acts, the logic which determines them is rapidly hidden under the obvious qualities of skill, of promptness, of clarity. . . . I cheat, of course, because I live among the relationships of ennui, of satisfactions, of pretentions, of human obligations. I animate the indecisiveness

in an endless motion and *vertige* which are the true atmosphere of Dada and surrealist poetry.

TEXTS

La poésie, seule interprétation plausible de cette
chiquenaude hors du réel.
—ARAGON, "L'Ombre de l'inventeur"

The English translations given here are neither "free" nor rhymed but rather literal; they are meant as a help for the reader who knows a little French, and not as creations on their own. Some of the short phrases intelligible from the context are left in French.

In general, the working division of poetry as verse is observed, justified here only in order to provide a more or less manageable body of material. It is certainly not meant to reflect a theoretical judgment, since in fact a great many of the prose works are obviously prose poems. Some of the most important of the latter are quoted here: Aragon's *Le Paysan de Paris*, Breton's *L'Amour fou*, Tzara's *Grains et issues* and his *Antitête*, Desnos' *Deuil pour deuil* and *La Liberté ou l'amour*; but the verse poems are especially prolific in the condensed forms of polarity and ambiguity.

---

which drags from one passion, from one act, from one idea to the other. (No. xxxi, p. 42.)

Later in the same work, the notion of the game is extended to cover human fate in its unpredictability ("God has amused himself by bringing off certain brilliant shots") and the interior divisions of personality ("Many spectators seated in a circle within me were watching a billiard game going on in the center . . .").

Compare Aragon's statement in the beginning section of *Le Paysan de Paris*: "I am at the roulette of my body and I play on the red. Everything distracts me indefinitely, excepting distraction itself. A sentiment as if of nobility impels me to prefer this abandon to everything else and I could not possibly understand your reproaches." (p. 12) For the surrealist notion of the game, see Audoin's talk at the "Décade du surréalisme," Gershman's "Toward Defining the Surrealist Aesthetic," *Papers on Language and Literature*, II (Winter 1966), and Beaujour's "The Game of Poetics" (*YFS* No. 41, 1969). Charles Fourier, one of the thinkers Breton most admired, wanted to replace the notion of work with the notion of play.

Liberal use is made of quotations throughout, but especially in the case of Eluard. His critics have so often refused to see any mingling of light and dark images in his works at exactly the same period (so often shown, for instance, how in the love poetry of his happiest times, all is sunny) that the actual juxtaposition of contraries must be demonstrated at length. However, the majority of the texts in this book were not chosen in order to illustrate the main theme of oppositions and resolution. They were first chosen for themselves, as characteristically surrealist according to a purely intuitive and personal judgment and only afterward examined and assorted by particular themes: it was in this *post facto* examination that the overall theme was seen, and not before. This is a deliberate effort to start from inside the surrealist "état de poésie," to follow the way of knowing and the way of extending experience which poetry represents for all these writers.

LOUIS ARAGON

Fausse dualité de l'homme, laisse-moi un peu rêver à ton mensonge.
—ARAGON, *Le Paysan de Paris*

"LE PASSAGE"

There could, from one point of view, be no more striking contrast than that between Dada and surrealist aesthetic theories on the one hand and a Marxist aesthetics on the other. At the outset, both the Dada and the surrealist movements were highly antipolitical, even if certain members did eventually become involved in political commitment. Neither movement would seem to have anything whatsoever to do with "socialist realism" of any variety since, though they attacked bourgeois principles, they appealed neither to the lower classes nor to the "realists." Dada, in attacking everyone and everything, in its deliberate provocation of the "gens de goût," could not conceivably help to form a constructive society after destroying the old. Surrealism, with its continued emphasis on the dream, its horror of *le travail* and of *le métier* and its latent appeal to a certain intellectual snobbism and a certain leisured class (the same class which can afford to purchase surrealist works) can scarcely be thought of as a valuable discipline for the "anticapitalist" mind. While it is true that Breton, for example, was always aware of the paradox implied in surrealism as a sort of parasite on wealthy society (see his letters at the time of his employment by Doucet) and always took a strictly "liberal" view of political events, that awareness in no way excuses him in the eyes of the "realists" for whom Aragon speaks. In any case, the distinction between surrealism and realism is a clear one: and though Aragon admits, in *J'abats mon jeu*, that his present style has been to a degree formed by his surrealist past, he never fails to point out the great difference between the content of his present writings and the content of surrealist works.[1] However, as one follows the path of Aragon's "passage," there is a stronger feeling of continuity than would have been expected, especially along three main lines—the emphasis on the simple or the concrete (which he later identifies with the *real*), the insistence on freedom from limitation (obviously associated with the concept of revolt), and finally the fascination with the possibilities and the weakness of language.

THE POETRY OF THE REAL

From the beginning of his critical writing, Aragon attacks artificial complication and heaviness, preferring in every case the simple to the elaborate. In an article of 1918 on the film,[2] he maintains that theatrical *trompe-l'oeil* and the luxurious scenery of castles and the like should give way to the modern simplicity of the newspaper and the poster. The great advantage of the cinema is that its stark black and white facilitate an intense emotional concentration on a small area, developing a more subtle and deeper sensitivity on the part of the spectator than do the various trickeries and complicated verbalizing of the theater. The simplicity Aragon is fond of has nothing to do with naïveté—it is an aesthetic preference,

[1] *J'abats mon jeu*, p. 92. Here Aragon speaks warmly of his surrealist youth and of his friends, from whom he has been estranged by insults and attacks: "Not on my part, haven't you noticed? Not once in almost thirty years. . . . Life has separated us, set some against others. . . . They will never be able to prevent me from thinking of them as my friends. Even with the political chasm between us which I am not about to cross. . . ." (p. 28)

[2] "Du décor," *Le Film* (September 1918). Reprinted in *Le Point*, LIX (1962).

based on a highly sophisticated judgment. For him, the essential is always the "mystery of the everyday," which he later calls the poetry of the real or the lyricism of reality. To some extent the most successful parts of all his poetry, whether early or late, treat the simplest things in the simplest form.

If he speaks of the morning, it is not to eulogize the inspirational aspects of the dawn, but to enumerate the trivial and material things ("the first croissant / the black coffee you drink by the percolator / the fresh newspaper")[3] which are for him as proper to the realm of poetry as are the greater subjects like social protest and the celebration of love.

Aragon's interest in the collage technique is directly connected to his preference for the real and the simple. For him it is a protest with modest means against the rich sentimentality of an artificial literature and the decadent sensuousness of more established forms of art. In the years around 1930, when Aragon is attempting to make surrealist theory coincide with Marxism, he sees collage as a lower-class ("pauvre") rebellion against bourgeois taste, playing the same role as that of the cinema in relation to the theater. Even in his earliest article on collage (1923) he considers it a realistic revolt of the simple object against the carefully created *taste* of "cultured" people; their criteria of beauty are upset by the intrusion of the ill-mannered object as it ruins the elegance of all decoration, revealing the illusion of the artificial façade. His collection of essays on this subject (*Les Collages*, 1965) indicates the importance he attaches to the technique, which for him is the best single method of incorporating reality into representation. The fact that the collages include not only real objects but proverbs, quotations from other authors, posters, and so on, is an even more garish manifestation of the bad taste, irreverent humor, and sarcasm distressing to the delicate sensitivities he despises. His loathing for "delicate" mannerisms and mentality is made perfectly clear in his famous poem "Front rouge" where he gives a sarcastic description of Maxim's restaurant in 1931:

[3] *Le Roman inachevé* (Gallimard, 1956), p. 14.

Les boissons se prennent avec des pailles
Délicatesse
Il y a des fume-cigarettes entre la cigarette et l'homme . . .
Et du papier de soie autour des paquets
Et du papier autour du papier de soie[4]
(The drinks are sipped with straws
Delicacy
There are cigarette holders between the cigarette and the
man
And tissue paper around packages
And paper around the tissue paper).

The well-arranged or artistic backdrop hides all that matters under its sham beauty, the "peristyles of your ridiculous palaces."[5] Again, the collage technique strips away all these artificial refinements and disorients the mind so that it can study the real relationships between itself and the world.

Aragon further insults good taste by his insistence on the "poetic shiver" or the poetic emotion as the true sign of understanding rather than intellectual insight or any such standard criterion, and by his frequently sentimental tone, used purposely to irritate "people of culture" who are not demonstrative in public. He irritates them also, and in an equally calculated manner, by inserting lines of flat and ordinary language in his poetry as another form of collage. To serve the same purpose as the real objects in a collage, which show up the unreality of the painted ones surrounding them, he recommends the use in poems and plays of clichés or "automatic crystallizations"; they mock the apparently original but actually static assumptions with which they are juxtaposed and the audience who must judge.[6] (Alienation of the reader or

[4] *Persécuté-Persécuteur* (Editions Surréalistes, 1931), p. 7.
[5] *Ibid.*, p. 35.
[6] Aragon makes a careful study of Tzara's use of the collage in his early play, *Mouchoir de nuages*, which Aragon considers "the most remarkable dramatic image of modern art" after *Ubu roi* and *Les Mamelles de Tirésias*. (The play uses Shakespeare's *Hamlet* as a "quotation" or "secondary theme" in the complicated sense Aragon explains.) In an unpublished letter to Jacques Doucet (October 30, 1922), speaking of his *Vingt-cinq poèmes*, Tzara says: "In 1916 I

the writer, artistic distance, crisis in communication—whatever it is called and whether it is willed or involuntary, the separation of all the writers discussed here from at least the major part of their audience is an undeniable fact.) Aragon admires Hugo for having deliberately provoked the fury of "reasonable" people by choosing an extremely unpoetic first line for his *Cromwell*: "Demain, vingt-cinq juin mil six cent cinquante-sept." Hugo is also to be admired for making his poetry a poetry of ideas, itself unacceptable to people of taste, according to Aragon. The most obvious contrast between a hero of "realism" and an apologist of taste is that drawn between the theoretician of dandyism, Baudelaire, and the populist painter, Courbet, who was to disturb the harmony of all the comfortable forms and aesthetic habits of the century, "that ideal concert of old and perfect instruments." Baudelaire, the anti-Courbet as Aragon calls him, represents the worst of established criticism in its endeavor to bind the

---

tried to destroy literary genres. I introduced into the poems elements which would ordinarily be judged unsuitable, such as sentences from the newspaper, sounds and noises. These noises (which had nothing whatsoever in common with imitative sounds) were intended as the equivalent of the efforts of Picasso, Matisse, and Derain, who used in their paintings different *materials*."

The various advertisements, signs, menus, and word / picture-games which abound in *Le Paysan de Paris* can be considered another sort of collage, but placed here as a testimony to the marvelous:

> BONJOUR, CHER AMI!
>
> Avez-vous pris
>
> vos biscuits
>
> M O L A S S I N E ?

MOLASSINE $\left\{ \begin{array}{l} \text{dogs \&} \\ \text{puppy} \end{array} \right.$ biscuits

The reader of Robert Desnos will have noticed a slightly different use of signs in his *La Liberté ou l'amour*: the billboards, the picture of Bébé Cadum, the calendar pictured on the wall which stop the motion of the text repeatedly.

potential energy of the artist in a tight "corset of good paint-ing."[7]

A parenthetical observation should be made here—for Aragon the element of intellectual simplicity or purity often appears linked to an element of intellectual cruelty. When Aragon recommends that film makers should "whip the public," he is orienting the spectacle in the same direction as Artaud's Theater of Cruelty. Of course the images of revolution are often images of cruelty seen by its participants as a kind of purity: Aragon praises a German Communist poster of a clenched fist as a "knife that penetrates every heart," and even in a mainly lyrical book such as *Les Poètes*, he considers his poetry a "slap" against the night or a "slaughtering of the beast."[8] There is a remarkable passage in *Le Roman inachevé* in which the desire for dominance is linked to the desire to inflict mental and physical pain:

Ah faire un mal pareil aux brisures de l'os[9]

(Ah to inflict a suffering like the breaking of bones).

Aragon then explains in what sense he feels himself "the prisoner of forbidden things"—the qualities and actions forbidden by social convention are precisely those he finds most tempting since they would most clearly prove his freedom.

AGAINST THE LIMITS

Freedom from limitations and boundaries of any kind, while a principal goal of the surrealist revolution, is accompanied, very early in the movement, by an emphasis on a *system* of freedom. Aragon maintains in *La Révolution surréaliste* that where there is no philosophic system, the word "liberty" loses its sense. In this respect man is, he says, "perfectly determined": he *must* be free.

Aragon's earliest poetry (*Feu de joie, Le Mouvement perpétuel*) is based on his determination to shake off all restric-

---

[7] *L'Exemple de Courbet* (Editions Cercle d'art, 1952), p. 8.

[8] See also his discussion of the "élan de la gifle" (the force of the slap) in his *Matisse-en-France* (Fabiani, 1943).

[9] P. 176.

tions. In a speech of 1925 to Madrid students,[10] Aragon predicts that a revolution will be born from the union of love and poetry, and in the same year he writes "Les Débuts du fugitif," a poem of protest against the narrow limits imposed by time, space, habit, and by the expectations of others. The poem begins with despair at the "exécution capitale" of human freedom:

J'ai abandonné l'espoir à côté d'un mécanisme d'horlogerie
Comme la hache tranchait la dernière minute

(I abandoned hope beside a piece of clockwork
As the axe chopped off the last minute)

and moves toward a final defiant statement about present and future personal liberty:

Je m'échappe indéfiniment sous le chapeau de l'infini
Qu'on ne m'attende jamais à mes rendez-vous illusoires[11]

(Under the hat of the infinite I escape indefinitely
Let no one wait for me at my illusory meeting-places).

[10] "Chroniques," *La Révolution surréaliste*, No. 4, 1925.
[11] From *Le Mouvement perpétuel* (Gallimard, 1926). Closely associated with the theme of escape is the notion of the lie, or the mask: see, for example, *Les Voyageurs de l'impériale* (Gallimard, 1947), pp. 21, 32, etc. In view of the importance of the themes of facade, artificiality, sincerity, and dizziness in Aragon's poetry and prose, the poem "Sommeil de plomb," from *Le Mouvement perpétuel* is worth quoting:

A la voir on ne croirait pas la ville en carton ni le soir
Faux comme les prunelles des femmes et des amis les meilleurs
Quel danger je cours
. . .
Vertige le décor devient le visage de la vie
. . .
Comme tu mentais bien paysage de l'amour

(To look at them you would never believe the town or the evening
   to be made of cardboard
False like the eyes of women and of good friends
What a risk I run
. . .
Dizziness the setting becomes the face of life
. . .
How you lied convincingly countryside of love).

But alternating with the desire for unlimited freedom and with the threat of suffocation (a shrunken sky, false horizons, doors that will not open, and stars crowding down like flies on the earth to challenge all human motion), there is a decided nostalgia for what the poet has left behind ("let me look one last time," "Paradise all has been scattered") and an intense awareness of solitude and strangeness. Here too the theme of the simple and the concrete is stated: the snatch of a popular song comes from a street by the sea,[12] representing, like the real objects in a collage, a strong feeling for the actual and making a textural contrast to the more bizarre images of runaway horses laughing in elevators like humans and pianos put on the sidewalk to await the rain. These latter images serve, like the flight of the fugitive himself, as escapes from the limits of confining reality; since it is exactly these limits which the poet regrets during the course of the poem, the emotional oppositions and the oppositions of images parallel each other. The poem equals in complexity and sentimental depth any of the more famous of Aragon's later poems.

---

[12] Aragon makes frequent references to songs, explaining: "All music takes hold of me." No matter how banal the melody, it is a part of poetry. And it is always poetry itself, "le chant majeur," which must defend the "musique de l'être humain" against its oppressors. The "vieille chanson de France" heard outside in the poem "Zone libre" from *Le Crève-Coeur* (London, Editions Horizon—La France libre, 1942) has the simple purity of the song sung by the girl in "Les Débuts du fugitif" and makes an unhappy contrast with the vacuous sentimentality of the song in "Vingt ans après" from the same collection, where:

> L'ère des phrases mécaniques recommence
> L'homme dépose enfin l'orgueil et la romance
> Qui traîne sur sa lèvre est un air idiot
> Qu'il a trop entendu grâce à la radio. . . .

And in an essay on Shakespeare (Editions Cercle d'art, 1965), he laments: "Ah, songs aren't what they used to be," but still acknowledges the witness they bear to the character of the people, as the knob on the radio can be tuned to "another town, other loves." Compare Breton's statement (*Arts*, October 24-30, 1952), in a discussion with Reverdy and Ponge, that the popular song is "a nervy little beggar who speculates on the most syrupy and unworthy traits of the human soul," and, on the positive side, Eluard's celebration of poetry as song in his speech "La Poésie de circonstance" (II, 931).

Most important among the refusals characteristic of "Le Fugitif" is that of usual habits and expected attitudes. To continue the path one started out on yesterday is, for him, a betrayal of the future:

Comment pouvez-vous revêtir vos habits de la veille?

(How can you put on yesterday's clothes?).

As in *Le Paysan de Paris* (1926), the predominant tone is one of youthful exuberance in its opposition to the stolidity of middle age. It is with the same pride that Aragon had declared in 1925: "The age of metamorphosis has begun." The belief in the possibility of constant transformation and in the power of the human mind to change all things is essential to surrealist hope and is in large part responsible for its spirit. Later, in the years of the Resistance, Aragon's often quoted "Les Lilas et les roses" wistfully echoes the youthful era of change by its "month of flowering month of metamorphosis."[13] And in 1956 the poem "Le Vieil homme" marks the final step in the disillusion of age, where the present in all its intensity is either negated or replaced by the distance of memory, where the possibility of change has gone forever:

Le printemps qui revient est sans métamorphoses
Il ne m'apporte plus la lourdeur des lilas
Je crois me souvenir lorsque je sens les roses[14]

(The returning spring is without metamorphosis
It no longer brings me the heaviness of lilacs
I think I remember when I smell the roses).

The one hope for the aging writer is his work, since writing is for Aragon a process which constantly renews both vision and the poet. As if he wanted to remind himself and us of this, he directs much of his poetry to the young and addresses many of his books to them. Yet he remains bitterly conscious of his age, which has only widened the gap between himself

---

[13] *Le Crève-Coeur*, p. 25.

[14] *Le Roman inachevé*, p. 168. (Compare the *fixity* and the absence of lilacs and roses in "Le Paysage" of Desnos, quoted in Chapter 6.)

and others, himself and things. "Le Vieil homme" laments his feeling of separation from people, his loss of hearing and even of interest—and worst of all, the loss of his perception of the nuances and the movement of everyday reality:

Le jour n'a plus pour moi ses doux reflets changeants[15]

(No longer does the day have for me its gentle changing reflections).

There could be no more pathetic contrast with the youthful invocations of the "trouble," the "ivresse," and especially the "vertige du moderne" in *Le Paysan de Paris*. They were invoked in order to upset the staid placidity Aragon imagined in those who are no longer young and to counter exactly this loss of interest by the spectator in the external world. But even in *Le Paysan de Paris*, Aragon wonders for how long he can retain the feeling of the marvelous, and it is that very doubt, expressed as an ambiguous conclusion to the introductory section, which sets the book in a complicated frame, typically surrealist.

In almost Proustian terms, Aragon speaks in this same work of a "metaphysics of places," conducive to dreaming, to the sentiment of the strange or the *insolite* which alone is capable of producing *le frisson*, the sign of extreme emotion which accompanies for him all manifestations of the marvelous: "I take no step toward the past without experiencing again this feeling of the strange which used to come over me when I was still wonder itself, in a setting where for the first time there came to me the consciousness of an unexplained coherence and of its extensions in my heart." (p. 19) As the passage on doubt was a prediction of loss in the future, this contrasting passage implies the possible recovery by a return to the past, of the feeling lost.

Aragon never abandons the concept of *le vertige*, although it can be momentarily effaced, as it is in the poem of the old man: "dizziness forgotten." (The term *vertige* implies both rapidity—which Aragon sees as the distinguishing element

[15] *Ibid.*, p. 168.

of poetry, itself the quickest possible transmission of ideas—
and total involvement.) Even within the poem the distance
felt between the poet and the world does not last; in the pattern of alternation characteristic of the poetry of surrealists
and ex-surrealists alike, it continues:

> Le frisson d'autrefois revient dans mon absence
> Le jour au plus profond de moi reprend naissance[16]

> (Yesterday's shiver returns in my absence
> Day begins once more in my inmost self).

Thus there is no sense of unrelieved despair. The old man
remains a poet, surrounded by the simplicity of the real. And
even in early poems like "Les Débuts du fugitif," the poet
does not always seem at ease in the world. There also a sense
of *distance* ("Jusqu'à la senteur du soir enfin qui m'est étrangère") made a sharp contrast with the almost sensuous presence of the marvelous. Later in *Le Roman inachevé* he experiences a distance even from himself:

> J'écoute au fin fond de moi le bruit de mes propres pas
>   s'éteindre
> J'entends ma propre chanson qui se fatigue de se plaindre[17]

> (I listen to my footsteps dying out in my depths
> I hear my own song tiring of its complaint),

and in *Le Voyage de Hollande* (1964) he pictures his long
passage through life as an unending labyrinth "where I am
endlessly pursued by myself." This is no longer the "labyrinth
without a Minotaur" of *Le Paysan de Paris,* where the poet
was unified with himself, even if lost, and where he had chosen
his own marvelous maze—but a far more negative one.

Worse even than a division of personality for a man who
has always fought against separatism and for continuity is
the sensation of limit which returns to haunt him. In the
twenties the limits were chiefly exterior and, for that reason,
could be transgressed, at least by the imagination. Now they
are felt inside the poet himself. "Le Vieil homme" clearly rec-

---

[16] *Ibid.,* p. 170.   [17] *Ibid.,* p. 182.

ognizes that the faith in unlimited horizons and actions was a transitory one, as strong as youth but just as fleeting. Now the range of possibilities has narrowed together with the poet's enthusiasm for testing them:

Chaque jour autrement je connais mes limites.[18]

(Each day I discover my limits in a different way).

Only four years earlier, Aragon had warned of the stagnation threatening the man who remains within "reasonable" bounds:

Honte à qui trouve sa limite et à qui sa limite suffit[19]

(Shame to the man who finds his limit and for whom his limit is enough).

But he had at the same time confessed his own lack of energy and audacity, corresponding to the shortcomings of the world outside him which is badly set up and in which nothing has changed:

Le monde est mal fait mon coeur las[20]

(The world is ill arranged my heart tired).

The poet feels now more than ever that he has wasted his strength to no purpose, and that he no longer has the will to push beyond his ordinary habits and the limits of the apparent world into the difficult and elusive world of metamorphosis and the marvelous, where only the youthful can be at home. The pessimistic current which, for Aragon in these last years, always seems to go along with the pride of poetic creation, finds its ultimate expression in this stanza from the *Voyage de Hollande*:

Est-ce qu'il faut un jour arriver au bout de ce qu'on pense
Au bout de ce qu'on fut au bout de ce qu'on est perdre sens
De ce qu'on sent qu'on dit s'arrêter au beau milieu des
    phrases[21]

---

[18] *Ibid.*, p. 168. [19] *Les Poètes*, p. 151.
[20] *Ibid.*, p. 161.
[21] *Le Voyage de Hollande* (Seghers, 1964), p. 51.

(Must you reach one day the end of your thoughts
The end of what you were the end of what you are lose
   the sense
Of what you feel you are saying stop halfway through the
   sentence).

As the appetite for revolt and adventure abates, the poet's
power of language diminishes. The tragedy is double—first
the sense of profound interior limitation and then, far worse,
the consciousness of one's inability to rebel against it any
longer.

MADNESS AND LANGUAGE

Depending in some degree on the other themes (the lyricism of simplicity and the necessary revolt against limitation)
is the third of Aragon's preoccupations, the love of and despair of language itself. Aragon consistently takes all language, that of art as well as that of literature, *au tragique*;
a serious representation of the world, it cannot be toyed with.
At the beginning of *Télémaque* (1922) he quotes Kant on the
difficulty of expressing thought, and this concern never leaves
him. In 1924[22] he declares himself a nominalist, maintaining
that there is no thought beyond words, which is again part
of his reliance on the concrete. If a thing cannot be expressed,
he says, then it *is* not. Verbal images are therefore the only
basis of poetry, of metaphysics, and of all philosophy, three
things he makes exact equivalents of each other. All thought
in the concrete world centers on the *je* and on the particular,
individual idea, against the tendency of the century which
Aragon describes as leaning toward the abstract. His extreme reliance on the particular makes difficult any general
communication; in his Madrid talk of 1925 Aragon states
this on a personal level:

> What first overwhelms me is that here I cease to believe
> in the omnipotence of the word. I am stranded on this
> cliff which is your ear. You have not been moulded by my
> words, you have barely given your polite attention to my

22 In *Une Vague de rêves* (privately printed, 1924).

language. My words, gentlemen, are my reality. Each object, the light and yourselves, your bodies, only the name that I give to this slippery aspect of the idea wakes it within me to this true life that the same sounds do not arouse in you.[23]

Is this a real crisis or a rhetorical one? In Aragon's own theory there can be no merely verbal crisis, since he claims, in the speech just quoted, that his language *is* his reality. But in any case he is able to say once more of himself a year later: "I who believe more than anyone in the omnipotence of words."[24] What is certain is that he expresses apparently serious doubts as to the efficacy of language with a noticeable frequency throughout his life, in his essays, his poetry, and his novels. At times these doubts are expressed in a very low and personal key, and only touch on a sort of verbal incapability Aragon senses in himself when he speaks of the authors he admires; in both *A la lumière de Stendhal* and *J'abats mon jeu*, he claims to find his own laudatory remarks artificial and mannered.

Although he never says so explicitly, it is possible that the feeling of artificiality comes from too great a familiarity with the subject: Breton warns that the modern passion for reducing the unknown to the known leads to a great sterility of mind. Neither in Aragon's *Paysan de Paris*, nor in his famous *Traité du style*—the former written in praise of *le vertige* and *le merveilleux* observed in the world around him, and the latter, as they are felt in the surrealist experiments with language—is there the slightest suggestion of artificiality. The *Traité du style* opposes the mannerism and formulas of literature to style, which is the irreducible, the unfixable. Even free verse, a category like any other, is less free than surrealist writing, since the latter is unhampered by any classifi-

[23] Compare Tzara, *Faites vos jeux, Les Feuilles libres*, No. 32 (1923), p. 150: ". . . for we live in a family with our various selves piled up like seashells on the ocean floor. The words that we consider precise and related to established reality awake no response in the receiving brain."

[24] *La Révolution surréaliste* (June 15, 1926).

cation. To the fugitive from all limits it is the unpredictable nature of the surrealist enterprise which matters. In the surrealist experiments he sees the traces of a totally unfamiliar *mobile*, of value precisely because it is unknown: "It is into the quest of this unknown that those who are undertaking the present experiment have plunged." (p. 195) But as Aragon leaves experimentation for communication, it is no longer the unknown he seeks, rather the exact words to express the known. The initiative is now with him.

Still, he always refuses to cut off any work from the future. In *Blanche ou l'oubli* (1967), he defines the novel as "not what was but what could be, what could have been. The intermediate moment where the word is emptied of its first sense, open to the new meaning but not yet occupied. Availability." The latter notion, expressed by the inclusive term *disponibilité*, is one of the keys to surrealism.

The surrealist refuses to localize himself on one side or the other of ordinary contradictions; his insistence on holding them all concurrently within his vision and his language is the richest source for the strength of that language and that vision. Many of the most convincing and least artificial passages are descriptions of a crisis in the visual realm (Breton's "La crise de l'objet") or in the mental and linguistic realm, as in the following passage from *Le Paysan de Paris*, where the initial atmosphere of doubt yields to the consciousness of abstract polarities in their mutual annihilation, and then to the complete absorption of the contraries and of the momentum their clash creates within the poet himself:

A great crisis is born, an intense uneasiness which gradually becomes more precise. The beautiful, the good, the just, the true, the real . . . many other abstract words go bankrupt at the same moment. Their opposites, once preferred, soon merge with them. One single substance of the mind finally reduced in the universal melting pot. . . . I shall be unable to neglect anything, for I am the passage from the shadow to the light, I am at the same time the west and the dawn. I am a limit, a mark. Let everything

mix with the wind, here are all the words in my mouth.
(p. 137)

No better description could be given of Aragon's surrealist
writing, or of its theoretical basis. The state of crisis, closely
related to the *vertige* he cherishes and the necessary condition for the experience of the marvelous as he has defined it,
and the subsequent universal merging, seen as a simplifying
or a condensation of the opposing elements, are felt as an
unlimited and *enlarging* range of experience and of personal
potential ("unable to neglect anything"). Here he is himself
the path and the passage, terms which are later to take on
such importance for him, as he discusses the "seriousness" but
also the "logic" of passing from surrealism to "realism" in
J'abats mon jeu and in his *Entretiens*. And, instead of having
to transgress limits which others have set, he himself forms
the limit. Finally, the entire range of oppositions becomes
the source of poetic language, to which it gives momentum
and breadth.

But the very intensity of these polarities leads directly to
the notion of madness, a transition whose frequency has already been mentioned. This notion haunts all efforts at expression:

non mais regardez-moi ce fou . . .[25]

(will you just look at this madman . . .).

In *Le Roman inachevé*, the poet's reason threatens to give
way under the *range* of things he cannot express: the source
of his strength is at once the cause of the most fatal weakness.
The title of this long poem reflects the anguish of the line
quoted above: "s'arrêter au beau milieu des phrases"—continuity of thought and language depends on an assurance of
one's own comprehensibility. *Le Fou d'Elsa* (1963) starts as
poetry and ends with actual "folie"; *Le Voyage de Hollande*
contains an ironically well-ordered complaint of obsession,
deformation, and disorder:

[25] *Le Roman inachevé*, p. 179.

Je suis ce possédé qui joue à pigeon-vole
Les secrets sourds-muets de son coeur mis en croix
Et cherchant vainement le soleil des paroles
Autre chose toujours exprime qu'il ne croit
N'étant de rien miroir de tout faisant image
Je tiens avec les mains des propos de dément[26]

(I am a haunted man playing children's games
The deaf-mute secrets of his heart crucified
And seeking in vain the sun of words
Always conveying something he does not mean
Mirroring nothing presenting an image of everything
I speak with my hands like a fool).

In fact, the impossibility of rendering anything exactly makes
of each poet a madman in that his vision of perfection cannot
be realized; he can never hope to mirror exactly what he sets
out to represent but can only give a distorted *image* of it. Far
from the surrealist conception of madness as a heroic and
nonconventional vision, this madness is a pathetic and human
shortcoming, still heroic perhaps, but not *useful*. Aragon has
worked this theme into many forms; the most moving is one in
which he does not speak to us directly ("Je suis . . ."), but
shows us indirectly his own vision of himself in his unre-
markable and even useless meditations as they contrast with
the ideal renaissance of the poet and his poetry:

. . . ô forcené qui se débat chaque nuit dans les lieux
communs qu'il s'est construit les dilemmes abstraits

. . .

ô forcené qui partait pourtant à la recherche d'une autre
vie ô Croisé d'un rêve moderne au bout duquel il y avait
le contraire d'un sépulcre[27]

(. . . oh madman who threshes about each night in
the commonplaces he has made for himself in the abstract
dilemmas

. . .

oh madman who was nonetheless setting out in search of

---

[26] *Le Voyage de Hollande*, p. 13.
[27] *Le Roman inachevé*, p. 178.

another life oh Crusader of a modern dream at whose end
there was not a tomb but its opposite).

Here the distance represented by his use of the third person
precludes all traces of self-pity, which is not the case with
either the "je" or the "tu" form, since both the latter link
the observer and the observed. Aragon is making a decided
and courageous effort at objectivity; whether or not it can
be considered the practical opposite of the surrealist value
of *presence* is a more difficult question.

It is not intricate rhyme or meter which complicates Aragon's most interesting poems, but the variations of mood
behind their sometimes simple appearance. Only the war poems such as "Les Nuits" are unmixed in their steady gloom,
their insistence on falsity and darkness. ("I drink a milk like
ink and the noon / resembles the carbon of swamps"; "Oh
night of total eclipse at high noon / Sad like kings in their
photographs.") The early poem "Les Débuts du fugitif," for
instance, seemed at first glance to be a poem on liberty, and
yet what we remember from it with most clarity may be the
sense of loneliness and the brief image of a girl singing by
the sea.

For many of the surrealists and particularly for Aragon,
the parallel exaltation and deception, precision and inexacti-
tude of language is a matter of deep concern. His most significant study of language is itself a poem. *Les Poètes* might
be, judging by its title and appearance, a series of descriptions
of various poets, and there are in fact passages on Desnos,
on the Czech poet Nezval, and so on. Nevertheless the pages
where the young poet dreams of Prometheus, and those
where Don Quixote soliloquizes are not very different in tone
from the "Discours à la première personne." It seems to be
a poem on the various challenges of language and the difficulties of poetry, and so it is. But it is at the same time a deeper
statement and a more desperate one on the uselessness of all
speech: "Language loses its power beyond the halo of our
breath." If the poet fails to extend his vision of reality to
the reader, he has failed in his entire enterprise and wasted not
only his passion but his life: "and I say that I have devoted

most of my time to the passage from the image to the word
and vice versa." He has based his hope on the faithfulness
and the force of language, and the hope has occasionally been
rewarded; after calling things by a name that "resembled
them," but is not theirs, he suddenly finds the odd name
which does belong to them:

> Le linge de couleur qui sèche à la mansarde des mots.

> (The colored linen that hangs to dry in the attic window
> of words.)

But Don Quixote, another incarnation of the Crusader in
Le Roman inachevé, laments the serious difficulty discussed
above, which arises through the independence of poetic language from the poet and from his dream:

> . . . chaque parole n'est plus
> Ce qu'elle était mise en branle Elle dit autre chose que ce
> qu'elle dit . . . tout vocable porte
> Au delà de soi-même une signification de chute une force
> révélatrice
> Où ce que je ne dis pas perce en ce que je dis
> Où plus fort est l'entraînement des paroles que le rêve qui
> les précède.[28]

> (. . . each word is no longer
> (What it started out to be It means something other than
> what it says . . . each sound carries
> Beyond itself a sense of falling a revealing force
> Where the unsaid penetrates into what I say
> Where the lure of words is stronger than the dream before
> them.)

We know from the autobiographical passages in this volume
that Aragon has always demanded perfection in himself and
others and that he characteristically despairs of ever attaining
it. He retains from his surrealist beginnings the tendency to
violent fluctuations of optimism and pessimism obvious in
Breton and his friends, and these come naturally into play
when he speaks of this problem of linguistic fidelity and po-

[28] *Ibid.*, "La Chambre de Don Quichotte."

tentiality which seems in the long run to have concerned him more than any other. So that in spite of his doubts as to the exactitude of language and as to its comprehension by the people to whom it is addressed, he can still say confidently in this same poem:

> Je suis celui qui met de l'ordre en la demeure énorme des hommes . . .[29]

> (I am the one who puts in order the enormous dwelling of men . . .).

Language can be an instrument of ordering as it can be a manifestation of disorder. In some measure, the will to perfection compensates for imperfection, and enthusiasm, for clarity. *Le vertige* which Aragon says he looks for in all he reads is also found in the act of writing as is *le merveilleux*:

> Jamais je ne perdrai cet émerveillement
> Du langage
> Jamais je ne me réveillerai d'entre les mots.[30]

> (Never shall I lose this wonder
> At language
> Never shall I wake up from words.)

And yet the most revealing lines of this poetic treatise on poetry go far beyond the problems of fidelity and communication to touch on an even deeper difficulty:

> je donnerais ces vers que j'ai tant aimés pour ce lièvre qui court et saute sur le mur
> A quoi bon le dissimuler.[31]

> (I would give these verses that I have loved so much for that spot of sunshine running and leaping on the wall
> Why should I pretend otherwise.)

For the poetry of reality is found in reality itself and not in poetry. The marvelous cannot be grasped and so the poet,

[29] *Ibid.*, "Le Discours à la première personne."
[30] *Ibid.*, p. 164.
[31] *Ibid.*, p. 160. The translation of the word "lièvre" follows Aragon's own explanation.

more sober than mad, more captive than crusader, is restricted
to the passage from the image to the word; *le vertige* invoked
in *Le Paysan de Paris* and all through Aragon's later writings
runs the risk of becoming at some point just another "vertige
verbal," capable only of producing poetry's opposite—literature.[32]

LOVE AS *"EPREUVE"*

In *La Revue européenne* of 1925 (February 1), Aragon
writes at length on the notion of love; first of all, he says, it
has always distinguished him in his own eyes from the crowd.
And then: "It is a necessity of my nature always to be involved with a woman. I can do nothing about it. To possess a
woman is perhaps less precious to me than her image possessing my mind and my body day in day out."

For years Elsa has been the focus of Aragon's work, representing for him all that Mélusine does for the surrealists
who idealize "Woman" as the most irrational, and therefore
the most valuable, source of inspiration in an overlogical
age. Aragon says more recently, in his *Entretiens*, that the
moral battle against fascism in France has been closely allied
with the exaltation of "Woman," and that he fights (as Breton does) for the "preeminence of woman." Since he has also
kept his faith in the concrete, it is fitting that his poetry should

---

[32] The first surrealist periodical had been called *Littérature*, and
though there is some dispute as to how completely this title was a
mockery of the word—*Lits et ratures* (*Beds and scrapings*), as one
cover read, or *Lis tes ratures* (*Read your erasures*)—or whether it
may have been less of a revolt against tradition than a symptom of
the respect the surrealists still kept for Gide, Valéry, and so forth,
the conception of the title as a mocking one seems the more likely.
To support this view, Garaudy quotes in his *Itinéraire d'Aragon*
(Gallimard, 1961, p. 13) an unpublished manuscript of Aragon where
the search for a title is described: "The title *Nouveau monde* (*New
World*), given to a journal which has appeared since 1885, was abandoned. Paul Valéry proposed to replace it by *Littérature*, this word
understood by us in its derisive sense, but generally taken as the
vindication of what Verlaine disdained . . . was immediately decided
upon for its provoking, disagreeable, pretentious, skeletal side. . . .
What distinguishes the birth of *Littérature* is the birth of a still ob-
scure opposition to cubist taste, a defense against this revival of
grace."

not focus on the abstraction Woman, but on Elsa in particular. He gives her name to his poems, writes Masses in her honor, declares in his "Prose du bonheur et d'Elsa" (1955) that he has learned to see the world in her way:

> Je te dois tout je ne suis rien que ta poussière
> Chaque mot de mon chant c'est de toi qu'il venait
> . . .
> Ma gloire et ma grandeur sont d'être ton lierre
> . . .
> Je ne suis que ton ombre et ta menue-monnaie.[33]

> (I owe everything to you I am but your dust
> Each word of my song came from you
> . . .
> I draw my pride and my grandeur from being your ivy
> . . .
> I am only your shadow and your small change.)

In *Elsa* (1959), he describes himself as the faithful black dog who has been at her heels for thirty years, taking refuge in the shade of her erect stature, his thought the shadow of hers. In 1964 (*Vita di Madonna Elsa*) he insists that he is her "scène" and her "théâtre," while she is his only landscape. The reader may feel that these expressions are too self-consciously humbling to be the straightforward translation of genuine sentiment, or that the sentiment is so exaggerated as to be improbable. This is one among many difficulties in the study of Aragon, but he claims to fear that his love poems will be read symbolically instead of literally, as they are meant; consequently, if we are to take him at his word, we must accept the poems as they stand. An author who entitles his autobiography *I Show My Hand* is making an explicit claim to sincerity. And even if we should remain skeptical, we must admit that genuine feeling can coexist with a poetic use of that feeling, the consciousness of one's attitude being in no way a *limitation* on that attitude. Whether or not Aragon or any poet is justified in using rhetoric for the conveying of

---

[33] In *Le Roman inachevé*, p. 237.

emotion, whether claims to sincerity are in this case valid or, if not, whether they are valid as a replacement for sincerity, none of this has any bearing on the poetry as we read it.

For Aragon, Elsa is a moral and intellectual guide; she has helped him break the ties to his past and given him, most important of all, "the new taste of a language of high noon." When he has despaired of language, she has encouraged him: "Let your poetry be hope." And still, by 1959, there frequently appears in his poems about her a kind of unhappiness. A writer herself, she leaves him to go off into a world of creation in no way linked to his:[34] there is, he says, no passport for him to her dreams, and her literary creations are the beings of her flesh, the products of a childbearing she undertakes apart from and even "against" him. Elsa is the cause of his poetic journey "par le pays de nulle part" (through the country of nowhere) and the only reassurance for his self-doubting; when she turns away to her own reading or dreaming, he is overcome by jealousy and fear:

Je tombe je me perds j'étouffe je me tue
. . .
J'ai peur de la contrée où les songes t'emmènent[35]

[34] Compare the description of Blanche in *Blanche ou l'oubli*: "I had become certain of this: she was writing *against me*" (p. 357). But there is now appearing a re-edition of both their works, with alternating volumes.

[35] *Le Voyage de Hollande*, p. 13. Compare *La Mise à mort* (Gallimard, 1965), where the narrator loses his image in the mirror while listening to his wife, a famous singer—as if her creation denied his real self and put in its place a new image of him: "I am convinced that as long as I stick to this image of me that she has imagined, I have almost nothing to fear" (p. 14). This novel, like *Blanche ou l'oubli* of 1967, is centered on the theme of the writer's eternal search for his true image in his writings ("If Anthoine looks for himself in mirrors—and all books are mirrors for him—I have eyes to see him living, such as he is, such as he was," says the wife). Compare Aragon's view of death as the absence of reflection in *Il ne m'est Paris que d'Elsa* of 1964: "Cette absence à jamais de moi dans le coeur profond des miroirs" / (My eternal absence from the depth of mirrors). Accompanying this theme, and connected with it, are the themes of reality and artificiality, and the theme of madness at the close of the book: "il vous a aimé *à la folie*" (he loved you to the point of *madness*), which is a rather precious reference to Aragon's own long poem, *Le Fou d'Elsa*.

(I fall I am lost I suffocate I kill myself
. . .
I am afraid of the country where dreams carry you off).

And in *Le Fou d'Elsa*, Aragon, here a madman less from
the fascination of language than from that of love, succumbs
to a despairing solitude he has both chosen and been forced
into. The poem which he creates denies him, and his sentiment causes him to wipe out all shadow and all "trace" of
himself:

> Maintenant je garderai pour moi mes constellations
>   noires . . .
> Où ferais-je mieux exercice de ne plus être qu'en ce poème
>   qui me nie[36]

> (Now I shall keep to myself my black constellations . . .
> What better practice for non-being than this poem that
>   denies me).

The "nuit de nous" he laments here is closer to the despairing
poem entitled "Night at High Noon" than to the exultation in
"a language of high noon." The poem negates the "being"
of the poet and the meaning of his poetic journey, now seen as
having been undertaken to no avail.

Since, for the reasons mentioned above, we cannot determine or even discuss whether this is jealousy, the pose of
jealousy, or a combination of both, we have to take seriously
the sadness here and the solitude it inflicts. It is odd that the
negative counterpart of Aragon's positive and more obvious
side should come out most clearly in this particular context,
but such a clear duality of sentiment is to be expected from
all the poets discussed.

The following poem, also from *Le Voyage de Hollande*, is
a poem of negation underlying an apparently tranquil poem
of love:

> Mon coeur battait comme une voile dans ta voix
> C'était un soir de toi quand les portes sont closes

[36] *Le Fou d'Elsa* (Gallimard, 1963), p. 413.

Et comme un vêtement sur la chaise repose
Tout le long passé nu des choses que l'on voit

C'était un soir pareil à tous les soirs absents
Quand le monde a de tout mémoire machinale
Il est trop tard déjà pour lire le journal
On n'entend plus la voix que de son propre sang

Il saigne quelque part un sanglot de jardin
Ou peut-être c'était un chien d'inquiétude
L'oreille longuement fait du silence étude
J'écoute sur mon coude et voici que soudain

Tu rêves.[37]

(My heart was flapping like a sail in your voice
It was an evening of you when the doors are closed
And like clothing on the chair
Rests all the long naked past of the things one sees

It was an evening like all the absent ones
When the world mechanically remembers everything
It is already too late to read the paper
One hears no voice but his own blood's

Somewhere a garden sob is bleeding
Or else a dog's uneasy sound
The ear studies the silence at length
I listen propped on my elbow and suddenly

You are dreaming.)

At first this appears to be a calmly romantic description of
an evening spent in quiet intimacy between two people happy
in each other's company: doors closed on the outside world,
the activity of the past put aside, the poet simply listening
to the silence after the outside noise (the vagueness of the
"quelque part" where the disturbance takes place deliberately
contrasted with the precise stillness of his room.) In this interpretation, the final "Tu rêves" is a perfect and gentle ending to a gentle poem—after the "soudain," anything might
have happened to upset the evening, but instead, Elsa has

[37] From "Du peu de mots d'aimer," *Le Voyage de Hollande.*

drifted off to sleep, simply transferring the peaceful atmosphere to another plane.

Looked at more closely, however, the poem reveals anything but a normal and peaceful atmosphere. Already in the
first line, because of the change forced on us when the ordinary "my heart was beating" becomes the unsettling image
of a sail *flapping* as if uncontrolled in the wind of the other's
voice, the reader is ill at ease. Throughout this "soir de toi"
the poet takes a completely passive role, as he does in saying
"I am forever your stage." The double nakedness of the
"passé nu," itself laid aside like a piece of clothing, is really
his—he no longer sees, reads, or talks. The personal pronouns
referring to him ("Mon coeur," "j'écoute") are all absorbed
either in the indefinite "l'on," "il," or in the predominance of
the other ("ta voix," "tu rêves") just as the unique quality
of the evening which could have redeemed it is denied by its
identification with all the preceding evenings just like it. Even
the sound heard outside is associated with bleeding, sobbing,
and anguish. Inside, the strong voice in the first line gave way
to the pathetic solitude of the poet in the eighth line; and
now, as a final culmination of the long series of negatives
and passives, while the poet, in a totally helpless attitude, lis-
tens to the unquiet stillness which has taken on a threatening
quality, Elsa turns away altogether. Since there is no indica-
tion of gender, of course it could be either who turns away
from the other; but we have all the other passages to confirm
this one. Elsa turns away from the unquiet stillness and from
the intimacy. For as a dreamer, she is *essentially* absent both
from the poet and the poem.

In his strange and self-conscious passivity before the absence or the presence of Elsa, Aragon seems at times less real
than she; it is almost as if she played the role of a "real" object in the collages he describes, placed there in order to
signal his own *pose* of reality. Does he place her in all his poetry as a simple tribute to her importance for him, in sincere
self-criticism, in a pose of self-criticism, or because he needs
a firmer center for his poetry than he himself can be?

Aragon has opened a question which is difficult to close. If he says that the poetic image is the sum of present and future knowledge and then casts doubt on the language by which that image is expressed and on the possibility of sharing it with another person, no matter how close the relationship, then neither the knowledge nor the poet can be of much use. "The feeling of uselessness . . . ," "I shall have been useful," "We will not have been useful": the problem so often debated by Aragon is never resolved.[38] But it is evident that in his critical works Aragon's answer is more clearly affirmative than in his autobiographical poetry. After all, the artist written on cannot turn away; Stendhal and Matisse, Hugo and Courbet are not only realists themselves, they are also guarantees of the reality of art. In the same way, Aragon's poetry on political themes—the greatness of France or of the Party, the injustice of the war in Indochina (and later Vietnam) or in Korea—shows no lack of affirmation because there is no questioning of language or of the poet's usefulness. When language is stating convictions firmly held, its power is never put in doubt by the poet, though the poetry itself is often exceedingly weak. But this is a vicious circle: when the subjects become more tenuous (that is, more personal) than the ones just mentioned, the danger is that the *vertige* safely experienced in the writings of others may challenge personal identity itself:

J'ai dépassé le lieu de moi-même le lieu d'être moi[39]

(I have gone beyond the place of myself the place to be myself).

This line of 1964 echoes the cry of *Le Paysan de Paris*: "What mattered to me so much, my poor certainty, in this great dizzi-

---

[38] This moral concern haunts all the surrealists. Compare Breton, *Les Vases communicants* (Gallimard, 1955), p. 113: "What self-complacency you would have to have, to think, on the intellectual plane, that you have accomplished something! Great philosophers, great poets, great revolutionaries, great lovers: I know. But if you aren't sure of ever attaining that greatness, what can you do to be simply *a man*? How do you justify the place you take up in your eating, drinking, dressing, sleeping?" This is in no way an *artificial* humility.

[39] *Le Voyage de Hollande*, p. 52.

ness where the consciousness feels itself to be just a landing in the abyss, what has it become? . . . A lost footing is never found again."[40]

It is significant that the general interior doubt of contemporary man which Aragon describes as so pathetic in some of his essays on art[41] should show through exactly in his own most personal poetry. Elsa is there to affirm the worth of the poetry and of the poet, and frequently she does; but also in other moments, she serves as a test for the success of the poetic image, apparently bearing a crucial testimony to "the painter's despair in front of reality." Just because Aragon has made her so real and so present even in her absence, when she turns away it is as if reality itself had turned away from the poet.

THE ILLUSION TRANSCENDED:
ARAGON'S FINAL ESCAPE

From Aragon "surréaliste," Aragon "réaliste" inherits a passion for language ("My words, gentlemen, are my reality") and a vivid sensitivity to its attractions and its dangers. If

---

[40] *Le Paysan de Paris* (Gallimard, 1926), p. 134.

[41] In his introductory essay to *Les Dessins de Fougeron* (Les Treize Epis, 1947) Aragon deplores the perverse taste that inclines us now more toward unfinished sketches than toward completed paintings, so that our critical sense is mostly occupied with decomposition and analysis rather than with construction and synthesis. He thinks nostalgically of the fervor of Dada, wishing there could be another movement with its energy to overturn the present values of art. Dada, he says, would be in its unsophisticated, undifferentiating negation a purer force than the insidious and corrupting interior doubt that in 1947 menaces the future of art. (He made these remarks, of course, before the advent of Pop or neo-Dada art.) Our negative aesthetic values he sees as symptomatic of our decadence of spirit, and what is worse, they implicate us in a graver future decadence. There have always been elements in the society exterior to the artist which tried to break down his creative will, but never before has there been such an interior suspicion of the worth of art. This situation must, he says, be taken seriously and not simply relegated to the aesthetic realm where it becomes the province only of artists and their critics. Picasso is an obvious model for Aragon's positive approach to criticism and his total involvement in the language of art, since, as Aragon explains, Picasso's artistic rebellion is waged precisely against interior doubt and against a superficial *manner* that leaves life untouched.

the extent or the precision of the verbal force is in some way doubted, his own sense of identity is threatened. Compensating for this lonely passion is an opposing one, for action in common, also inherited from surrealism. The sense of the concrete on which Aragon based his surrealist philosophy continues to serve as a basis for his poetry and his thought: *real* objects or *signs* of the real (see note 6), phrases from other poets (or close allusions, "How narrow the sky is at the end of the day"),[42] and quotations from Elsa's novels are inserted in his poems, lending them support in the exterior world, justifying by their presence his sense of the "everyday marvelous" and of the particular as superior to the abstract. And it is his reliance on the image, the form of the concrete central to the poetic theory of both surrealism and realism, that constitutes the main guideline to his "passage." Aragon retains the surrealist theory of language according to which the poetic image is at once the résumé of present knowledge and the prediction of future knowledge, the principal link between the mind and the world: "Poetry enables me to attain reality directly, by a kind of shortcut. Poetic emotion is the sign of knowledge grasped, of a consciousness which travels nonstop."[43] Writing, for the surrealist, leads to knowing: in *Le Con d'Irène* (1928), Aragon said explicitly that he never thought without writing, that writing was, in fact, his only way of thinking. That has been true for him ever since.

The elements which separate him from the surrealists are more political than poetic. It is in order to serve a specific cause that he chooses to use rhymed verse and traditional forms, more easily comprehensible to all. He quotes, as do all the surrealists, Lautréamont's famous statement: "Personal

---

[42] See Baudelaire's *Le Voyage*:

Ah! que le monde est grand à la clarté des lampes!
Aux yeux du souvenir que le monde est petit!

(Ah! how large the world is in the light of lamps!
In the eyes of memory how the world is small!)

[43] "Chronique du Bel Canto," *Europe*, No. 13 (January 1947), p. 109. Compare Tzara's idea of poetry as an *act* and as a way of knowledge (*moyen de connaissance*) in his *Grains et issues* (Denoël et Steele, 1935).

poetry has had its time of trickery and of relative contortions." But is *Les Poètes* really less personal a poem than "Les Débuts du fugitif"? He champions Lautréamont's positive *Poésies* against the unhappy romanticism of *Les Chants de Maldoror*—but Breton himself stands against contemporary *misérabilisme* and prefers "positive" images to "negative" ones. It is true that Aragon left the surrealist advocacy of the revolutionary power of words, images, and moral positions, for that of a party doctrine. But the surrealist revolution is always intended to affect a wider realm than the realm of language: compare the relative positions of the surrealists and the Communist Party on the 1968 events in France. All the themes of surrealism remain in Aragon's late works: the protest against all limitations, exterior and interior, including the attempt to transcend oneself ("se dépasser") in the exaltation of woman; the passion for the particular, the real, and the concrete; and the incorporation in them of creative dreaming. In this context, the emphasis placed on Elsa's dream:

> . . . voici que soudain
> Tu rêves

takes on once more the positive force that the poet's jealousy and loneliness had seemed to remove from it. And his statement: "J'ai dépassé le lieu de moi-même le lieu d'être moi" may be seen from a less simplistic point of view than before as the ideal position for a surrealist poet—to transcend the obvious limits of personality into the unlimited imagination. Here the uncertainties as to the validity of language are no longer obsessive, since the communication of the dream is less important than the simple celebration of the dreamer and of the act of dreaming. Breton celebrates *Nadja*, but she remains alone; Aragon celebrates Elsa and her creations, but in the moment of creating, she is a stranger to him. We do not see her doubts, only her strength which *appears* to deny him.

In his fondness for allusions, which he shares with past and present surrealists, Aragon is perhaps suggesting a parallel—that we can no more follow him in his "passage" and in the intimacy of his creative work than he can follow Elsa, although we *seem* to be able to do so through his own indications. The author of *J'abats mon jeu* may not be so unlike "Le fugitif":

Je m'échappe indéfiniment . . .
Qu'on ne m'attende jamais à mes rendez-vous illusoires.

One might conclude that the essential duality in the work of Aragon is not an obvious one, but an implicit one, of which the poet himself is certainly aware; the distance lies not between one area of his thought and another, not between his theory and his verse, but between himself and his appearance or his double.

ANDRE BRETON

*J'irai aujourd'hui jusqu'à dire, quand le surréalisme à son
tour comme toute chose, s'est "classé," est devenu à la mode,
entré dans les anthologies, qu'on ne rend pas justice à André
Breton, comme poète, et pour la prose qu'il écrit. On ne dit
pas, ce qui est pourtant vrai, tandis que n'importe qui,
n'importe quoi est porté aux nues, que ce langage aura été
l'un des plus purs qu'on ait écrit dans notre pays. Même s'il
aura trop souvent servi à ce contre quoi je donnerais ma vie.*
—ARAGON, *J'abats mon jeu*

POETRY AS FUSION AND EXTENSION

While poetry is, for Aragon, a way of knowledge, it is for
Breton a miraculous widening of experience and an "exaltation" of life. The famous statement on surrealist language
which Breton calls "Les Mots sans rides" (1924) demands
that the full significance of language and its essential youthfulness be restored, so that it can intensify and expand everything it touches. It is not simply a matter of juxtaposing the
words to create new elements, but of rejuvenating the word
itself. All the surrealist word games, puns, anagrams, and
aphorisms with double meanings are part of this attempt to
heighten the power of language and to widen its scope.

Along with the word play goes the play of images, the
goal of both being "to multiply the short-circuits," as Breton

says in the second manifesto (1930), that is, to sabotage as frequently and as definitively as possible the usual "realistic insanities" and to show what is on the other side of the accepted reality. The surrealist image is necessarily shocking— it destroys the conventional laws of association and logic, so that the objects which compose it, instead of seeming to fit side by side naturally and normally, "shriek at finding themselves together." But the same electrical force that splits up the habitual relationships of the ordinary world has the power to fuse all that has previously been separate.[1] Breton will frequently use the metaphor of electricity in his theoretical writings, with all its implications of intensity, shock, fusion, and a highly dramatic quality proper to surrealism. He thinks of poetry as a "conductor of mental electricity" and his criterion for the success of art is the achievement of a particular "fusion of the mind and the heart in a verbal or plastic mold which shows itself in some way to be electrically appropriate to it."[2]

If the surrealist image must be so intense as to be shocking, it must also be new, not only to the observer or reader but to the artist or poet himself. The certain way to fall out of surrealist grace is to lose one's power of vision and then capitalize on an earlier originality, as do di Chirico and Dali. For art to be a constantly destructive and revivifying force, it must reject its own former discoveries as persistently as it rejects "normal" or unchanging modes of thought. Anything once seen is no longer vital, anything once known can no longer seem miraculous. The task of the artistic eye and the poetic imagination is to perceive and express only novel relationships between the most heterogeneous entities and thus destroy forever "the false laws of conventional juxtaposition."[3] There is no reason to assume that after the pear comes the

[1] Just as the image can miraculously fuse together the most opposed entities, the man to whom an extraordinary (that is, surrealist) imagination has been given acts as the mediator between hostile forces. See Breton's essay on Max Ernst (*Le Surréalisme et la peinture*, Gallimard, 1965).

[2] *La Clé des champs* (Editions du Sagittaire, 1953), p. 49.

[3] *Le Surréalisme et la peinture*, p. 200.

apple, or after the lobster, the spidercrab. Why not confuse these laws? Why should we not hope that some totally unexpected thing might appear instead, to show up the limits of the traditional categorizations? Breton demands at this point "the free and unlimited play of analogies," the only possible key to the mental prison in which we have shut ourselves. Again, the term "play" emphasizes the mobility implied in analogical perception.

What is perhaps Breton's most interesting statement of the value of art occurs in his essay on Arshile Gorky. Without sentimentalism of vocabulary or overblown rhetoric, the surrealist use of analogy is forcefully described, and naturalistic or "inventory" art is rejected. Breton makes it very clear that he includes in this rejection the direct picturing of any object, even if it comes from a vivid oneiric memory. The goal is always to create a new kind of vision, not to transcribe a vision already glimpsed. Nor is a startling technique an excuse for an imitative subject matter:

> I say that the eye is not *open* as long as it limits itself to the passive role of a mirror—even if the transparency of that mirror offers some interesting peculiarity: exceptionally limpid, or sparkling, or bubbling or faceted. . . . It was created for the purpose of throwing a line, of laying down a conduit[4] between things of the most heterogeneous appearance. This line, pliable in the extreme, should enable one to grasp in a minimum of time the relationships which link, with no continuity to explain them, innumerable physical and mental structures.[5]

All of this holds true for the art of literature, and this theory of analogy, of multiplicity, and of unity is the basis for all surrealist art. It is an art which unites without reducing, an art in which the linkings are necessarily spontaneous and generative of other linkings. The idea of art as a simple and

[4] Compare with Tzara's concept of the "images conductrices" or conduit images. The theory of *linking* is of primary importance in surrealist writings (see Introduction).

[5] *Le Surréalisme et la peinture*, p. 199.

irresponsible mirror is of course just as violently opposed by Aragon, who claims, in "A la lumière de Stendhal," that Stendhal's famous passage on that subject was only a cover for his real audacity. According to both Breton and Aragon, even the most accurate reflection is not true art, since it is neither creative nor dynamic.

Breton's essay on the artist Matta explains why our world is particularly appropriate to poetic recreation by analogy. We have new values and a new space; corrupted charlatans like Dali profit from this with facile brilliance, but Matta pictures far more seriously "the disintegration of exterior aspects; because, for the man who knows how to see, all these aspects are *open*, open not only like Cézanne's apple to the light but to everything else, *including the other opaque bodies*, because they are constantly ready to fuse, because in this fusion *alone* can a key be cut which is the *only* master key to life."[6] Such a fusion can only take place in an atmosphere of complete animism, where nothing is old or static, since the artist, his medium, and the world he remakes are all constantly changing. In the new universe where the law of chance has replaced the law of causality and where all possible events tend to become probable, every conflict is eventually resolved. Matta's control over his medium is equivalent to possession of the essential secret of reality. Instead of the traditional picture of a body in relation to surrounding bodies, Matta reveals interior man in all his sudden possibilities, and the revelation itself enables the possibilities to be more fully realized. In the new space, the new artist is never tempted, for instance, to copy a landscape in different lights like the impressionists, whom Breton ridicules for their "deadly boring variations on the exterior image"; he feels compelled instead to impose the form of his interior vision on what actually surrounds him. Breton quotes Reverdy: "Creation is a movement from the interior to the exterior and not from the exterior over the facade." Breton's poems, even the first ones, written long before his theories on art were formulated, show the same traits he will require of all surrealist poets and

[6] *Ibid.*, p. 187.

artists. The interplay of words and images is complex, particularly in the techniques of fusion and generation of new words and images, and the poems are in no way descriptive of any conventional vision of reality. It is as if Breton himself had already his *modèle intérieur*, later to be exteriorized into surrealist theory, his original poetic personality determining to a great extent the character of the movement he was to lead.[7]

The short prose poem called "Age" (1916) is typical of Breton's earliest poetry. Some of the other poems in the collection *Mont de piété* are like Mallarmé in tone, or like Valéry; this one is closer to Rimbaud, beginning: "Aube, adieu! Je sors du bois hanté, j'affronte les routes, croix torrides." / (Dawn, farewell! I leave the haunted woods, I brave the highways, sweltering crosses). But the images already show the striking juxtapositions Breton discusses in his article on Ernst:

[7] A further thing to be noticed besides the variations on the surrealist image and perception in Breton's early poetry is that the gravity of the poet's personality carries over occasionally into his verse. Near the end of the poem "Tournesol," well known because Breton quotes it later as a prediction he unconsciously made of future events, comes a significant line:

Je ne suis le jouet d'aucune puissance sensorielle . . .

(I am not the plaything of any sensual power . . .).

Everything, despite its frivolous appearance, is to be taken seriously. When he says in "Les Mots sans rides" that "Words have finished playing. They are making love," Breton is fighting as he always does against any possibility that his and his friends' poetry be considered in any way linked with "l'art pour l'art," or play for play's sake. We know very well that the surrealist games are played in earnest, and how Breton always insisted on rules and on consequence. Surrealist play can never be gratuitous, it is always to an end. Passive submission to the dictates of the subconscious is serious and valuable because it is supposed to be revelatory of deep and repressed desires, but the weakness of character implied in submission to one's senses ("le jouet") was abhorrent to Breton. It has been pointed out to what extent game is an essential part of surrealism, and a continuing theme in all these poets: "Faites vos jeux"; "J'abats mon jeu." It must, however, always be taken in earnest and not just in fun; this is also true of "la fête," as in the expression "The poem must be a feast of the intellect." Surrealist theory emphasizes spontaneity and freedom, and yet they are always accompanied by a grave consciousness of responsibility.

Chemises caillées sur la chaise. Un chapeau de soie
inaugure de reflets ma poursuite. Homme . . . Une glace
te venge et vaincu me traite en habit ôté. L'instant revient
patiner la chair.

Maisons, je m'affranchis de parois sèches. On secoue!
Un lit tendre est plaisanté de couronnes.

Atteins la poésie accablante des paliers.[8]

(Shirts clotted on the chair. A silk hat starts off my chase
with its reflections. Man . . . A mirror avenges you and
treats me as a conquered prey, naked. The moment returns to cast a patina on the flesh.

Houses, I free myself from dry walls. Someone is shak-
ing something! A tender bed is mocked with crowns.

Reach the exhausting poetry of landings.)

Perhaps the images make more "sense" and are more obviously linked than will be the case in his later poems. Shirts
thrown on a chair in heaps are not unlike clotted cream, the
tightly stretched silk of his hat can reflect him as the mirror
does and he has indeed taken off his shirt and hat ("habit
ôté"). But "l'instant revient patiner la chair" is a good example of one of the forms of the surrealist image Breton will
later describe, that in which an abstract thing ("l'instant")
is put in a matter-of-fact combination with a tangible object
("la chair"). That the brief moment can bestow the patina
of age (as in the title) to the bare flesh as if it were a statue,
is as unlikely as the contrast between "Homme" and the
slightly undignified "poursuite."

"Maisons, je m'affranchis" repeats the lofty tone of "Aube, adieu! Je sors. . . ." But dry walls are the exact opposite
of the traditional (and trite) haunted woods; and in the pun-
ning spirit of Dada and surrealism, they are the prosaic end-
product of the "bois." Similarly, "On secoue!" is as impersonal and down-to-earth as the "j'affronte les routes" of the
first line is proud and lyrical; it is also a sort of nasalized
version of "Au secours!" (Help!) or a pseudo-pun. The

---

[8] In the collection: *Poèmes* (Gallimard, 1948).

"plaisanté" of the next image introduces a joke cruel or customary, depending on the sense of the "couronnes": either they are literally crowns whose spikes puncture the "tendre" bed and its occupant, or they are simply the traditional boughs (wreaths) placed on the nuptial bed. Just as the surrealist image is a "strong" one if the components are greatly removed from each other, so this is a strong pun, since the two meanings of pain and of ornament are totally opposite to each other in feeling but united in the obvious Freudian sense also congenial to surrealistic thought. "Paliers" in the last line offers another stable everyday element —contrasting with the lyricism of the woods, the fountains, and the necklace of bubbles in the first part of the poem, are the more commonplace shirts, chair, mirror, house, bed, and staircase of the second part. Fleeing (or chasing?) his naked reflection and the dry walls and the probably uncomfortable bed, the man should reach the landing, ordinarily a place of rest or at least of stability; is "la poésie accablante" ironic or is it a genuinely overwhelming sensitivity to the poetic? The reader is already put off by the switches in personality—if the "je" of the beginning and of "ma poursuite" in the second part observes the shirts and the mirrored reflections, does "Homme" refer to the reflected self? Does this sufficiently explain the change from "te venge" to "me traite" as the change from the man in the mirror to the man before the mirror? And he will certainly not know whether to interpret "Atteins" as a serious or mock command, addressed to himself or to the man in the poem. And worst of all, this complex assault on our reason is couched in a deliberately frivolous style, full of exaggerated alliterations (aube, adieu!; chemises, chaise, chapeau, chair; caillées, couronnes; venge, vaincu; poursuite, patiner, parois, plaisanté, poésie, paliers). The poem is just as complicated, as irrational, and as alienating to the reader as any later poem, and perhaps more so. Most of Breton's early poetry lacks the sentimental undertone of his more famous work, but it is no less a demonstration of many-level vision and language. It is surrealist in form if not in content.

"Plutôt la vie," in the 1923 collection *Clair de terre*, shows the same fondness for double meanings as the poem just discussed. Surrealist play at its best is supposed to produce in the reader an involuntary sense of surprise which is disturbing to his ordinary perception of the universe and to his ordinary verbal framework. "Clair de terre" replaces the ordinary "clair de lune" as "plutôt la vie" replaces the ordinary "plutôt la mort," so that the positive present terms substitute for the distant clichés. The poem contains many such tricks:

Plutôt la vie que ces établissements thermaux
Où le service est fait par des colliers
Plutôt la vie défavorable et longue
Quand les livres se refermeraient ici sur des rayons moins
    doux
(Rather life than these thermal establishments
Where necklaces wait on you
Rather life long and unfavorable
Even if the books were to close here on shelves not so
    soft).

The nightmare world to which even life is preferable is made up of things serving the wrong purpose, of necklaces (a half-pun on students, "écoliers") doing the housework and soft bookshelves holding up the books, the latter image having the same disquieting effect as the soft watches of Dali, Méret Oppenheim's fur teacup, Man Ray's nail-studded iron, or "these overripe stones" ("ces pierres blettes") we are forced to imagine earlier in the poem. To introduce the most uncomfortable images by a "these" is to engage the reader in the poem, to make him consider at close range the stones turning soft like fruit. The qualities by which we ordinarily define our universe, like the hardness of stones and the stability of bookshelves, have given way to less stable qualities suited to the new space where, says Breton in his article on Matta, there is "a constant interchange of the visual and the visionary." If the poet sees the stones as soft, they *are* potentially soft. In his optimistic essay "Il y aura une fois" which introduces the poems of *Le Poisson soluble*, Breton states the credo of the surrealists: "the imaginary is what tends to become the real." The *tension* between the imaginary and the real furnishes the power for the surrealist image.

The state of grace surrealism detects in children, madmen, and primitives is this complete fusion of the mind and the world usually missing in the sane or cultivated adult mind. Since whatever the child thinks, already *is* for him, he lives always in an atmosphere of directness which is the envy and the goal of the surrealist creator. The reader of surrealist texts is forced to participate in the word play and the image play as fully as the poet if he does not wish to be excluded from the world newly created by the childlike vision of surrealist poetry.

DOUBLING AND DISTANCE

In *Les Vases communicants* (1932) there are three images of primary importance. There is the optimistic image of the constantly widening circle of possibilities, including and conferring unlimited expansion upon everything that exists; the explanatory image of the communicating vessels itself, with the secondary image of a capillary tissue connecting the interior world to the exterior world; and the most essential and most complex image of two men, one consciously immobile at the center of the whirlwind ("Removed from the contingencies of time and place, he really appears to be the pivot of this whirlwind itself, the supreme mediator")[9] and the other immersed in his immediate circumstances, the fog made up of "the density of the things immediately perceptible when I open my eyes." Since these men personify sleep and wakefulness, they are really an extension in human terms of the communicating vessels of interior vision and the exterior world. (Surrealist man is, of course, a combination of both, a resolution of the "real" and the "unreal.") When Breton announces, later in this same essay, that poets must find a way to "put man back at the heart of the universe, to abstract him for a moment from the events that would decompose

[9] *Les Vases communicants* (Editions des Cahiers Libres, 1932), p. 120.

him, to remind him that he is, for all the sorrow and joy external to him, an indefinitely perfectible place of resolution and echo,"[10] he is returning to the same image. In some senses, this is the basic perception for him, and all the other images he uses to depict the surrealist universe depend on this one; a decade later he will explain that the image itself is the art of burning the candle at both ends, of extending the nocturnal vision from the physical realm to the limitless moral or mental one.[11]

The constant insistence upon contraries and complements, discussed above and exemplified here—that of the waking and sleeping states, the exterior and the interior worlds, the real and "the other side of the real," the subject and the object—is closely connected to the emphasis Breton places on the experience of division within the self (*le dédoublement du moi*). His attitude toward it is less negative than that of Aragon, for whom it appears to suggest an unwanted symptom of age and loneliness. Since Breton is convinced that surrealist behavior cannot coexist with the stability of personality we judge normal, he considers the shock that the realization of this personal duality produces to be a necessary one. In his introduction (1933) to Achim von Arnim's *Contes bizarres*, he demands that "The Self be treated in the same way as the object, that a formal restriction be invoked against the 'I am.' "

From the romantics and from Rimbaud surrealism inherits many things, and in both it finds the consciousness of the double discussed in the Introduction. Along with the interior crisis of personality goes an exterior crisis of the object, in which the real and the imaginary qualities have become interchangeable; the human cognitive process is upset and the "déséducation des sens" which Breton adds to Rimbaud's "dérèglement des sens" is begun. In his *Situation surréaliste de l'objet* (1935), Breton advocates the effort to disorient or "dépayser la sensation" as a step to this "dérèglement"; Aragon admires the collage particularly because of its ability to

---

[10] *Ibid.*, p. 128.
[11] In *Les Etats-Généraux*. Quoted in Breton, *Poèmes*, p. 219.

disorient the onlooker, and Breton claims that poetry can do the same thing. He gives several rules for a poem to follow in order to disquiet the reader, the main one being that it should have no specific subject, neither rational nor speculative, neither tangible nor emotional. He also reiterates his faith in the unstabilizing power of the metaphor, which alone is sufficient to distinguish poetry from prose. The intensification of personal instability and the revolution against conventional relationships in the exterior realm are in large measure interdependent, the internal and external vision being closely related. Breton glorifies the concept of *le vertige* as do all the surrealists, for whom it is the necessary and disorienting prelude to novel experiences of sensation and perception. In the poem "Pleine marge" of 1940, he suggests that only the man of violent actions can know that feeling in its most vivid form:

. . . la part de vertige
Faite à l'homme qui pour ne rien laisser échapper de la
    grande rumeur
Parfois est allé jusqu'à briser le pédalier.
(. . . the portion of dizziness
Allotted to the man who, so as to let none of the great
    noise escape
Has sometimes broken the very pedal-boards.)

And in *Les Etats-Généraux* of 1942 he claims, like the Aragon of 1925 and all the years since, that of all the things he has known, *le vertige* is the most beautiful. Here, in a different mood from the stateliness of his prose and the occasional egotism of his poetry, Breton suggests the actual insignificance of the individual personality, since the memory may be only a product of the imagination. There is no justification for the individual's belief in his own nature as a fixed, reliable starting point for experience. Such uncertainty about the continuation of the self is a necessary product (and cause) of *vertige*: linked to the consciousness of duality, it will never be absent from surrealist thought even in its moments of highest optimism.

Breton and the other surrealists, although they try to regain the child's attitude of *presence* and immediacy, are constantly haunted by the sense of inner disunity and by the more obvious outer division between man and his surroundings. Breton's consciousness of isolation and distance pervades his writings from 1924 to 1932. In *Poisson soluble* (1924) the poet imagines himself alone behind a window, all he observes contributing to his sense of *ennui*:

Les heures, le chagrin, je n'en tiens pas un compte raisonnable; je suis seul, je regarde par la fenêtre; il ne passe personne, ou plutôt personne ne *passe* (je souligne passe). Ce Monsieur, vous ne le connaissez pas? C'est M. Lemême. Je vous présente Madame Madame. Et leurs enfants.[12]

(The hours, the pain, I keep no rational account of them; I am alone, I look out of the window; there are no passersby, or rather no one *passes* (I underline passes). You don't know this gentlemen? It's Mr. The Same. May I introduce Mrs. Mrs. And their children.)

In *Le Revolver à cheveux blancs* (1932), windows separate the watcher within from odd and vaguely threatening spectacles:

Je suis à la fenêtre très loin dans une cité pleine d'épouvante
Dehors des hommes à chapeau claque se suivent à intervalle régulier[13]

(I am at the window far off in a terror-stricken city
Outside, men in opera hats follow regularly on each others' steps).

Or, as "windows of hell," they frame bizarre and erotic gestures for the benefit of someone watching from without; or again, they are frames for the marvelous:

[12] "Moins de temps." Related to the image of the window is that of the curtain, which fascinated Breton in the work of di Chirico, Hopper, and Hirshfield: see his interview with Nicolas Calas in the single issue of *Arson*.
[13] "Non-lieu."

Les belles fenêtres aux cheveux de feu dans la nuit noire
Les belles fenêtres de cris d'alarme et de baisers[14]

(Beautiful windows with their flaming hair in the black night
Beautiful windows of warning cries and kisses).

The probable reference to red curtains ("flaming hair") is simply a positive interpretation of the "windows of hell" in the poem just mentioned, since the cries and kisses could refer to the same kind of sadistic-erotic spectacle (although the two poems differ in every other way). The oppositions in color (red, black) and possibly also in emotion (cries, kisses) form the structure of the spectacle in each case, all three of these poems demonstrating a theatrical impulse within the poem characteristic of much of Breton's poetry. But the spectacle already contained within the poem is suddenly moved from an impersonal distance to the interior and the personal, as the ordinary glass of all the windows takes on the marvelous, and therefore illogical, quality of crystal. Gathered within the poet, the windows form one crystal "blue like wheat." This is a perfect example of Breton's claim that for the poet, as for the child, distance has no meaning. All perception becomes presence.

In this same collection the associated and familiar theme of the double is strikingly presented in the poem "Rideau rideau," where the poet's life is played out on the scene of a theater, the baroque spectacle including not only the actor playing Breton, but another man in a Breton mask, and on a level below the stage, a silhouette of Breton outlined on a white wall in fire, with a bullet in his heart. In a less dramatic form, "Les Attitudes spectrales" indicates the voluntary and inevitable split between the poet and the world and the parallel separation within the poet himself in a light manner completely devoid of self-pity:

Je n'attache aucune importance à la vie
Je n'épingle pas le moindre papillon de vie à l'importance

[14] "Noeud des miroirs."

Je n'importe pas à la vie
Mais les rameaux du sel les rameaux blancs
Toutes les bulles d'ombre
Et les anémones de mer
Descendent et respirent à l'intérieur de ma pensée
Ils viennent des pleurs que je ne verse pas
Des pas que je ne fais pas qui sont deux fois des pas
Et dont le sable se souvient à la marée montante
  . . .
J'avais déjà cet âge que j'ai
Et je veillais sur moi sur ma pensée comme un gardien de
    nuit dans une immense fabrique.

(I attach no importance to life
I do not pin the slightest butterfly of life to importance
I do not matter to life
But the branches of salt the white branches
All the bubbles of shadow
And the sea anemones
Descend and breathe inside my thought
Tears well up which I do not shed
Steps I do not take which are steps twice over
And which are remembered by the sand in the rising tide
  . . .
I was already as old as I am now
And I watched over myself my thought like a night
    watchman in an immense factory.)

Here all the objects which penetrate his contemplation give
the impression of delicacy or lightness, as if any harsh or
heavy elements must be deliberately eliminated from the poem. Even the suggestion of sadness which enters ("des
pleurs") is quickly covered over by his denial of personal
concern ("que je ne verse pas"). As the poet is detached
from the action, he is equally detached from his own thought:
only the sand remembers the steps which have been taken.
The facile word play matches the lightness of the images:
"attacher . . . épingles," "des pas . . . pas . . . sont deux

fois des pas." This poem extends the separation within the poet to the point where he can convincingly speak of his eyes having watched himself burning, a theme expanded in the quiet and beautiful "Vigilance." In the latter poem, the poet dreams of setting fire to his own room and himself sleeping within it, so that free of material obstacles he may enter the world of primary unity both invisible and unaware of the dragging steps of the living and the unpurified:

Je vois les arêtes du soleil
A travers l'aubépine de la pluie
. . .
Je ne touche plus que le coeur des choses je tiens le fil
(I see the bones of the sun
Through the hawthorn of the rain
. . .
At last I touch only the heart of things I hold the thread).

In this pure and serious atmosphere there is no trace of *ennui*. The initial suffering is only seen, not felt, and the isolation from the passersby is voluntarily chosen by the poet who is finally able to replace his unhappy consciousness of duality and of distance by a sense of unity and presence. The *absence* sensed as early as 1923 in his poems ("Je n'y suis guère, hélas")[15] is now denied by the value he had seemed at that time to refuse:

La vie de la présence rien que la présence[16]

(The life of presence nothing but presence).

Like the man immobile in the middle of the whirlwind in *Les Vases communicants*, published in the same year as this poem, he rediscovers the calm vision at the center of things where play is no longer necessary to expand the perception and where all separations are resolved within an infinite series of possible links continuously recreated by the poet's imagination: "Je tiens le fil."

---

[15] "Plutôt la vie" from *Clair de terre*.   [16] *Ibid.*

ANTICIPATION, PRESENCE, UNITY

It is to this faith in a new sort of unified vision that the surrealist's "lyrical behavior" bears witness. Intensely aware of the necessary and marvelous passages that form spontaneously between the interior and the exterior worlds, he lives in a state of *attente*, of openness to all chance events, where the element of surprise is always valued for its own sake and the predictable, always despised.

"Regardless of what happens or does not happen, the anticipation is magnificent." This sentence concludes Breton's description in *L'Amour fou* (1937) of the *disponibilité* which characterizes the surrealist attitude, unhampered as it is by the logical connections which cover over "the paths of desire" for nonsurrealists. For Breton, woman as the incarnation of irrationality is the eternal marvelous; in this book he says quite simply that *l'amour absolu*, which takes place on the same level as *l'amour fou* and as Benjamin Péret's *amour sublime*,[17] is man's only guarantee that all his endeavors are not undertaken in vain, and in *Arcane 17* (1945), he maintains that earthly salvation can come only through the redemptive power of woman. The notion of madness and immoderation—that is, absolute love of any sort, whether of a person or an idea—excludes the possibility of prudence and restraint: "Liberty only consents to caress the earth out of respect for those who have not been able to live, or have only been able to live badly, because they have loved her to the point of madness."[18] In principle the often imprudent attitude of the surrealist places him, as we have seen, in an illogical and natural state of mind,[19] where surface convention and acquired culture yield to spontaneity and where the most extreme passion reveals itself as unique wisdom. The unlimited power of immoderate surrealist love suppresses dis-

[17] Mary Ann Caws, "Péret's *amour sublime*—just another *amour fou?*," *The French Review* (November 1966).

[18] *Arcane 17* (New York, Brentano's, 1945), p. 27.

[19] But Breton would not have used the word "state" ("état"), which for him indicates immobility; the surrealist mind is better characterized by the concept of a *force vive* or a living force. See *ibid.*, p. 165.

tance and makes impossible, at least for a time, the unemotional detachment of *l'ennui* and the proud loneliness of despair found in such passages as Breton's "Le Verbe être." In *L'Air de l'eau* (1934) there are two love poems which exemplify surrealist poetry at its best and surrealist vision in its simplest and most moving form. The first poem begins with the paradox "Every time for the first time" ("Toujours pour la première fois"); since at each moment he falls in love with the woman *again* (dynamically opposed to the static condition of *still* loving her) as if he were actually seeing her for the first time, he can say that he scarcely knows her even by sight ($=$ recognizes her). Her appearance seems to change and so his love for her is always new, in spite of what we might call the "real" conditions within the surrealist vision. "Reality" here assumes a less narrow sense, for as the woman enters an imaginary house and disappears behind imaginary curtains, the poet who watches her from his window is suddenly aware of:

La déchirure unique
De la façade et de mon coeur
Plus je m'approche de toi
En réalité

(The unique rending
Of the facade and of my heart
The more closely I approach you
In reality).

His emotional distance is thus overcome, and this also for the first time each time he sees her. The less simple qualities of the poem depend on a certain lyrical (irrational) form of observation and association, intelligible on an aesthetic and emotional plane. The odd angle at which the curtain is hanging, for example, reminds him of the way a group of jasmine pickers he once saw on a road near Grasse seemed to stand on a diagonal; and then the unexplicit element of threat in the position of the curtain and of the jasmine pickers leads the poet to imagine, or rather, to see the woman surrounded by dangers and by dangerous temptations, by branches that

might scratch her in the woods and rocking chairs balanc-
ing precariously on bridges. The fact that she is inside a
house (imaginary or "real") is in no way a protection from
this sort of danger existing on the level of genuine feeling,
against which there is no defense.

All the poems of this collection are complex in *vision* but
simple in tone, as is all surrealist love poetry and all surrealist painting at its best; the following poem, like the one
just discussed, is introduced as an event of the imagination:

Je rêve je te vois superposée indéfiniment à toi-même
Tu es assise sur le haut tabouret de corail
Devant ton miroir toujours à son premier quartier
Deux doigts sur l'aile d'eau du peigne
Et en même temps
Tu reviens de voyage tu t'attardes la dernière dans la grotte
Ruisselante d'éclairs
Tu ne me reconnais pas
Tu es étendue sur le lit tu t'éveilles ou tu t'endors
Tu t'éveilles où tu t'es endormie ou ailleurs
Tu es nue la balle de sureau rebondit encore
Mille balles de sureau bourdonnent au-dessus de toi
Si légères qu'à chaque instant ignorées de toi
Ton souffle ton sang sauvés de la folle jonglerie de l'air
Tu traverses la rue les voitures lancées sur toi ne sont plus
        que leur ombre
Et la même
Enfant
Prise dans un soufflet de paillettes
Tu sautes à la corde
Assez longtemps pour qu'apparaisse au haut de l'escalier
        invisible
Le seul papillon vert qui hante les sommets de l'Asie
Je caresse tout ce qui fut toi
Dans tout ce qui doit l'être encore
J'écoute siffler mélodieusement
Tes bras innombrables
Serpent unique dans tous les arbres

Tes bras au centre desquels tourne le cristal de la rose
    des vents
Ma fontaine vivante de Sivas

(I dream I see your image indefinitely superposed upon
    yourself
You are seated on the high coral stool
Before your mirror always in its first quarter
Two fingers on the water wing of the comb
And at the same time
You come back from a trip you linger last in the grotto
Streaming with sparks
You do not recognize me
You are stretched out on the bed you wake up or you fall
    asleep
You wake up where you have gone to sleep or elsewhere
You are naked the elderberry bounces again
A thousand elderberries hum above you
So light that you are not aware of them
Your breath your blood saved from the insane jugglery
    of air
You cross the street the cars rushing toward you are no
    more than their own shadow
And still the same child
Child
Caught in a bellows of spangles
You jump rope
Until at the top of the invisible staircase
There appears the only green butterfly haunting the Asian
    summits
I caress everything that was you
In everything that you are still
I listen as your innumerable arms
Make a melodious whistling
Snake unique in all the trees
Your arms in whose center turns the crystal of the rose
    of winds
My living fountain of Siva).

In the poet's dream the woman is presented in a series of
limitless vertical images, indicative of the optimistic vision
of surrealism; the tendency is always toward *la fête*, toward
the celebration of woman and of life, in the same way as the
superréel is opposed to the subreal, or *sousréel*, of a "miser-
abilistic" prosaic world. The mirror does not give off sunlight
but the more romantic moonlight, and is itself a moon as
eternally young as the face reflected in it; such condensation
of the image is typical of surrealist poetry and art, both of
which demand from the onlooker more than he is commonly
willing to give. The metaphor here exemplifies Breton's
statement: "For me the only *evidence* in the world is that
provided by the spontaneous, extra-lucid, insolent relationship that is established, under certain conditions, between
one thing and another thing which common sense would never
think of bringing together."[20] Consequently, for him the
word "therefore" is detestable and "the most exalting
word is the word LIKE, whether it is pronounced or implied."[21] In the example under discussion, as in the
image of the "pierres blettes" described before, the "like"
is silent; had Breton said "your mirror like a moon," the poem would have taken on a different tone. When the comb
is compared to a bird, the image is made as delicate and as
suggestive as possible, a wing of water implying at the same
time the suppressed and linking element of a wave of hair.
Like Mélusine, the mermaid and the sorceress of surrealism,
this woman is not bound by the limits of time and place
("time having no power over her") for she is also still swim-
ming with the sparks of water on her and she is also naked
on the bed: the poet cannot be sure what is part of his dream,
what of hers. He is strange to her like the elderberries, which
multiplied instantly as her image did and are even more
delicate than she is. Saved first from their giddiness (as in the
poem "Toujours pour la première fois," the implied threat
here is vague) by being unconscious of them, she is then
saved again from an ordinarily "real" danger by being more

[20] "Signe ascendant" in *La Clé des champs*, p. 112.
[21] *Ibid.*, p. 114.

real than the cars, only shadows of themselves in comparison to her—in both cases, her existence is shown to be so
miraculous as to deny the reality of any other presence. Surrealism is by no means inclusive; it is deliberately and pas-
sionately exclusive of all that is foreign to its way of thinking.

In all senses more *present* than other women, Mélusine,
"la femme-enfant," while lying on the bed in the *pose* of a
woman is also skipping rope like a child, calling forth a vision which *really* appears, unlike the staircase that remains
unseen since it is not part of the marvelous universe of the
poem. In the mythological-sexual reference at the end, the
image of the fountain repeats the water of the comb-wing and
of the grotto, reminding us that, as well as possessing the
usual feminine qualities—fertility (the fountain) and vanity
(the comb, but with the added nuance of frivolity and delicacy given it here)—surrealist woman goes beyond the sensual to the marvelous proper to surrealism (the grotto). No
ordinary addition of some qualities to others, this combination is rather a miraculous union of opposites and ambiguities.

Breton's love poetry stands out from his other poems by
its extraordinary strength: the poems in *L'Air de l'eau*, for
instance, are as complex and as eloquent as *L'Amour fou*, as
compelling in vision and as unified in feeling. That this latter
quality goes precisely against one of the rules given, the year
after the publication of *L'Air de l'eau*, for disorienting the
senses is a typically surrealist contradiction. Surrealist love
itself is, like surrealist poetry, the supreme "place where all
contradictions are resolved"; the nature and the quality of
the surrealist love poems answer, perhaps better than anything else, the underlying question about the efficacy of the
surrealist revolution in art. For these poems, like the work
of all the artists Breton most admires, recreate the primary
state of unity which is the highest goal of surrealist hope.

OPENNESS AND RESPONSIBILITY

Through his own vision and through the marvelous power
of surrealist love, the surrealist poet overcomes his sense of

disunity and estrangement, at least temporarily. By 1940
Breton can write, in his universe without windows ("univers défenestré") a poem as open and generous as "Pleine
marge":

> O grand mouvement sensible par quoi les autres parvien-
> nent à être les miens
> . . .
> De quelque manière qu'ils aient frappé leur couvert est
> mis chez moi
> (O great sensitive movement by which the others become
> mine
> . . .
> However they may have knocked their place is set at my
> table).

Nor is this movement of charity directed solely toward other
surrealists; the recreated world is eventually to be shared
with all, even those least likely to understand it:

> Et même des êtres engagés dans une voie qui n'est pas la
> mienne
> Qui est à s'y méprendre le contraire de la mienne
> (And even those traveling along a path that is not mine
> The very image of the path opposite to mine).

After the passionate self-analysis of some of the poems of
Le Revolver à cheveux blancs and the hallucinatory visions
of the love poetry in *L'Air de l'eau*, the poet is now turned
toward the world and in *Les Etats-Généraux* of 1943 he is
able to place even "le risque," or the romantic current of
surrealist adventure, with its "imposing apparatus of temptations" into a more general and less credulous perspective.
This poem has as its theme the harmony of universal de-
pendence, the equality of all peoples and "the imperceptible
and yet irresistible inclination toward the best." It is, like
many of the poems of Aragon, unashamedly sentimental and
optimistic. The "exaltation of life" Breton so frequently in-
vokes and which inspires all his extraordinary images merges

here with an undisguised humanism, as the *separation* occasionally sensed by the poet is transformed into a more lasting involvement.

Surrealist optimism is never free of responsibility; for Breton, as for Aragon, art matters desperately because it is the only moral counter to destruction. In 1928 Breton says there is no reality in art—but he will never take this as a sufficient justification for a divorce between art and the world around it. The "surréalité" pointed to by certain painters and writers, even when it is represented by the means of and in the spirit of play, is to be taken seriously. When Breton discusses the freedom of art and its responsibility in his *Prestige d'André Masson* (1939) he makes very clear the distance between his point of view and Aragon's as well as the similarities between them:

> To be sure we have not the slightest intention of ever making artistic themes depend strictly on actuality; we persist in believing that above all art should be love rather than anger or pity. At the same time we refuse as tendentious, as reactionary, any image that the painter or the poet proposes to us today of a stable universe where the trivial pleasures of the senses can be not only enjoyed but exalted. Their so-called art appears here and now as *not situated*; for the problem is no longer, as it used to be, whether a canvas can hold its own in a wheat field, but whether it can stand up against the daily paper, open or closed, which is a jungle.[22]

For Aragon, "Art ought to be read like the paper." For Breton, art must not depend on daily events, but it must be just as significant as any of them. He is condemning not only the "art for art's sake" which has no bearing on the world (*nonsitué*)[23] but all egotistic art of sheer pleasure and description, no matter how realistic and how tasteful. If he attacks the notion of taste as strongly as Aragon, it is not

[22] Reprinted in *Le Surréalisme et la peinture*, pp. 151-52.
[23] Breton had already insisted in 1928 that a painting must be able to "hold its own in the face of famine."

in the name of the common man who cannot enter the delicately arranged paradise of the elite—in fact, Aragon's vicious poems in *Persécuté-Persécuteur* exemplify the anger and pity Breton wants to avoid. Breton discerns in mere taste a frivolous quality akin to sensuality and incompatible with the *sérieux* of surrealist concerns. Furthermore the notion of "taste" depends on the assurance of a fixed universe for its fixed values, in opposition to the mobile universe of the surrealist vision. Surrealist art is not the prisoner of any predetermined way of seeing things. The judgment it implies is always a fresh one, fitting the criteria of the moment while not inflexibly committed to any system or structure; it is neither dissociated from the actual world nor subordinate to it. The surrealist revolution is meant to take place in all realms and to retain its validity in all situations.

THE AMBIGUITY OF THE SURREALIST ADVENTURE

But there is always another side to the optimism; Breton remains conscious of the sharp dualities he has never ceased trying to reconcile in the unitary reality he calls "L'amour la révolution la poésie." The words he addresses to Charles Fourier (*Ode à Charles Fourier*, 1947) are addressed also to himself:

Toi qui ne parlais que de lier vois tout s'est délié

(You who spoke only of linking look how everything has come apart).

Poetry is able to form no more than an ephemeral link between the disparate surfaces, even in the newly open universe Breton describes; poetic fusion, in which he places all his hope, may not last:

Car les images les plus vives sont les plus fugaces

(For the most vital images are the most fleeting).

The ending of the poem *Sur la route de San Romano* (1948) has often been quoted as an example of surrealist faith:

L'étreinte poétique tant qu'elle dure
Défend toute échappée sur la misère du monde.

(The poetic embrace as long as it lasts
Prevents any sight of the misery of the world.)

Yet in the light of the above quotations, the "tant qu'elle dure" here may imply, as strongly as the "fugace," the ephemeral quality of surrealist poetry, based as it is on the quick and spontaneous image. Of course this is also the basis for its beauty.

Fourier, a visionary hero like the surrealist artist and the surrealist poet, thought he could defeat habit and human unhappiness, but things do not really change for the better:

Dieu de la progression pardonne-moi c'est
    toujours le même mobilier

(God of progress forgive me it is
    always the same furniture).

In *Xénophiles* (1948), Breton reaches the lowest possible depth of surrealist despair:

Ceux qui s'avancent sont ridicules
Les hautes images sont tombées.

(Those who go forward are ridiculous
The lofty images have fallen.)

Breton and the other surrealists put their entire confidence in the reconciling power of the image ("The image never deceives")[24] and in the creative strength of the interior vision. When the images fall and the vision fails, they have no recourse.

But without the extremes of exaltation and despair surrealism could not be the "place of resolution" Breton considers it. The vagueness of the terms used in his theory and his criticism—"révélation," "interrogation," "solicitation," "création," "représentation," "figuration"—leaves room for all the ambiguities of art; the odd mixture of genuine emo-

[24] In *Hommage à Saint-Pol-Roux*, reprinted in Alain Jouffroy, *Saint-Pol-Roux* (Mercure de France, 1966), p. 274.

tion and visual precision in his poetry and their interdependence engages the reader, as surrealist theory says it
should, in a disquieting world of separations and unity, total
contradictions and partial understanding. Many of his images
are clearly based on the obvious or implied dualities of soft
and hard, clear and dark, absence and presence, one and
many, elaborate costumes and nakedness, and so on. Like his
theory, Breton's poetry betrays a constant awareness of opposites, sometimes deliberately provoking them to upset the
habitual perceptions of the reader, sometimes temporarily re-
solving them into a new and always ambiguous compound.
That the ambiguity should persist even within the newly
created unity is as essential to the character of surrealist art
as is the ephemeral nature of the images. For the vision to be
always fresh and the visionary to be always active, the art
he creates must not be allowed to stultify him with its perfection or its permanence. All surrealist effort is directed
against the stability to which we are accustomed—if it were
ever to produce its own form of stability, it would instantly
betray its revolutionary nature:

> Et la route de l'aventure mentale
> Qui monte à pic
> Une halte elle s'embroussaille aussitôt[25]

> (And the highway of the mind's adventure
> Which climbs straight up
> At the slightest pause it becomes overgrown).

[25] "Sur la route de San Romano."

TRISTAN TZARA

"TZARA-DADA":
THE CRYSTAL AND THE IMAGE

It is often assumed that Dada is a totally pessimistic and destructive movement, of which surrealism is the positive and constructive opposite. But Tzara's own view of poetry as he states it in 1919 can scarcely be described as negative: "Vigor and thirst, emotion in response to the formation which is neither to be seen nor to be explained: poetry. . . . A will to the word: a being on its feet, an image, a construction unique, fervent, of a deep color, intensity, communion with life."[1] In fact, the values held in highest esteem by Dada are exactly those values which recur in surrealist pronouncements—first of all, the intensity, enthusiasm, and strength ("Here we have the right to proclaim, for we have known the shivering and the awakening. Returning drunk

---

[1] Tristan Tzara, "Note sur la poésie," *Sept manifestes Dada* (Pauvert, 1963), p. 104.

with energy we stab the trident into the heedless flesh.")[2]
Then, the rapid motion and the primitive, spontaneous vitality ("To accelerate this quantity of life";[3] "Dada is a quantity
of life in a transparent transformation, effortless and gira-
tory")[4] closely connected to the emphasis on liberty, possibility, and extension "of a shining gold brilliance—an in-
creasing, expanding crescendo of beating wings"):[5] the
luminous atmosphere of "abundance and explosion" in which
the Dada artist creates is the obvious forerunner of the surrealists' "convulsive beauty."[6] Tzara's image of purity as the
clear glass corridors which he directly contrasts with the bourgeois idea of morality ("the infusion of chocolate in the veins
of all men")[7] depends on the notion of interior necessity
and dynamic precision: ("To be severe and cruel, pure and
honest toward the work one is preparing to place among
men, new organisms, creations that live in the bones of light
and in the fabulous forms of action"),[8] and on the notions
of immediacy and bareness ("Simplicity is called Dada").[9]

One of Tzara's essays on art in 1917 ends with a passage
which brings together in one place several of the most important themes and images of surrealism—the fountain and
the crystal, both representing freedom and clarity, purity and
transparency, the theory of the image which combines all of
them, and finally, the necessary evolution toward an interior
surreality:

> The diversity of today's artists forms the jet of water into
> a great crystalline liberty. And their efforts create bright
> new organisms in a world of purity aided by the trans-

[2] "Manifeste Dada 1918," *ibid.*, p. 24.

[3] "Conférence sur Dada," *ibid.*, p. 139.

[4] "Manifeste sur l'amour faible et l'amour amer" (read at Galerie
Povolozky, December 12, 1920), *ibid.*, p. 69. As originally published
in *Cannibale*, I (April 25, 1920), this statement reads: "Dada est une
quantité de vie en transformation transparente orange et giratoire."
The later suppression of the "orange" is characteristic of Tzara's procedure for constructing simple and lyric formulas.

[5] Tzara, "Note sur la poésie," *Sept manifestes Dada*, p. 105.

[6] See the final sentence of Breton's *Nadja*.

[7] Tzara, "Note sur la poésie," *Sept manifestes Dada*, p. 33.

[8] *Ibid.*, p. 106.   [9] *Ibid.*, p. 142.

parencies and the materiality of construction of a simple image as it takes shape. They continue the tradition; as it evolves, the past pushes them slowly like a snake toward the interior and direct consequences, beyond surfaces and reality.[10]

Like Breton in his essay on the "Crisis of the object," Tzara points out in an essay on African art that exterior reality must be dissolved before the interior depths can be seen: "by means of purity we first deformed and then decomposed the object."[11] Like Breton in his article on the art of Oceania, Tzara here praises "simple, rich, luminous naïveté." And like Breton in his eulogy of the crystal, Tzara here praises the genuine work of art (which he calls "Latin" art) as a spontaneous, effortless creation of active simplicity, contrasting with deliberate and laborious *work* (or "German" art), developed by a purely mechanical, exterior process of syntax. This preference fundamental to both Dada and surrealism is the best explanation of the constant use of the single and spontaneous image instead of the more elaborate metaphor which needs to be worked out.

At first reading, Tzara's early Dada poetry, such as *Vingt-cinq poèmes* (1918) and *De nos oiseaux* (1923), seems to consist of unusual images gratuitously linked to each other in an order invisible to the logical mind and in complete accord with Dada principles of rapidity and vitality. There is no immediately apparent structure exterior to the images which would hold them together in a definite form and thus mute the impact of their collision; the type of linking which becomes apparent on a second reading is only thematic and therefore totally flexible. It is usually thought that Dada poetry is a sort of random catalogue, that the words pulled out of a hat according to the famous method advocated by Tzara are in no way joined to each other, that his statements about the poem formed by the random words and its necessary ressemblance to the man making the poem are only another Dada joke. Yet one of the primary elements of the

[10] *Ibid.*, pp. 85-86.   [11] *Ibid.*, p. 87.

Dada joke, like its parallel, the surrealist game, is its seriousness; its particular type of humor lies precisely there. Tzara
always claims for Dada creations an essential interior ordering, a "constellation" of necessary clarity below the obvious surface. Of course we are meant to look at the surface
as at a spectacle, and Dada poetry is full of references to
vision: "Look at me"; "see." According to Tzara, the inner
order is only apparent to the intuition; whether the thematic
links that can be perceived are signs of the subsurface order
or accidental manifestations of the continuity of certain Dada
attitudes, we cannot know—but the links are incontrovertibly
there.[12]

In brief, if the early Dada poems are examined, these main
themes, all of which are exact parallels to the themes of the
Dada manifestos and critical essays, are to be found: vivid
color, motion, a certain direction or grouping, definite geometrical figures, and light or its variants. (The specialist
might be interested to note that of the 26 poems of the
Vingt-cinq et un poèmes, all 26 contain at least one reference
to color, 25 to movement, 23 to light, 21 to a principle of
ordering or direction, and 20 to a geometrical figure; many
contain 6 or 7 references to one or more of these themes.)
The images or themes might, of course, be differently characterized, but in any case, they are all related to the spectacle Dada is supposed to be, and to its motion and invisible
purity of order. But these thematic links never fall into any
fixed (non-Dada) or predictable form or succession, nor
could they ever be said to soften the literally *spectacular*
shock of the images against each other: they are, rather,
intensifiers for those images.

In the later *L'Arbre des voyageurs* (1930) there is an
equally rich profusion of brilliant imagery, which is only
partly absurd. The fact that the American with "pointed
leaves" holding a "marriage in her beak" in one poem and
the ear feeding on the sound of a "muscled waterfall" in
another have certain possible supports in reality (that is, a

---

[12] Mary Ann Caws, "Motion, Vision, and Coherence in the Early
Dada Poetry of Tristan Tzara," *Studies in Contemporary Literature*,
special issue of *The French Review* (Fall, 1969).

stereotyped picture of a brittle, ambitious girl for the first, and a curved surface of water as it flows over the stones for the second) in no way subtracts from the power of the images or from the spontaneity of the poetic imagination: they are witnesses to its correspondence with the world outside it. The same statement could be made about much surrealist imagery.

On another level, it is also clear that surrealist word play is prefigured by Dada word play, as they are reflections of the aesthetic theories of the movements and intended to expand the range of possible significations of vocabulary and to intensify the poetic effect by doubling it in sense and in sound. Some of the puns and more obvious tricks of sound Tzara uses in his poetry, both early and late, are decidedly trivial ("dévastant le champ vaste," "les volets volés," "venir à venir," "les filles du fil de fer," "des longues files de filles de la plaine"). But at their best the word experiments can result in passages of singular beauty, where each sentence leads to the next in an unbroken lyricism. The following passage, based entirely on a pattern of rearrangement, makes an interesting contrast with Breton's solemn "Eloge de cristal" ("The work of art, like any fragment of human life considered in its most serious aspect, seems to me of no value unless it presents in all its exterior and interior facets the hardness, the rigidity, the regularity and the luster of crystal"):[13]

Crystal of the most beautiful pleasures, bitterness with the tired hair (moldy). Crystal with haggard eyes, with the haggard hair of wind, bitterness with the beatings of a rusted insect, its drum. Crystal of hearts, of temples and of sounds, bitterness rusts the drum of insects. Insect crystal with haggard eyes, the bitterness with the rumpled hair rusts the bitterness with haggard eyes of our most beautiful desires of the heart, temple and noise. Crystal with the most beautiful desires, bitterness rusts hearts, temples, and noises. Haggard crystal, bitterness rusts the

[13] André Breton, *L'Amour fou* (Gallimard, 1937).

most beautiful insect, the angel. Crystal of love and bitterness, the crystal, the white, the angel and the precision.[14]

The obvious oppositions here, such as bitterness / beauty,
insects / angels, rust / precision, haggard / pleasures, and
moldy / crystal, are interwoven in a linguistic complexity of
repetitions, transformations, and modulations which sometimes carries over into Tzara's critical writings. These odd,
oblique images, which are finally as convincing as more
regularly "poetic" ones, are frequent in the language of Dada:
for example, the white of angel (made from the sounds of
blanc mange and replacing the ordinary "eggwhites"). The
image of temples makes a typical double connection with the
elements of the poem: with the religious motif—angels—and
with the motif of exhaustion—haggard, rumpled, and tired, as
in the greying temples.

Frequently the chief difference between Dada and surrealism (or between the theoretical writing of their most
prominent exponents, Tzara and Breton), seems to be only a
difference of tone or of style, since the themes they deal
with are so similar. One has only to compare Breton's majestic eulogies of *le point sublime* with Tzara's deliberately
modest statement that Dada is the meeting place of contradictions, "the point where the *yes* and the *no* meet, not solemnly
in the castles of human philosophies, but very simply on
street corners like dogs and grasshoppers."[15] At other times,
even their styles are similar, especially in the more "poetic"
writings. After the initial period of Dada and before the
period of his political commitment, Tzara lays as heavy a
stress on the romantic themes of solitude and ennui as Breton.
In 1923, the hero of *Faites vos jeux* takes pride in his melancholy: "I held on to my unhappiness with a secret jealousy
as if it were a precious and impassioned possession, con-
secrated by a grief in which I believed myself the unique
sufferer."[16] His *Minuits pour géants* in *L'Antitête* (1933)

[14] "Filatures de jonques" from *Monsieur AA l'antiphilosophe* in
L'Antitête (Cahiers Libres, 1933).
[15] *Sept manifestes Dada*, p. 143.
[16] In *Les Feuilles libres*, No. 32 (1923), p. 252.

laments in a tone more classically lyric than shocking, marked with passive human melancholy rather than with the impassive antisentimentalism of Dada, with the distress of uncertainty, loneliness, and deception:

> The creaking furniture, the barking dogs, the worry, the anguish of waiting, when no one will come and never any joy except for those who are at home in their minds, the furniture creaks and those who never find any home except where the dogs are ceaselessly barking. . . . The one who has understood. Nothing, never again anything, anything but ravages.[17]

The transpositions of repeated phrases ("the creaking furniture. . . the furniture creaks; the barking dogs. . . the dogs are ceaselessly barking") reinforce the melancholy exactly as they did in the preceding quotation centering on the crystal and the bitterness which doubles it. Nevertheless, the images here are usual human images, in no way oblique, and the feeling behind them is obviously genuine. Unlike the preceding passage, this prose poem uses the technique of combinations to reinforce the sentiment. (Such similarity of technique and dissimilarity of tone between the poetry of two periods was also evident in the case of Breton.) In "Désespéranto" (also from *L'Antitête*) Tzara declares the same enthusiasm for the notion of *ennui* as Breton: "Tedium, before it reaches death, when I abandon myself to it completely, is my most delightful waking state." Here the violent energy and the sense of action are less prized than the acute intensity of consciousness to be found in the endless waiting which Tzara describes as full of charm.

As for the many other points of similarity between Breton and Tzara already mentioned, they are not by any means confined to Tzara's early Dada period. In 1932 Tzara asserts that his activity and his interests are those of the surrealists, and they remain so until 1934. The prose parts of his *Abrégé de la nuit* (1934) are very close in tone and content to Breton's *Vases communicants*, especially in the description

[17] *L'Antitête*, p. 119.

of the salutary deforming action of the dream on the world of everyday thought ("night in the fermentation of its profound possibilities").[18] In order to destroy the system of ready-made ideas about the relation of man to nature, Tzara would have the individual "withdraw, for a moment, from the coincidence of movements";[19] in similar fashion Breton's immobile man is "withdrawn from the contingencies of time and place."[20] He must make every effort to escape the tyranny of normal perception, determined as it is by the narrow and schematic laws of intelligence, so that he can attain and keep the necessary openness of vision; here Tzara continues to use the same images of transparency and brightness he had used in the Dada period, as he speaks of a "more luminous life . . . which will dazzle us by the lightness and facility ("légèreté") of its understanding of things and of beings."[21]

From this point on, Tzara lays a decided stress on the definitions of poetry or art itself. In his essay on Max Ernst and his "reversible images" (1934) he speaks not just of the dream but of all forms of poetry as an ideal means of deformation, always leading to new types of knowledge. In *Grains et issues* (1935), poetry becomes the supreme method for bringing about the required "transparency of things and beings."[22] It is at the same time the act of knowledge and the way of knowing. Like the dream, it exalts thought and goes beyond it. In fact, thought and poetry seem to have somewhat the same relationship as that indicated by "communicating vessels," since Tzara calls for the absorption of one in the other as the goal of a necessary and significant revolution.[23] He treats his own images as though they were thoughts, joining in this way the realm of poetry and the realm of knowl-

[18] *Abrégé de la nuit* in *Midis gagnés* (Denoël, 1939), p. 31.
[19] *Ibid.*, p. 30.
[20] André Breton, *Les Vases communicants*, p. 187.
[21] *Midis gagnés*, p. 31.
[22] *Grains et issues* (Denoël et Steele, 1935), p. 128.
[23] Exactly opposed to Breton's image of the "communicating vessels" is Tzara's theory that nights should be enlarged "to the detriment of days, in broad daylight." Specifically, he predicts that "the content of days will be poured into the demijohn of night." (*Grains et issues*, p. 9.)

edge. There is no possible separation in Tzara's essays between the idea and the image—so that, for instance, the mirages perceived by the mind when it is paralyzed by the strength of the sun actually themselves augment the understanding and the vitality of the man who sees them, "of the man who is subjected to the nondeceitful action of the phenomenon, to its very instant of radiance and of presence, [and who] is so affected by its truth that he mortally compromises his whole being, which commits itself entirely to the process of recognition."[24] Such a *crisis of the senses* serves exactly the same purpose as the diseducation of the senses proposed by Breton. Having himself undergone this upset of the logical mechanism, the poet learns to disturb the mental workings of his readers, to confuse their formerly sharp intellectual and sentimental perceptions and thereby to enlarge the circle of reality for them. So that Tzara's claim in this essay, "I have blinded the paths of feeling," is a justifiably proud one.

His will to unite elements, ordinarily considered separate (like the image and the idea, poetry and thought) extends to other realms also. Like Breton and the other poets connected with surrealism, one of the ideas to which he refers with the greatest frequency in all the periods of his life is that of the *union* of all things, however contrary in appearance. He calls poetry a way of living, a "condition of existence." Attacking, in *Le surréalisme et l'après-guerre* (1947), his former friends the surrealists from whom he had separated for permitting what he considers a divorce between their action and their theories, he insists on a *unicité* of action, which he describes as "action confused with dream,"[25] or, in his presentation of Rimbaud (1948), as a state of activity "where the terms of absence and presence are both unthinkable separately and where dream and action are linked in one unique projection."[26] As an ex-surrealist, he sees the surrealists overcome with despair at the duality of man and the world and he calls for a humanistic hope in the power of man

---

[24] *Ibid.*, p. 12.

[25] *Le Surréalisme et l'après-guerre* (Nagel, 1947), p. 34.

[26] Introduction to Arthur Rimbaud, *Oeuvres complètes* (Lausanne, Editions du Grand-Chêne, 1948), p. 18.

to rearrange his world by his creative will, to make the "immense transparency" of his work mirror that of his life in all its purity and integrity. For this reason he explains the work and the life of all his heroes of poetry and of art—Apollinaire, Reverdy, Rimbaud, Corbière, Picasso, Ilaire Voronca—in terms of luminosity and transparency ("the being of sun," "a gallop of clarity," "the lofty burning," "the clarity of the future," "the struggle for greater clarity"). If most of the essays are not conducive to a profound reexamination of the artist under discussion, they are at least in every way consistent with Tzara's own theoretical writings on art.

In the case of his own works, as one would expect, he refuses again to make any separation by periods. As Aragon republished his earliest surrealist writings and reinterpreted his essays in the light of his later political commitment, Tzara was unwilling to permit even his very first poems, written in Romanian between 1912 and 1915, to appear under the title *Poèmes d'avant Dada*. As he explains, such a title: "would imply a sort of rupture . . . which has, to tell the truth, never existed," in his poetic personality; "for there has always been a continuity through more or less violent and significant jolts, if you like, but still a continuity and an interpenetration, firmly linked to a latent necessity."[27] Tzara neither dwells on his "passage" like Aragon, nor totally dissociates himself from Dada either in his surrealist period, as does Breton, nor afterwards, as do other former Dada poets. That the reader should accept this underlying but absolute linking of all Tzara's work is essential to an understanding of his theories and of his poetry, both of which continue to exemplify certain qualities enunciated by the spokesman of Dada, "Tzara-Dada," and demonstrated in his Dada poetry.

THE "CONDUIT" IMAGES OF
LIGHT AND DARK

A description Tzara once gave of modern poetry ("Gestes, ponctuation, et langage poétique" in *Europe*, January 1953) is the best clue we have to his own poetry. There he speaks of the "*poetic fields* which are electrically charged by certain

[27] *Les Premiers poèmes* (Seghers, 1965), p. 21.

conduit images with the help of meanings recalled, of assonances and auditive echoes." The reader who is troubled by the profusion of assonance, alliteration, repetition of key words and key sounds, and various other sorts of word play must realize that these poetic devices furnish the verbal echoes Tzara has always used to reinforce his images in the memory. By means of these images the poet sets up a "current of induction" which flows in the way he determines. Tzara's insistence on transparency and on the family of images with which it is associated is a deliberate "charging" of his poetry to make possible the eventual creation of a *poetic reality*, that is, a reality as convincing in the realm of poetry as the objects surrounding us are in theirs. And in this interior reality, we have only his images for landmarks.

Tzara's first French poems bear a surprising resemblance to his latest poetry both in their structure and in their feeling. In his long poem of 1915, "L'Orage et le chant du déserteur," the simplicity of form and the sharpness of images as well as the insistence on light and darkness, all constants of his poetry like the accent on mobility and on vision discussed in the last section, show up clearly:

La lumière a jauni comme dans une tulipe,
De quels draps les nuages ont-ils arraché les ténèbres bleues
Où je fus mordu par les serpents de la pluie
. . .
Afin que ma lumière arrive aux lointains illuminés?
Sous des immensités de tristesse,
Ainsi que le tonnerre sous des voûtes asphyxié,
Je suis un voyageur à l'âme obscurcie,
Obscurcie.
Pour moi seul la nuit n'est pas belle.
. . .
Pour moi seul la nuit n'est pas belle,
Pour moi seul.

(Light has yellowed like a tulip,
From what sheets have the clouds snatched the blue shadows

Where I was bitten by the serpents of rain
. . .
So that my light reaches the bright distances?
Under immensities of sadness,
Like thunder stifled under vaults,
I am a traveler with a darkened soul,
Darkened.
For me alone the night has no beauty.
. . .
For me alone the night has no beauty,
For me alone).

The brief and very simple repetitions of the darkness and
the individual solitude intensify the emotion without arrest-
ing the movement of the poem. With its hope concentrated in
the series of "lumière / éclair / illuminé" and then denied by
the series of "obscur / noir / nuit—tristesse—asphyxié," as
both themes are stated first on the general and then on the
personal level, this poem is already characteristic of Tzara's
poetic vision. More important, he already identifies language
with the most powerful source of illumination, and this is a
faith he will never lose:

Il fait si noir que seules les paroles sont lumière

(It is so dark that only words are light).

Already he has identified language with the source of light
and of optimism: the interruption or suffocation of light will
always indicate his deepest moments of pessimism. He explains in 1923 that only the sight of the sun could prevent
the "fermentation du dégoût" to which he was so strongly
attracted, and that he can remember from his childhood only
the scenes illuminated by the brightest sunlight because of
his extraordinarily bad vision. In Tzara's *Indicateur des
chemins de coeur* (1928), the images of sun resemble those
of his earliest poetry and prose: although they are menaced
by ambiguities, anxieties, and by the fear of death as well as
by conventional morality. "The infusion of chocolate" he
dreaded now gives way to graver dangers. The mournful

refrain of a transparency broken or shattered as it penetrates the "glass of our existence" is built on an effective image of extreme Dada-surrealist despair. The cracked crystal stands in dreadful contrast to the purity of shining glass corridors and to the spontaneous perfection of a cube of crystalline rock salt.

The extremely diverse and unequally brilliant images of Tzara's masterpiece *L'Homme approximatif* (1931) are themselves appropriate to the theme of approximation. Taken together they form a full-scale portrait of multiple-natured and imperfect man as he wanders aimlessly about in the "à peu près" (the almosts) of destiny, with labyrinths hanging on the shadow of his steps and others weighing heavily on his back, without direction outside and in ("lost inside myself lost"). Even the space of his existence is rented; the only continuity he possesses is the series of worries he puts on in the morning like underclothes. Inconstant in his relationships with others, he is no more constant with himself, changing into "another self at every turning." He haunts the stores where bric-à-brac is sold, hoping to find there forgotten remnants of himself, some of the "fragments of life" fallen behind in his trivial movements. Always conscious of the "deadly punctuations" which mark his flesh, he feels his horizons limited to the border of a watch face and his prospects gambled away in a universal lottery, feels insignificant and shrunken into himself. Or again, swept by frenzied currents of air, with rats scurrying in the attic of his head,

> l'homme trait l'éternelle soustraction de chaque tranche en lui-même
> qu'il lui reste à mûrir de sa dette noire envers les durs soleils
> rit de face et pleure à l'envers (49)

> (man milks the eternal substraction from each slice in himself
> that remains for him to ripen in his black debt toward the harsh suns
> laughs with one face and weeps with the other).

Mocked by space and time, impoverished and confused, this man who is all of us ("approximate man like me like you reader and like the others") often betrays his incomplete nature by his inconclusive style, where one line of verse breaks off unfinished and the next line begins a totally different idea:

sans amertume sans dettes sans regret sans
les cloches sonnent sans raison et nous aussi (13)

(without bitterness without debts without regret without
the bells ring without reason and we too)

peu de lait peu de sucre peu de
à l'ombre des fumantes ronces sous les arcades de ton
   coeur (49)

(little milk little sugar little
in the shadow of the smoldering brambles under the
   arcades of your heart)

et si je m'égare c'est que je
chevaucheuse de cascades le temps a couru ses risques
   et les primes (50)

(and if I lose my place it is that I
straddler of waterfalls time has run its risk
   and the premiums).[28]

---

[28] The final result is actually a deliberate choice on the poet's part, since the line originally continued into another line: "I was strong." In his revision of the poem, he inserted a line irrelevant to these two between them, to break the logical and emotional continuity. This is a frequent procedure: for instance, to the sentimental interjection "Oh my God," he adds in a revision, "my violin." The simple image "humble peasant habitations" he changes afterwards to "humble peasant hesitations," keeping the sound but not the sense. A net which originally brought up "rings and rubies," in an ordinary logical sequence, brings up instead "rings and rockets," the change satisfying the requirement of the unexpected image and intensifying the upward direction on which the image is based; the poetry becomes at once more interesting and more difficult. The five-year period in which Tzara wrote and rewrote *L'Homme approximatif* was probably the period of his greatest poetic development, when he discovered ways of complicating and extending the simple elements of his first poems.

In a similar manner, the frequent repetitions of lines, and of words ("et sur les autres silences . . . et sur tant d'autres," "consolation . . . consolation") may be considered repeated attempts at, or approximations of, completeness.

Insofar as he is not even completely man, but "un peu animal un peu fleur un peu métal un peu homme," approximate man belongs not only to the human realm but to the world beyond man which is as incomplete as he is; in fact, the whole sweep of the poem is determined by the constant mixture of human and natural elements. An important series of images represents a serious state of imperfection: like man, the night and the moon are described as shriveled, and, like him, the mirror and the drinking glasses are broken. Elsewhere the rain is disheveled, the wind grieves, the valley is uneven, stars are incomplete, eternity has a gap in it, and a god is inconsolable. But the desolation of the outside world may be only a human interpretation, since the mind often serves as an intensifier of catastrophe. At other times natural objects are the only consolation for the sadness and impoverishment that haunt man's dwellings, and it is their "inexpressible plénitude" that compensates for human shortcomings and human wants. Unable to rely on his own constancy, man can count at least on the unfailing cycle of nature, on the "retour des choses / infatigable retour." Here he learns to renew his vision and expand it.

Far less flexible than man's vision, and far more important to the poet Tzara, is his language. From the sound of the bells and of the chains, felt more than heard at the beginning of the poem ("this language which lashes us") to the stammering sounds of hell at the end, the theme of nonhuman expression runs through the poem, and it is always counterbalanced by the theme of the human word. Ideally, our language would be the instrument of our eventual completeness, since it relates "apparences et architraves." In the word are gathered at once light ("the word alone suffices for seeing") and strength:

et passion sur le glacis du glaive transparent
cinglant fouet d'éclairs ramifié de bistouris
parole—au bord du précipice dans les siècles durcie
jet de venin fusant des cimes avortées—
glorifie des haines la lumineuse tension (91)

(and passion on the slope of the transparent blade
lashing whip of lightning branched with lancets
word—at the edge of the precipice in the centuries
hardened jet of poison fusing aborted summits—
glorifies the shining tension of hatreds).

Language alone provokes the drunkenness which can deliver
us from what Tzara calls the "lazy habit" of living. Our faith
in the word has even retarded our adventures into other
spheres: "word that I wait for . . . / around the hive of your
chance sweetness / we are so many bees whose flight your
promises have checked." And yet this faith is often disap-
pointed. The language approximate man has chosen, perhaps
the only one he could have chosen, is a language befitting his
imperfect nature, full of words that are "rotten unhealthy
moth-eaten." It is both static and nonvisionary:

aveugles sont les mots qui ne savent retrouver que leur
place dès leur naissance
leur rang grammatical dans l'universelle sécurité
bien maigre est le feu que nous crûmes voir couver en eux
dans nos poumons
et terne est la lueur prédestinée de ce qu'ils disent (113)

(blind are the words who from their birth can only find
their place again
their grammatical place in universal safety
feeble is the fire that we thought we saw kindling in them
in our lungs
and dull is the predestined gleam of what they say).

The "perfect chords" of language to which man lifts himself
are implicitly negated by the profusion of musical scaffoldings
thrown helter-skelter everywhere. The delicate and unrealiz-
able vibrations of which he speaks at one moment contrast

with the leper's rattle and with the bugles and fireworks that besiege and insult the mouth at other moments, as well as with the electric flood of music so harsh it breaks the tympanum of the drum: "l'armée des mots nos ennemis" is a threat to human peace. And whatever sounds the poet does succeed in uttering may be instantly swallowed up in the "common grave of noise" that the ground extends under the heavens.

As an absolute opposition to the imperfect character of human life and language (including, of course, the language in which the poem is written), *L'Homme approximatif* offers a theme of distant perfection and "brightness forever immeasurable," of luminous forgetfulness and an eternal warmth of sun raining down upon the earth its "chantante nourriture de lumière." Contrasting with the brief and strikingly incomplete lines already mentioned, there is a lengthy passage, comprising at least three of the nineteen sections of the poem, in which the outstanding images are linked by the color white—so that "la blancheur invincible immaculée" joins tufts of souls, swans gargling sprays of water, birds, glaciers, clouds, the white finger of the stone thinker, a woman's body, fog, and the frequent recurrences of the more general statement: "outside all is white" or its variations. The unforgettably simple affirmations of the natural and human realm find a celestial and sterile counterpart in the often reiterated "up there all is stone." The "rigid clarity" of the absolute has none of the approximate character of man, and the changing spectacle of nature and of man's own desperate attempts at courage seem tarnished by its light,

. . . l'éternelle incandescence
qui assourdit l'apparence des choses et leur simulacre
    d'héroisme (113)

(. . . the eternal incandescence
which dulls the aspect of things and their seeming
    heroism).

The only possible link seen at first between celestial perfection and earthly incompleteness is an exterior one. The wolf lost or bogged down in the confusion of the forest bears the same relation to ordinary sheep as does Tzara's hero of language to ordinary unheroic man; in these years Tzara frequently compares the poet to the wolf, in his revolt against his circumstances, for his "state of turbulence." Lycanthropy, he says, is an "affective mode" of the poets' consciousness. Some day the wolf might find a shepherd in whose calloused and confident hands he can place his hope after his faith in his own expression has been deceived. This unmoving shepherd, so great that he occupies everything, can guide him to a linguistic perfection far above his former hesitations and approximations. But at last the poets, the brave "cultivators of colors and of skies," are granted a sudden perception of "man bearing in his fruit the burning and propitious blossoming of morning." No longer passively led by an immobile shepherd toward the "celestial pastures of words," man now takes upon himself the responsibility of guide along with the commitment of the pilgrim toward purification and perfection, in a Dada-surrealist resolution of the inner and the outer reality. When, in the final section of the poem, the slow furnace identified with man's spirit and his hope rises to a litany of fire, and when there is a new and decided stress on the notions of height, strength, violent gestures, and infinite presumption, all modest approximate language and all principles of human logic are rejected (or redeemed) simultaneously: "harmony—let this word be banished from the feverish world that I visit." With them disappear the timid distinctions of limited earthly vision, as the tones of hell are heard among the "dizzying salvoes of stars." And finally the extended accumulation of seemingly disparate images receives an absolute retrospective unity as the epic tone of the poem prevails over the pathetic human theme of approximation.

Infinite in "the holy variety" of his species, as magnificent as he is miserable, man is now able to move toward completeness without physical motion. The universal refrain, "and others and so many others," which returns throughout the poem and particularly in the next to last section gives way to the heroic vow concluding the long journey which is the poem:

et rocailleux dans mes vêtements de schiste
j'ai voué mon attente au désert oxydé du tourment
au robuste avènement de sa flamme (158)

(and rugged in my clothing of schist
I have pledged my waiting to the oxidized desert of torment
to the unshakeable advent of its flame).

In the most difficult way possible, the poet here takes upon himself the will to immobile perfection and the necessary torment of purification. His attitude of waiting and his garments of rock are a human echo of the permanence and the static completeness of the preceding refrain: "all is stone." The certain flame he accepts at the end is the response to and the double of the nocturnal peace he implores near the beginning:

paix sur le dehors de ce monde renversé dans le moule des
    unanimes approximations
et sur tant d'autres et sur tant d'autres (36)

(peace on the outside of this world inverted in the mold
    of unanimous approximations
and on so many others and on so many others).

But the universe which was the subject of the former outward vision of the poet is now absorbed into his interior landscape. Pilgrimage and waiting, torment and repose, flame and stone, Tzara and his reader, language and absence of language, imperfect attempts and absolute commitment—all the elements of the journey meet in the space and time of the poet's own mind. And since it is only an outward witness to the interior realization, and is formed of the imperfect matter of human language, the poem itself is finally no more than an approximation of the inward journey "beyond surfaces and reality."

Où boivent les loups (1931) mixes images of suffering and darkness, of a black thirst and a night for blind men, of shadows, dead men, and dying laughter, of velvet griefs and nights flowing under the tears on the cheeks of summer, with brighter images of the depth of the sun and its "peaceful imprint the radiance of its surging word." But most of the

images of hope here are predictions rather than certainties,
where the main actions are expressed as problematic and
where all the forms are future in implication (both forms
italicized in the following examples):

les vagues *en quête* de nuits de cristal

(the waves seeking crystal nights)

—

un jour *peut-être jaillira* la lumière

(one day perhaps light will spurt forth)

—

le front *enfin* levé de la boue comme un enfant au sein
tu *partiras* dans ton audace de blancheur immémoriale

(with your forehead finally raised from the mud like a
    child at the breast
you will set off in your audacity of immemorial whiteness).

A year later, in "Le Puisatier des regards" (1932), images of
sun and light are everywhere—"lèvres de soleil," "la spon-
gieuse lumière sans bruit," "soleil aveuglement lent," "re-
tours lumineux"—together with the negation of all distance
and deceit ("les portes se démasqueront"), of all loneliness,
emptiness, and blindness:

même sous la meule de sommeil il n'y aura plus de solitude
tout sera plein profondément dans l'odeur de foin et de
    soleil[29]

---

[29] "Le Puisatier des regards," in *Où boivent les loups* (Cahiers
Libres, 1932), p. 157. Several passages in *L'Homme approximatif*
have this same tone of certainty and presence:

matin matin
matin scellé de cristal et de larves
matin de pain cuit
matin de vantaux en folie
matin de gardien d'écurie
matin d'écureuils et de polisseurs de vitres fraîches à la rivière
matin qui sent bon
haleine attachée aux stries de l'iris

(morning morning
morning sealed with crystal and with larvae
morning of baked bread

(even under the millstone of sleep there will be no more
    loneliness
all will be deeply full in the odor of hay and of sun).

In this atmosphere of *presence*, even the barest words become
"des paroles de soleil." The benevolence of nature would
seem to guarantee man's spontaneous and silent identification
with things. But in Tzara's characteristic manner, the images
of sun will be juxtaposed with their contraries in a moment
yet to come, if not in the present:

> et il y aura encore du soleil sur les robes et dans les cheveux
>   pétris à la campagne
> au bord d'un ruisseau dont la clarté sera de sang
> et de perdition seront le feuillage et le goût.[30]

> (and there will still be sun on the dresses and in the hair
>   kneaded in the country
> beside a stream whose brightness will be bloody
> and doomed will be its branches and its taste.)

More serious than the inevitability of future oppositions is
the grim warning expressed earlier in the poem that even
words will come to an end, a warning justified as the poet
is finally imprisoned by silence. Loneliness waits for him not
only on the crystal mountains and in the glass corridors,
where the encounter would be heroic, as it is in the flaming
desert of *L'Homme approximatif*, but at the end of bronze
streets, where the vertical dimension and the transparent
purity are utterly lacking. The hero does not struggle against
the silence waiting to enslave him, and there is not even an
aura of elevation or mystery to his fate, for the silence is
spun by "the bastard and quavering fingers of an old woman."
The words of sun and the language of youth are more seri-

---

morning of shutters in madness
morning keeper of the stable
morning of squirrels and of cleaning windows cool in the river
sweet smelling morning
breath clinging to the striation of the iris). (p. 124)
[30] *Ibid.*, p. 158.

ously threatened by a complete cessation of interior power than by the natural fall of outside darkness. Silence is perhaps more perfect than nonsilence, just as it is less human: this is of course the problem suggested by *L'Homme approximatif,* the man who makes successive attempts at human language and then commits himself to a perfection beyond the space of language and silence. But the stylistic technique of repetition continues in the poetry of Tzara himself as in that of his fellow Dada-surrealist poets: the linkings of images by a theme, the refrains, and the litanic form[31] can all be considered recurring *approximations* or steps toward a perfect language, the accumulated efforts of the surrealist poet toward a perfect poetry in a formal journey parallel to the metaphysical one.

In the volumes *La Main passe, Mutations radieuses, Midis gagnés,* and *Entretemps* of the years 1935 to 1940, when Tzara's poetry begins to take on a strong political orientation, the same themes continue and are amplified, acquiring a "realistic correlation" and a more *apparent* structure. There is the familiar insistence on fullness, vitality, and luminosity:

Le sel et le feu t'attendent sur la colline minérale de l'incandescence de vivre[32]

(Salt and fire await you on the mineral hill of the incandescence of living)

—

Vivre vivre à pleins bras de lumière[33]

(To live live with armfuls of light).

—

[31] Tzara occasionally resorts to more subtle forms of repetition. For example, the highly emotional sentence in *Grains et issues* which ends in the words "nos heures de vitres et de clairières" (our times of windows and of clearings), so that the sound "clair" in "clairière" (or "clear" in "clearing") repeats the concept of the clear window. This is certainly a more interesting technique than the puns and halfpuns (for example, in the title *La Bonne heure,* a play on "le bonheur").

[32] From "La Main passe," in Tristan Tzara, *Morceaux choisis* (Bordas, 1947), p. 212.

[33] *Midis gagnés,* p. 96.

Espoir ton jour est grand ouvert[34]

(Hope your day is opened wide).

And as before, there is an equal insistence on the threats of
blindness, despair, and death, where the "trop de lumière"
(excessive light) is replaced by the "soleil tari" (the dried-
up sun).

j'ai connu aussi la détresse des cristallins[35]

(I have also known the distress of crystalline lenses).

l'étincelle aux bras cassés[36]

(the spark with broken arms).

In these poems, however, Tzara begins to stress the necessity
of the interweaving of hope and despair, no longer in a formal
conception or in a mere poetic balance, but as the basis of
life itself as man can best perceive it. The darkness and the
light seem at first to exist side by side: "l'aveugle dort la
flamme règne"[37] (the blind man sleeps the flame rules).
But in reality, one is *within* the other, as in the game of *l'un
dans l'autre* already discussed: "Sale vie mélangée à la
mort"[38] (dirty life mixed into death). This theme is responsible for many of the most memorable of Tzara's poems and
images, such as "midi éclaté dans l'obscurité de sa force"
(noon exploded in the darkness of its strength):

même tard dans l'abîme se lèvent des promesses de vitres[39]

(even late in the abyss arise promises of windows)

———

taciturne tu écoutes le désir remuer au coeur de l'hiver
chaque ombre à son âme reconnaît la lumière[40]

(silent you listen as desire stirs in the heart of winter
each shadow knows the light in its soul).

[34] "Matin en vue," *Morceaux choisis*, p. 240.
[35] "Perdu en route" in *Entretemps* (Le Point du jour, 1946).
[36] *Ibid.*
[37] "Avoir le temps" in *Entretemps.*
[38] *Midis gagnés*, p. 63.
[39] "Perdu en route" in *Entretemps.*
[40] "Maturité" in *Entretemps.*

The hope of "the man of the day after" lies in "the man of today." From now on Tzara's titles, such as "Salut," "Matin en vue," *Le Signe de vie, Le Poids du monde, Terre sur terre, Miennes, A Haute flamme, La Bonne heure, Le Fruit permis*, and *Juste présent* are the strong positive equivalents of the former *Minuits . . . , Désespéranto, Abrégé de la nuit*, and, above all, of the tragic *L'Homme approximatif*.

MOTION AND ITS CENTER

There is nothing particularly original in the identification of light and dark with the feelings of hope and despair. In the writing of Tzara and of Eluard the profusion of images of this sort is striking, but in neither is it the primary basis for the value of the work itself. What is interesting in the case of Tzara is that the group of images he uses to carry the specific "poetic charge" both reflects and determines the values he emphasizes in his prose essays.

The "rayonnement" Tzara attributes to Picasso, for instance, is a function of Picasso's concern for continual creation and his involvement with movement in general. The notion of rays being sent out in successive moments is an essential part of the compliment Tzara pays him, implying as it does not a steady light but a constant renewal of energy. And if there is one concern that stands out among the others in the long essay *Picasso et les chemins de la connaissance* (1948), it is that of possible change. The static rendering of an object or, as such things are always parallel in surrealist and ex-surrealist critics, the static interpretation of a situation, would deny to the object or the situation the volume or the density which is its most important characteristic. The object pictured must show, according to Tzara, a sliding of levels, an oscillatory movement that affects not only its contours, but its whole form. Picasso is more than anything else the artist of motion, who can spontaneously capture all the slight variations that he sees by the rapidity of his perception and by his attitude toward each artistic representation as an experiment with knowledge itself, like Breton's attitude toward poetry. Tzara here modifies his famous statement about Dada, "thought is made in the mouth," so that it becomes an expression ideally suited to Picasso's way of creation, "thought is made by the hand."

In his own poetry, Tzara refuses the concept of stability and unchangeable order; the most superficial study of his manuscripts shows that he often experiments with the location of a line or a group of lines, and that this is especially true for what might be called the key lines, those which include the most often repeated images, such as that of fire, or which form part of a litanic series. Many "necessary" lines may come into the head at once, but their position can be rearranged without destroying any *a priori* fabric of the poem. Furthermore, some of the parts of *L'Homme approximatif* originate in simple sets of bizarre words, listed by association (geological, botanical, etc.) which Tzara then combines in various groups which are to be shifted about as the poem grows. A particular and preconceived *form* would scarcely be appropriate to a poem on approximate man and his language.

The emphasis on motion in all the Dada manifestos and in the Dada poetry is striking; in a poem of 1917, even "the crystal dissolves in motion." But Tzara shows a permanent concern for all manifestations of movement. In *Le Désespéranto* he maintains that the will to action is more interesting than the act accomplished, and that desire is far more important than the attainment (compare Breton's "abandon the prey for the shadow"). He insists here also that the stable appearance of things, if overturned, would show an intense verbal activity as the starting point of all matter: "Under each stone, there is a nest of words and it is from their rapid spinning that the world's substance is formed."[41] And when Tzara explains his conception of poetic humor, which is for him the total comprehension of life and of its dualities, he is careful to distinguish it from the surrealist image and its formalized components which he considers far less mobile. He goes so far as to call the surrealist image a formula and to accuse the surrealist attitude of being essentially static

[41] *L'Antitête*, pp. 183-84.

rather than dynamic. Tzara never ceases to be a Dadaist in
spirit, insofar as Dada represents a state of ceaseless and
unformalized activity: "The poem forces or digs a crater, is
silent, murders or shrieks along the accelerated degrees of
speed."[42] The poet's task, as Tzara envisions it, is to "*break
the winter of things,*" to "*shake* the laugh from the apple-
tree," or to "*seize* the flux of wings at the moment of transparency."[43] All of these expressions reveal his concern that
poetry should be *active*—not a passive perception of the
world but an involvement in its seasons and changes of mood
and rhythm. He calls this "la fidélité de vivre" and opposes
it to the stupid gaping of the man who only watches as the
procession of other lives goes by.

References to journeys and to the desire for greater mobility are everywhere in Tzara's writings. The painfully slow
progress of the poet is at times described in terms of genuine
humility:

ainsi je vais feuilletant des paysages à suivre
déchirant déchiré fidèle
de bois mort de chair de terre
mal loti persévérant
d'une station à la prochaine

je suis cheval je suis rivière
j'avance mal je vis quand même.[44]

(so I go leafing through landscapes to come
tearing torn faithful
made of dead wood of flesh of earth
badly off persevering
from one station to the next

I am a horse I am a river
I go on clumsily but somehow I live.)

The desire for movement is at times expressed in more
heroic terms. Tzara undertakes his pilgrimages "against the

---

[42] "Note sur la poésie," *Sept manifestes Dada*, p. 106.
[43] Emphasis added.
[44] "Anecdote" in *Terre sur terre* (Geneva, Editions Trois Collines,
1946).

current" or "on the path of the stars of the sea" (where he hurls himself into "the pursuit of I no longer know which pain"), or again, he simply follows "an odd star," lonely and empty-handed except for his torn hopes, toward the Magi in rags who are always late in coming.[45] His perpetual and sometimes lamentable flight is complicated by frequent images of delay, places of tedious halts and waiting, like hotels and stations: his play *La Fuite* (1941) and his prose poem "Gare par temps d'égarement" from *Miennes* (1955) both picture an enclosed space, filled with people dressed in "tatters of waiting," consumed by a desperate desire to flee. Worse than all, however, is the forced acknowledgment that all escape is finally impossible: "the painful flight which had set you against your own body. What were you fleeing but your own footsteps?"

But nevertheless, in the center of all the movement, the urge to motion, and the despair it necessarily entails, Tzara is still conscious of the luminous and isolated vision of the immobile man. In another poem from the collection *Miennes*, where he talks of the active enthusiasm for living he felt in his childhood along with his "adorations always in motion," he remembers seeing once on the top of a hill a motionless horse in an "arrested universe" like a perfect image of solitude—at the same moment he saw himself suspended in time, with his sensations petrified in that one instant. He became suddenly aware of the interlocking of dualities and of the possible multiplicity and extension of perception, by the deliberate subtraction of the subject perceiving from the spectacle: "Life and death completed each other, all doors open to possible prolongings. For once, without participating in the meaning of things, I saw. I isolated my vision, enlarging it until it could penetrate through its boundaries infinitely."[46] Implied in this passage is a statement on the image as Tzara conceives it, a statement all the more interesting for its nonproclamatory nature. Tzara's reflections on and examples of the Dada-surrealist image are less often

---

[45] *Ibid.*, p. 166.
[46] "Le Cheval" in *Miennes* (Caractères, 1955).

quoted than those of Breton, Eluard, and Aragon, but they
are none the less significant. In fact, it could be said that as
much of the particular quality of Breton's writing depends
on sharply marked dualities of sentiment, Tzara's is distinguished by an accumulation of startling images, often contrasted with one simple image standing out from the rest by
its very simplicity (in the same way that the horse alone
on the hill stands out among the other memories.)

THE IMMEDIATE VISION

Of all the values Tzara finds necessary to good poetry,
simplicity seems always to be the most important for him,
together with the qualities of entirety, immediacy, and necessity he sees as its primary components. In his essays on Rimbaud, Reverdy, and Apollinaire, Tzara praises the deliberate
bareness of their poetry; he explains that Reverdy juxtaposes
his images or superimposes them in layers without disturbing
the nudity of structure essential to his art,[47] while Apollinaire
refuses even the most elementary word play in favor of
"the exact, real, totally unpromiscuous nudity of the word
which is only itself, intended in its round force, with no background of allusions, or, rather, with none of the seductions of
sublimated imagery."[48] Apollinaire is from every point of
view the exemplary poet for Tzara, who describes him in an
essay of 1917 as the very spirit of action in his fondness
for rapidity and for the unexpected ("the explosive star
everywhere")[49] combined with his spontaneous and un-
quenchable curiosity for the new. With his irrepressible enthusiasm and energy Apollinaire encouraged laughter, which
Tzara defines as human goodness. But above all he embodied
this quality of simplicity, which is the basis of his modernism
and his poetic realism. Tzara points out in his preface to an

---

[47] In "Hommage à Pierre Reverdy," *Le Point* (July 1946). It is
interesting, in view of Tzara's own practice of isolating images, that
his article on Reverdy should be entitled: "De la solitude des images
chez Pierre Reverdy."

[48] Preface to Guillaume Apollinaire, *Alcools* (Club du Meilleur
Livre, 1953), p. 3.

[49] *Sept manifestes Dada*, p. 91.

edition of *Alcools*[50] that its original title was *Eau-de-vie,* and that in rejecting that title, Apollinaire rejected preciosity and euphemism ("water of life") for frankness ("alcohol"), aristocratic delicacy and nuance for brutal plebeian reality. Preferring the crude shock of the image to the rhetoric of the metaphor, the individual spoken language to the general and the symbolic, he represents the tendency of the modern world, "young, nonchalant, and sunny," as totally opposed to the era of the "poètes maudits" as light is to darkness, straightforwardness to elaboration, and the immediacy of the Dadaists and the surrealists to the alienation and "misérabilisme" they see around them. The prose and verse passages in which Tzara laments Apollinaire's death are appropriately simple and clear even though they are contemporary with the Dada writings generally supposed to be deliberately difficult and even incomprehensible:

"La Mort de Guillaume Apollinaire"

nous ne savons rien
nous ne savions rien de la douleur
la saison amère du froid
creuse de longues traces dans nos muscles
il aurait plutôt aimé la joie de la victoire
sages sous les tristesses calmes   en cage
ne pouvoir rien faire
si la neige tombait en haut
si le soleil montait chez nous pendant la nuit
pour nous chauffer
et les arbres pendaient avec leur couronne
—unique pleur—
si les oiseaux étaient parmi nous pour se mirer
dans le lac tranquille au-dessus de nos têtes

ON POURRAIT COMPRENDRE

la mort serait un beau long voyage
et les vacances illimitées de la chair des structures et
des os.[51]

---

[50] *Alcools,* p. 3. See note 48.   [51] *De nos oiseaux* (Kra, 1923).

("The Death of Guillaume Apollinaire"
    we know nothing
    we knew nothing about pain
the bitter season of cold
digs long furrows in our muscles
we would have preferred the joy of victory
        prudent under the calm sadness   caged
                                unable to do anything
        if snow fell upwards
if the sun rose toward us in the night
                        to warm us
    and the trees hung downward with their crown
                        —unique tear—
    if the birds were among us to see their reflection
    in the tranquil lake above our heads

            WE COULD UNDERSTAND

    death would be a beautiful long voyage
and an endless vacation from flesh from structures
    and from bones).

Here Tzara's successful expression of the tragedy depends
entirely on his poetic understatement. It is a combination of
simple devices, such as repetitions ("rien . . . rien . . . rien,"
"si . . . si . . . si . . .") and sudden changes of subjects and
tenses, which give the poem continuity and a certain struc-
tural and emotional complexity; the half-repetition "nous ne
savons rien—nous ne savions rien" is characteristic of Tzara's
more serious word play. The present tense used in the beginning line to negate any knowledge possibly acquired in the
rest of the poem and then used to describe the actual bitter
weather and the corresponding physical and mental helpless-
ness of Apollinaire's friends, contrasts with the imperfect
tense referring directly to the time of the loss. The claim that
they knew nothing about suffering until this event occurred
renders their general ignorance all the more pitiful now
since it implies the uselessness of all events as contributions
to understanding. The only line applying to Apollinaire him-

self is isolated (like the unique simple images mentioned before) by its tense and its tone, which are not echoed anywhere else in the poem, "Il aurait plutôt aimé la joie de la victoire," and it is the parallel of the line in the prose lament, "Sa saison aurait dû être la joie de la victoire." Tzara's insistence on the energy of Apollinaire underlines the impossibility of action on the part of his fellow poets, imprisoned in their own unhappiness. In its childlike vision opposed to actual fact, the second part of the poem resembles the early poem of Breton that begins "If only it were sunny tonight." For Tzara, as for Eluard and Breton, the clear eyes through which the child is able to see the world have all the purity which should illuminate poetic perception: "childhood, childhood, I call upon you."[52] And as a result of this vision, the phrase "On pourrait comprendre" acquires an overtone of irony in addition to its primary anger and bewilderment. This poem is touching in its restraint and in its use of minimal devices, none of which are dramatic, but whose combination produces a poetry of genuine emotion without falling into the sentimentality scorned by Dada.

Such apparent simplicity marks a great deal of Tzara's poetry; even in the epic grandeur of *L'Homme approximatif*, the passages of the greatest strength are not the complicated ones. In his love poetry, short lines and easily grasped images predominate,

> tu reviendras ma bien lointaine
> je sais les herbes veillent en toi[53]
>
> (you will return my faraway one
> I know the grasses keep watch in you),

occasionally interspersed with the sort of unlikely images favored by Dada-surrealist theory (snow as distant love, landscapes of slow-rising bread, and the like). These latter images, participating in the same rhythm and feeling as the

---

[52] *A Haute flamme* (Jacquet, 1955).
[53] "Le feu défendu," *L'Arbre des voyageurs* (Editions de la Montagne, 1930), p. 90.

other lines, do not alter the tone or lessen the emotional
force of the poetry: rather, they intensify both.

Even the longer poems with their more universal scope
show the rigor and bareness of structure that Tzara the critic
points out in the poets he admires. The images of crystal,
sun, and fire, together with the themes of presence and
vision, birth and language, give a sense of continuity to all
his poetry, early and late. A typically political poem, "Sur une
aurore grecque" (*Terre sur terre*) begins with a catalogue
of positive objects and optimistic sentiments:

> voici le sable voici mon corps
> voici le marbre et le ruisseau
>
> (here is the sand here is my body
> here is the marble and the stream).

A glass of wine is touched by the "word of moon," the
crystal is mingled with the sensual and the human ("le
battement de cristal qui vous traverse"), but suddenly a
group of menacing images intrudes—a crow blocks off all
the routes of freedom, a dream is seen as rotten,

> et le sang est mort souillé
>
> (and the blood has died dishonored).

The poem ends, however, with the reassurance (admittedly
"oriented" in a political sense, "la faucille et la colère sont
les maîtres du monde") of eventual rebirth. When the time
comes, the crows are once more replaced by images of sun,
crystal, and flame:

> le rêve revenu
> dans sa grandeur incendiaire
> les rois mages vers de nouvelles naissances
> il est dit sur la montagne que déjà leurs feux s'allument
> au coeur visible du silence
>
> (the dream returned
> in its incendiary grandeur
> the magi toward new births
> it is said on the mountain that already their fires are lit
> in the visible heart of silence).

In spite of the elementary framework of repetitions ("Voici
. . . voici, mais . . . mais, le soleil . . . le rêve") there is a
decided expansion and development within the poem, so that
at its conclusion the reader has a strong impression of time
elapsed since the first introduction of presences ("voici le
sable . . ."). The Magi, figures whom Tzara characteristically associates with the themes of birth and rebirth, offer a
nobility and objectivity that the more personal "voici mon
corps" does not at first seem to have. The poem has moved
from a material and subjective description of present things
toward an abstract future possibility. In other forms, this
pattern of expansion and vertical progression is frequent—
for example, in "La Source voilée" (1956), where a deeply
personal despair ("Where I go there is no more light")
yields finally to the lofty spectacle of the "burning moments
on the heights of man." Tzara's poetry, like that of Eluard,
characteristically opens out from the individual perception of
the simple to the most positive universal vision.

Tzara's long poem of 1955, *La Bonne heure,* displays a
complete range of the brighter images. The light and the
burning are new and turned toward what is to come ("aux
flammes neuves," "tout le feu de l'avenir"), and even the
difficulties of human language and of human desire are resolved, as the "mots brisants" or destructive words give way
to an inner bareness and purity, where transparency is seen
as the heart of desire. But once again the laughing faces, the
golden windows thrown open, all the spectacles of offering
and clear vision ("crystal eyelids") are followed by a stark
listing of opposed images, in which the signs of life are
juxtaposed in brief lines with those of death. Ruined fruits,
extinguished hearths, toothless laughs, and trampled city
squares present a far more horrible picture when they are
condensed into this minimum of space. There are no words
surrounding the juxtapositions to soften the conflicts, so that
what may at first appear a simplistic catalogue proves to be
on closer examination, a poetic process directed at intensity
of feeling. Any momentum which might have spread out in
the space of a longer line is arrested within it, as time and
space lose their potential meaning,

les heures souillées
les pas verrouillés

(the tainted hours
the locked steps),

as the present is cut off from the future and from possible
freedom. The streets are broken, and so there is misery outside to walk on instead. Horror invades even the inside of
the human mind, the intellectual haven traditionally safe at
least from physical misfortune:

les chevaux éventrés
dans l'arène des têtes

(the disembowelled horses
in the arena of heads).

The alternations of bright and dark fall into many patterns, some far more subtle than others. But the distinguishing mark of Tzara's poetry which remains constant from the
time of Dada is the sharp condensation in one or a few
lines of the sort of image which perfectly illustrates the
merveilleux of Dada-surrealist poetry, fusing transparency
and all its allied qualities of luminosity, intensity, elevation,
and immediacy into a perfect whole. In the 1961 poem
"Juste présent," the poet sees, with the clarity of a child's
vision ("les vertus enfantines des yeux clairs à venir") and
with the full range of human experience:

la meute des brumes dissipée
l'incandescence du temps
et le sourire haut de l'homme tout autour
sur le coup de midi

(the flock of mists dispersed
the incandescence of time
and the lofty smile of man everywhere
at the stroke of noon).

Here in these lines is concentrated, in the single and simple
image of the "sourire haut," all the force of the most powerful Dada and surrealist inspiration.

The bare simplicity of this kind of image exemplifies both the Dadaist and the surrealist attitude toward artistic creation and appreciation. Art cannot be constructed, and it cannot be verbally explained; it depends for its strength on spontaneity and can only be seen directly: "Art is at present the only construction complete in itself, of which there is nothing more to say, since it is to such an extent richness, vitality, sense, wisdom. Understand, see. Describe a flower: relative poetry more or less paper flower. See."[54] Description of art is no more valid than art as description—none of the surrealist writers really *describes* art any more than the surrealist artists describe objects. Dadaism is, like surrealism, an art of presence.

It is however true that Tzara, when he wants to distinguish the Dada attitude from the surrealist attitude, chooses exactly this point for his argument. In his *Propos sur Braccelli* (1963) he explains that whereas Dada is absolutely subjective and gratuitous, surrealism has always been fascinated with the "mécanisme" responsible for the work of art and with the manner in which the creation reveals human personality. So that for surrealism, the work of art must be *symptomatic* of a certain state of consciousness and cannot content itself with simply existing. Dada, he implies by contrast, is a nonformulated, spontaneous, unapplicable pleasure of pure creation and free activity. From such a perspective Dada seems to be, far more than surrealism, a pure art of *presence* uninvolved with prior motivations or with any possible network of manifestations, symptoms, or second-order phenomena. Dada insists above all on the richness of the instant of art, of the image as image in its momentary and spontaneous density—in its simplicity. "Simplicity is called Dada."

PROFUSION, MEASURE, AND CLARITY:
"LA FACE INTÉRIEURE"

The necessary complement to Tzara's simplicity is the emphasis he places on the notion of *plénitude* ("fullness" or

[54] "Note sur l'art," *Sept manifestes Dada*, p. 85.

"completeness"). It is this quality that he respects in Matisse (his "tranquille plénitude"), or in the work of Picasso, revealing as it does the artist's love of life and his hope so firmly entrenched in "this earth." Matisse fills his paintings with a "radiant sun already prefiguring the infinite expansion of existence and the dream," and Picasso serves the revolution of which Tzara often speaks by uniting alienated man once again with his own natural profundity, from which society has estranged him, and restoring to his impoverished spirit the vigor appropriate to it. Tzara's faithfulness to the principle of simplicity never entails a passive agreement in the narrow sense, for he is equally faithful to the spirit of his *L'Homme approximatif*: "Harmony—let this word be banished from the feverish world I visit." The concept of *plénitude*, then, is not only compatible with the extreme variance of light and dark images constant in Tzara—it is in just this dramatic play of differences visible to the poet that the concept acquires its greatest scope and intensity.

As early as 1931, the theme of *plénitude* can be plainly identified in Tzara's poetry and essays among all the other lesser but related themes. Tzara describes *L'Homme approximatif* aware of his own possibilities as

> l'homme portant dans son fruit la brûlante et propice
> éclosion du matin[55]
>
> (man bearing in his fruit morning's burning and
> propitious blossoming).

The burning and the brilliance of the morning sun are of course closely allied to all the images of clarity and intensity which provide the major focus for Tzara's early poetry, whereas the image of ripening fruit and the adjective "propice" announce the atmosphere of his later poems. All the themes of presence and of the bounty and wisdom of the natural world are already indicated here by phrases such as "objects are still there a consolation alongside feelings" and "the slow consciousness of plants and of things." As time

---

[55] *L'Homme approximatif*, p. 118.

goes on, Tzara begins to stress the *juste* in place of the *merveilleux*: "juste fruit," "juste présent," "juste aube" are all perfectly fitting in a human sense. Instead of the wish that night turn into day, or trees hang upside down, there are repeated assertions of the completeness of life as it is and as we perceive it (*Le Signe de vie*), a life where poetry is exactly appropriate to the word it magnifies and to the nature of the man who writes it: "the fire of the word sewn to the fruits of the earth."[56]

The poems of *Terre sur terre* could all be placed under the heading of the rhetorical question posed in one of them: "What is this space that radiates in me?"[57] Here the contrasts of light and dark images are less important than the force of the whole to which they contribute.

These poems use what Aragon would call "the poetry of the simple" as the thoroughly convincing basis for a celebration of man at once natural and mystical:

> j'ai vu de près parmi les aveugles le mystère de la naissance
> vent et pluie et vin et fruits
> le soleil de l'aveugle un enfant dans la neige
> et à dire l'avenir toute la force de l'homme
> offerte de chair comme le sel et le pain
> à la plus belle à la merveilleuse à la flamme future
>
> . . .
>
> seule lumière seule
> pure entre les hautes déchirures
>
> j'ai vu de près parmi les aveugles le soleil de la naissance
> et la fleur première
> le pain rayonnant sur le comble de l'ombre
> et des montagnes d'oiseaux fraîchement confiants
> revenir à la source
> le chant et le silence mon beau pays de joie
>
> (I have seen among the blind the mystery of birth
> wind and rain and wine and fruits
> the sun of the blind man a child in the snow

---

[56] "Vltava," *Le Signe de vie* (Bordas, 1946).
[57] "Une Route Seul Soleil."

and for telling the future all the strength of man
offered in flesh like salt and bread
to the most beautiful the marvelous to the future flame
. . .
the only light the only one
pure between the high lacerations

I have seen among the blind the sun of birth
and the first flower
the bread shining on the peak of shadow
and mountains of birds freshly confident
coming back to the spring
both the song and the silence my beautiful country of joy).

Here the clarity, allied with a certain majestic fullness, is
of a slower pace than the "galop de clarté" by which Tzara
characterized the spirit of Apollinaire. The poem is no longer
a spectacle but a witness to what the poet himself has seen
and comprehended, as mystery ("à la merveilleuse à la
flamme future") and as the ordinary course of nature. The
smallest elements of man's daily life (bread, wine, salt) are
elevated with those of the natural world (wind, rain, fruits)
in a splendid pagan communion of the future (birth, the
future flame). Once more the emotional texture of the poem
depends on a contrast of elements: blindness and vision,
rain and sun, man and child, radiance and shadow, song and
silence—and these uncomplicated, undramatic, and obvious
elements form a poem of great depth and epic vision. The
title of the final poem in *Terre sur terre*, "Acceptation du
printemps," is indicative of the frame of mind that precedes
all these poems (in accordance with Tzara's definition of
poetry as the quality of mind or the sentiment that precedes
the actual verse). Man here takes for his own the rhythm
and the richness of the outside world in a manner more
natural than emotional. The importance Tzara gives to this
acceptance, or this relation between man and nature is obvious in the preponderance of the whole family of images
related to the earth, its produce, and the weight of its presence
—images implying possession, fulfillment, maturity, and con-

viction—and of the titles and phrases which correspond to this set of feelings: *Le Poids du monde, Miennes,* "the words heavy with gardens / the substance of their certainty," "the heavy radiance of things," "an afternoon of earth," "this path is of the earth and could never disappear." The poet has great confidence in his poetry and in its power to create an entirely new epoch by its optimism and its strength:

> je parle d'un temps neuf luisant
> et d'une fraîcheur bleuie
> . . .
> les portes sont ouvertes ivoire des fruits murs
> je parle de constance

> (I speak of a new time shining
> and of a coolness tinged with blue
> . . .
> the doors are opened ivory of ripe fruits
> I speak of constancy).

Here brightness and freshness of vision are closely joined to the necessity of patience and fidelity. These latter and seemingly more "mature" virtues themselves furnish in due time the luminous center for the surrounding darkness:

> au coeur des déchirures
> l'attente se fait flamme

> (at the heart of the lacerations
> the waiting becomes flame).[58]

Tzara closes the poem with a humanistic prayer to the profusion and the perfection of the natural and simple world:

> que la terre advienne sur terre
> et se multiplie la graine de son règne

> (let earth come on earth
> and let the grain of its kingdom multiply).

The long poem of 1953, *La Face intérieure,* gives what is perhaps the best and most complete summation of all Tzara's

---

[58] Compare with the ending of *L'Homme approximatif.*

favorite images of earth—of its seasons and its fruits, of the dualities of presence and absence, pain and hope, misery and grandeur, the word and the cessation of the word. More than any other of his poems it is a poem of *plénitude*; though it uses many of the same elements as the poem quoted at length from *Terre sur terre*, it is clearly larger in scope, directed not toward the natural mysteries of birth and the future seasons, but toward the actual construction of eternity. The elemental and simple objects of the former poem—rain, sun, bread, salt, wind, birds—are replaced by, or rather absorbed in, the larger reality of man's possible greatness and vision, his stubborn determination, and his refusal of the death of language:

> des yeux clairs de bâtisseurs de villes
> bâtisseurs d'intarissables villes.
>
> (the clear eyes of the builders of towns
> builders of inexhaustible towns.)

And still the patterns of opposition remain, as the "présence des hommes" balances the "absence des choses," and the "yeux clairs" redeem the misery seen at every window and the hideous spectacle of man before his prey, "la cruauté faite homme." It is plainly from these opposed elements that the plenitude of vision is developed, taking its full range from the doubles of cruelty and clarity, language and the positive, *constructed* silence of a new beginning:

> bâtisseurs de villes immémoriales
> hautes frondaisons vous bâtisseurs d'étés
> rayonnantes figures aux fronts de plénitude
> comme les fruits intacts de l'humaine mesure
>
> invraisemblables présences des quatre coins du monde
> bâtisseurs de silence au recommencement du monde
> vous êtes là quatre points cardinaux de la vérité du feu
> transparences retrouvées aux sources du romarin.
>
> (builders of immemorial towns
> high foliage you builders of summer

shining faces with foreheads of fullness
like the whole fruits of human measure

unlikely presences of the four corners of the earth
builders of silence at the resurrection of the world
you are there four cardinal points of the truth of fire
transparencies found again at the springs of rosemary.)

The clarity and the assurance of totality so highly prized by
Tzara throughout all the periods of his poetic and critical
evolution is finally perceived in its simple presence within the
concrete world of natural objects, whose inner surface and
depth (*La Face intérieure*) is identical with their exterior and
universal reality. From one point of view, nothing could be
further from the obvious anti-natural violence of Dada. But
that point of view is perhaps not the one closest to the more
profound spirit of Dada as Tzara expresses it.

PAUL ELUARD

Je reste mon propre miroir
Je mêle neige et feu
—ELUARD, *Médieuses*

Miroirs brisés miroirs entiers
—ELUARD, *Poésie ininterrompue I*

A force de mêler le blé de la lumière
Aux caresses des chairs de la terre à minuit
—II, 121

Murs ensoleillés murs opaques
    . . .
Ruines naissances le soleil bat en ton coeur
—ELUARD, *Le Livre ouvert I*

ORDER, PARTICIPATION, TRANSFORMATION

The same themes of purity, spontaneity, and intensity which are all-important in Tzara's Dada manifestos and Breton's surrealist declarations pervade all the writings of Eluard—poetry and prose, early and late. It is true that the "absolute liberty" he continues to champion after his break with surrealism does not depend, as it did at first, on the idealistic requirement stated in *La Révolution surréaliste* (No. 3): "no word will ever again be subordinated to matter." But the new framework of political interpretation does not alter in any way Eluard's tone or his imagery. This continuity is perfectly understandable when one reads in his *Anthologie des écrits sur l'art* such quotations from the young Marx as: "The essential form of wit is gaiety, light,"[1] "Art is the highest joy man can offer himself."[2]

Eluard's own poetry does not change, nor does his definition of poetry. Poetic fidelity, he says in his preface to *La Poésie du passé* (1951), requires clarity of vision, reflection of that vision, and action: it requires "keeping your eyes open on yourself and on the world, on the front of the mirror and on the back of the mirror in order to hold off the night." The vocabulary and the concepts are much the same as they were twenty years earlier, with an emphasis on light, on the image with its metamorphosing power, and on the future community of men united in a common vision: "Weak man transforms himself into radiant man. . . . The image is his virtue. He dissolves himself and gives himself a new form, he knows how to live and to bestow life, he is common."[3] Each of the main elements of this excerpt is essential to the whole of Eluard's system of values: the luminosity of the new (surrealist) vision, the potential self-transformation of man by his vision, in which he participates continuously, and the necessity of sharing it.

"Radiant man" is the being who refuses to limit himself to the old world of reason, which Eluard considers a dull and disordered world. Poets and painters, the "ordonnateurs," see a new bright and irrational order in things, an order which their vision reinforces. The natural and luminous arrangement Eluard values is clearly not the tempestuous *ordre* of Dada: "We admire the order of things, the order of rocks, the order of hours. But this shadow which disappears and this sorrowful element which disappears."[4] Here man does not impose the narrowing grid of his rational interpretation

[1] Karl Marx, quoted in Paul Eluard, *Anthologie des écrits sur l'art* (Editions Cercle d'art, 1952), p. 93.

[2] *Ibid.*, p. 97.

[3] *La Poésie du passé* (Seghers, 1951), p. 14.

[4] "Baigneuse du clair au sombre," *Les Nécessités de la vie, poèmes* (Gallimard, 1951), p. 46.

on the simplicity of nature. The lost contact between the object perceived and the mind perceiving it is reestablished as the artist sees everything afresh and, offering the vision to others, doubles the clarity for himself: "Que fleurisse ton oeil / Lumière" (I, 579) / (Let your eye flower / Light). The motto *donner à voir* is not an empty oral pun; it is equally valid in its two meanings ("to give to have" and "to offer vision"). To see and comprehend clearly and to help others see and comprehend is the highest possible achievement. Furthermore, seeing and understanding are the same thing for Eluard: "voir, c'est comprendre" (I, 526).[5] So there is no gap between the visual and the mental for him; his poetic theories are all based on this simplicity of sight and thought and on this union or reunion of disparate or disordered elements: "J'établis des rapports. . . ."[6] Such relationships (*rapports*) as he establishes apply to the human as well as to the object world: by linking the elements of one, he links those of the other. The search for a "fil conducteur" is common to all the surrealists.

In "Le Miroir de Baudelaire" (*Minotaure*, 1, 1933), Eluard discusses the poetic technique of comparison, the surrealist technique *par excellence*, and warns that the power to compare is not to be taken for granted by all poets since the resemblance between two things is determined more by the character of the mind that perceives it than by the objective relationship that may exist or be *created*. (If he had used the verb "identify" instead of the verb "establish" in describing the role played by the poet in making the comparison, he would have implied that the resemblance was certain, in which case the image would not demand the effort essential to surrealism. For the surrealist image cannot be simply stated by the poet or passively observed by the reader; they must both actively participate in it, even if the action is spontaneous and subconscious.)

Like Tzara, Eluard considers poetry a form of constant mo-

[5] "La Nécessité," *La Vie immédiate*. Compare Tzara's: "Comprendre, voir."
[6] *Avenir de la poésie* (G.L.M., 1937).

tion. Participation precedes comprehension: "All that really matters is to participate, to move, to understand."[7] Only the man who actively engages himself in the world about him with the whole force of his imaginative vision is able to escape his paralyzing solitude and accept his active responsibility for other men. The poet who is "on earth" cannot take a safe distance from the suffering of others but must participate in it:

Où donc est la muraille poétique du bien-être
Que nous la renversions
Et que nous prenions pied dans ce monde impossible[8]

(Where then is the poetic wall of well-being
So we can knock it down
And take a stand in this impossible world).

In his *L'Avenir de la poésie* (1937) Eluard points out as Baudelaire's most significant contribution his realization that the "I" always points to an "us," that ultimately poetry should depend on a universal equality of happiness. Here the last two points of Eluard's poetic program are clarified and united. As the poet *realizes* or *creates* the unlikely resemblance which is the image he recreates himself, the observer, and the whole community of men—that is, he makes himself "common." In this sense poetry is not, as Eluard says once more in *Les Sentiers et routes de la poésie*, an object of art, limited to personal aesthetic enjoyment, but an *object to be used*, a conception based on Lautréamont's dictum so often quoted by the surrealists: "Personal poetry has had its age. . .". The dark images of individual uselessness should yield to the bright ones of a common universe: "And the good of all men has no shadow."[9]

In his *Anthologie des écrits sur l'art* (1952), Eluard expresses the hope that drawing will some day become a social fact like language and writing, and that eventually all the forms of communication will pass from the trivial social plane

[7] *A Pablo Picasso* (Geneva, Editions Trois Collines, 1944), p. 31.
[8] "Aujourd'hui," *Poèmes politiques* (Gallimard, 1948).
[9] *Poésie ininterrompue*, II (Gallimard, 1953), p. 36.

to the universal plane on which "all men will communicate by the vision of things and they will use this vision to express the point that is common to them, to them and to things, to them as it is to things, to things as it is to them."[10] His old formula: "voir, c'est comprendre" is now expanded: "To see is to understand and to act; to see is to unite the world with man and man with man."[11] Men are separated in an epoch of moral misery, and artists like Picasso understand that the most essential task is to encourage the enthusiasm that can unite them in a new and optimistic perception. Picasso, better than anyone else, is able to demonstrate a "poetic reason" for the infinite series of relationships he sees between things which is the artistic equivalent of the childlike vision. Adult or logical thought makes a sharp distinction between concrete things and their abstract relations, whereas animals and primitive man, insane persons and children, immediately establish simple emotional relationships based on sympathy and antipathy. But their instinctive power of comparison is the only alternative to the alienating or civilized rational age. The ideal vision presented by the poet approximates the pre-rational instinct of a child who sees and understands simultaneously, in an immediacy strange to the "normal" sensibility of the adult mind. This natural poetic closeness to creation is the answer to physical and mental human isolation. It is no more difficult for the poet of the marvelous to make a fire in the snow than to "blend the swimmer with the river" as Picasso does. In an essay on Max Ernst, Eluard speaks of the artist's power to transmute everything into everything else, and the strength of his own poetry is based on exactly that power. Following the principle enunciated by Breton[12] that in our world the aspects of all things are open and therefore interchangeable, Eluard sees one woman as a hundred and any object as any other: on this openness of vision depends the sense of multiplicity essential to his poetic uni-

[10] Quoted in *L'Art poétique*, J. Charpier, ed. (Seghers, 1952), p. 664.

[11] *Anthologie des écrits sur l'art*, p. 8.

[12] "Préliminaires sur Matta," *Le Surréalisme et la peinture* (Gallimard, 1966).

verse, his consciousness of the "multiplied dimensions of future strength" (ɪ, 1101). Each separate object, valuable in itself ("L'unique soleil") contains an unlimited potentiality of expansion: "Une seule goutte d'eau / Multipliait ses halos" (ɪɪ, 431) / (A single drop of water / Multiplied its haloes). From "une aurore unique" comes a succession of days. All things are *ressemblantes* in the poetic perspective, and so they repeat each other in an endless series of reflections: a town can be "repeated" like a poem, because it "resembles." Eluard does not specify what it resembles, since to specify would be to limit, while the goal of his poetry and of surrealist poetry in general is to go beyond the limits.

All relationships between things, no matter how modest, are flexible and infinite, infinitely generative of new forms of vision. If a tiny bird walks "dans d'immenses régions", the sun is likely to sprout wings. In Eluard's poetry, water forms hills and men inebriate the wine; there are no fixed frameworks. Through the principles of constant transference and uninterrupted communication, the world of nature expands the human world:

Les arbres nous grandissaient (ɪ, 47)

(The trees enlarged us).

To an even greater extent than Breton, Eluard occupies himself with a poetic investigation of the paradox "one within the other." Breton wants his life and works to have the spontaneous brilliance of the crystal, but Eluard values above all else *La Vie immédiate*, that is, "to participate, to move, to understand," not to be separate but to be *ressemblant*, to perceive things not as discontinuous, but as joined. In an early essay on Ernst, Eluard describes the inseparable nature of the exterior and the interior, of "matter, movement, need, desire."[13] There is no distance between man and the objects of his vision, and ideally none between things actual and imagined, the concrete and the abstract: they are in fact identified with each other. This belief is sometimes reflected in a

[13] Essay of 1934, printed in *Beyond Painting* (New York, Wittenborn, 1948).

continual telescoping of images, as in the poem "Coeur à pic" (from *Cours naturel*), where human images are mixed with natural ones:

> Villages peuplés eau pleine
> . . .
> Lampes de pain enfants de feuilles
>
> (Towns of people water full
> . . .
> Lamps of bread children of leaves),

where the abstract powers of language and vision, as well as intangible feelings, are identified with the physical landscape:

> Moulins des miroirs et des yeux
> Iles des seins sillons des mots
> Neige câline de la force
> Mares fanées de la fatigue
>
> (Windmills of mirrors and of eyes
> Islands of breasts furrows of words
> Caressing snow of strength
> Faded ponds of fatigue).

This poem is genuinely a meeting-place of the dissimilar and the contrary, since phrases of fullness, abundance, light, and strength join those of secrecy, darkness, and disaster in a permanent poetic union, effectively illustrating Eluard's desire that the "transparent image" should reflect and be a reflection of the *point confluent* at the heart of the real.

Art is the principle of exaltation, but also of participation and transformation: one of the highest compliments Eluard pays to an artist is his description of Dominguez's work as "lofty paintings hot with metamorphosis." To accept seriously the basic principles of *ressemblance* and interchangeability implies the acceptance of a further, more difficult irrationality—that a man can be at once his own being and another:

> Je fus rocher dans l'homme l'homme dans le rocher
> Je fus oiseau dans l'air espace dans l'oiseau[14]

[14] "Mes heures," *Le Livre ouvert II*.

(I was a rock in man man within the rock
I was a bird in air space within the bird).

The poet's imaginative ability to identify himself with what
he sees is no more important than his psychological capability of transforming himself into a different personality, of
recreating himself entirely through the "mediation of all beings."

Je suis le spectateur et l'acteur et l'auteur
Je suis la femme et son mari et leur enfant
. . .
Car où commence un corps je prends forme et conscience
Et même quand un corps se défait dans la mort
Je gis en son creuset j'épouse son tourment[15]

(I am the spectator and the actor and the author
I am the woman and her husband and their child
. . .
For where there is a body I take on form and consciousness
And even when a body is undone in death
I lie in its crucible I wed its torment).

The poet's consciousness begins with the consciousness of
any other being, his form begins with any other form. What
is stylistic condensation or juxtaposition in Tzara's transcription of the natural world becomes, in Eluard's, a deliberate
suppression of *personal* distance, which leaves the space of
the poem untouched. The unceasing metamorphosis of the
individual, and of individuals together, is the primary manifestation of what Eluard calls *La Poésie ininterrompue* of

---

[15] "D'un et deux, de tous," *Les Derniers poèmes d'amour* (Seghers,
1966). See also his *Poésie ininterrompue*:

Je suis ma mère et mon enfant
. . .
Je suis mon rayon de soleil
Et je suis mon bonheur nocturne. (II, 26)

(I am my mother and my child
. . .
I am the ray of my own sun
And I am my nighttime happiness.)

the "undivided world" ("le monde sans rupture"). This vision rests on the denial of separation and on the absolute
power of poetry. For Eluard, as for all the surrealists, the
poet creates his own past and his own space: "J'avais mon
paysage et je m'y suis perdue" (I, 1199)[16] / (I had my
landscape and lost myself there). He wills a vision of constant motion in the universe equivalent to the human hope
"of always being mobile." (II, 898) The most valuable
images or objects are those capable of forming a "moving
mirror" for man, a reflection of his motion and the inspiration for his belief in a constant becoming. Breton's concise
statement: "Always for the first time" has an exact parallel
in Eluard's credo: "To be at the beginning," or "The celebration is always new," and the leitmotif running through Eluard's poems—"Grandir est sans limites" (I, 406) / (Growing is limitless)—is the ideal of surrealism itself. When space
and time are annulled by poetic reality or surreality, there
is no limit to the force of surrealist poetry, to the field of
surrealist vision, or to the faith of surrealist love. At the
height of this faith, the poet can claim that he and the woman
he loves are future, that all his fellowmen, who are also
poets, are "en avant," and that in the world surrounding
them, "rien n'a des limites" (I, 124) / (nothing has limits).

One might expect at least the concept of nonlimitation to
be without shadow. But there is an opposite perception even
here, and it arises not in the exterior world, but in the in-
herent human reluctance to accept unlimited possibility.
Eluard's confession is, as always, simply phrased because it
is meant for everyone who has or has once had his confidence in the potentiality of poetry:

Je souffre d'être sans limites. (II, 681)

(I suffer from being limitless.)

[16] Compare with Desnos' poem "Le Paysage," where again the
poet is in some sense a prisoner of his own landscape. Eluard's poem is
addressed "à celle qui répète ce que je dis"—thus the feminine form.
Note also the theme of repetition and reflection.

A LANGUAGE OF BALANCE AND TRANSPARENCY

Eluard is so naturally a poet that he states his theories of art more convincingly in his poems themselves than in any of his prose writings. His notion of the image as a "perfect contact" and as a "confluent point," of the poet as the double of the beings he observes and whose truth he guarantees, and as the person uniquely responsible for the spiritual and actual inventory of the real ("Tout dire," "Je rends compte du réel," "Et je veux dire ce qui est")—these form an integral part of his verse. They *are* poetry as much as they are reflections upon it, in the same way as the reflection of love implies a parallel identification. All Eluard's theories are mingled in a relationship which endlessly mirrors the aim of poetry or of art, an aim of multiplicity, expansion, and endless communication.[17] It is hard not to see this refusal to stand outside his own poems, this quiet integration of theory and poetry, as a further example of his basic modesty and understatement, the necessary and oddly touching opposite (or double) of his requirement that poetry have the volume of a shout of joy, and the irreversible force of a wave.

In *Cours naturel* (1938), a title that indicates a certain acceptance of things as they are, Eluard meditates at length on the language which is the point of contact between the order of man and the order of the world, on its value and on the realm of poetic creation which is as unlimited as the realm of vision. All words are marvelous by their nature, all are *equivalent*: for Eluard, the poet's task is also to make equivalents of all possible questions, their answers and their echoes. Poetry is a principle of balance ("ma limite et mon infini") and a realm of potential rearrangement over which it is man's privilege to reign:

[17] In fact, Eluard deliberately chooses a simple form so as not to place a barrier between himself and any reader; the poem should be equivalent to the song—instantly comprehensible. (See Eluard's note on poetry as song [II, 931], and Chapter 2, note 12.)

O mon empire d'homme
Mots que j'écris ici
Contre toute évidence[18]

(O my empire of man
Words that I write here
In the face of all the facts).

The structures man controls in his language exert a powerful
influence over the natural elements; at the "first limpid word,"
material obstacles and awkwardness disappear to make way
for the constantly renewed possibility of a fresh and even
facile beginning in clarity.

"Image, oh perfect contact . . ."—along with the consciousness of multiplicity runs a parallel consciousness of immediacy; the contact between the object and the person who
sees it is reestablished so that the poet is in no way separate
from his world. He has the power to create a special universe
outside himself and contrary to all usual perception, which
is, however, a universe that closely resembles him ("Tonight
I shall build an exceptional night / Mine") and reflects his
vision like a perfect mirror, multiplying his image and giving
him the sense of community with his fellowmen. The most
perfect example of this ideal (and perhaps also real) community and its poetic vision of liberation is expressed in the
often-quoted and majestic poem "Sans âge," also from *Cours
naturel.* Entirely constructed about the themes of creation,
fraternity, childlike innocence and freshness, and around the
parallel images of purity and light, joy, warmth, and language, "Sans âge" can be read either as a poem about surrealism or about Communist fraternity, or about the fraternity
of poets, or better still as an example of the similarity between
all three:

Nous approchons
Dans les forêts

[18] "Quelques uns des mots qui, jusqu'ici, m'étaient mystérieuse-
ment interdits." Michel Sanouillet, in his *Dada à Paris*, discusses at
some length Eluard's passion for words.

Prenez la rue du matin
Montez les marches de la brume
Nous approchons
La terre en a le coeur crispé
Encore un jour à mettre au monde.

———

Le ciel s'élargira
Nous en avions assez
D'habiter dans les ruines du sommeil
Dans l'ombre basse du repos
De la fatigue de l'abandon

La terre reprendra la forme de nos corps vivants
Le vent nous subira
Le soleil et la nuit passeront dans nos yeux
Sans jamais les changer

Notre espace certain notre air pur est de taille
A combler le retard creusé par l'habitude
Nous aborderons tous une mémoire nouvelle
Nous parlerons ensemble un langage sensible.

———

O mes frères contraires gardant dans vos prunelles
La nuit infuse et son horreur
. . .

Moi je vais vers la vie j'ai l'apparence d'homme
Pour prouver que le monde est fait à ma mesure

Et je ne suis pas seul
Mille images de moi multiplient ma lumière
Mille regards pareils égalisent la chair
C'est l'oiseau c'est l'enfant c'est le roc c'est la plaine
Qui se mêlent à nous
L'or éclate de rire de se voir hors du gouffre
L'eau le feu se dénudent pour une seule saison
Il n'y a plus d'éclipse au front de l'univers

———

. . .

Le prisme respire avec nous
Aube abondante

Au sommet de chaque herbe reine
Au sommet des mousses à la pointe des neiges
Des vagues des sables bouleversés
Des enfances persistantes
Hors de toutes les cavernes
Hors de nous-mêmes.[19]

[19] Compare with this poem the shorter but similar "Facile" from the 1936 collection *Les Yeux fertiles*, which exemplifies, in a similar way, the vision described in Eluard's speech of 1937, *L'Avenir de la poésie*, of a "reciprocal" poetry, based on equal happiness for all. Both poems are based on the themes of approach, of unique intensity, bareness and brilliance, equivalence and fraternity, and they share the same rhythms and the same imagery:

Nous avançons toujours
. . .
Nous vivons d'un seul jet
Nous sommes du bon port
. . .
Nos baisers et nos mains au niveau de nous-mêmes
La jeunesse en amande se dénude et rêve
L'herbe se relève en sourdine
. . .
Toute brume chassée
. . .
Notre ombre n'éteint pas le feu
Nous nous perpétuons.

(We always go forward
. . .
We live all at once
We are assured
. . .
Our kisses and our hands at our own level
Youth like an almond disrobes and dreams
The grass rises in secret
. . .
All mist dispersed
. . .
Our shadow does not put out the fire
We perpetuate ourselves.)

Furthermore, each poem has a section (not quoted) in which the village of doubting and impure men is abandoned by the poetic hero: "We have forever / left behind us hope that exhausts itself / In a town fashioned of flesh and of misery"; "Where have I left you / With your hands in the lazy oil / Of your former deeds / With so

(We draw nearer
In the forests
Take the street of morning
Climb the steps of mist

We draw nearer
The earth is impatient
Once more a day to be born.

———

The sky will open out
We were tired
Of living in the ruins of sleep
In the lowly shadows of rest
Of fatigue of abandon

The earth will assume once more the form of our living
    bodies
The wind will submit to us
Sun and night will pass into our eyes
Never changing them

Our certain space our pure air is sufficient
To fill the delay dug by habit
We will all begin a new memory
We will speak a sensitive language together.

———

O my contrary brothers holding in your eyes
The night infused with horror
. . .

I move toward life I have the look of man
To prove that the world is made to my measure

---

little hope that death wins out / Oh my lost brothers."

    Jean-Pierre Richard, in his brilliant commentary on Eluard (*Onze études sur la poésie moderne* [Seuil, 1964]), underlines many other dualities than those mentioned here. He speaks, for instance, of the virgin moments which are totally offered, of the light abolished and recreated, of the objects both illuminated and illuminating. And in his interpretation of "Sans âge," he stresses the opposition between the "pointe" and the expression "hors de," an opposition which reveals Eluard's passion at once for the finite and for the open.

And I am not alone
A thousand of my images multiply my light
A thousand similar gazes equalize the flesh
The bird the child the rock the plain
Mingle with us
The gold laughs to find itself outside the chasm
Water fire bare themselves for a single season
There is no more eclipse on the forehead of the universe
—

. . .

The prism breathes with us
Abundant dawn
Queen at the point of each grass blade
At the summit of moss at the peak of snow
Waves sands overturned
Lasting childhoods
Outside all caves
Outside ourselves.)

In this setting of absolute activity, man is stronger even than the nature which surrounds him ("le vent nous subira") and the force of the poem is entirely dependent on the theme of human confidence. The vocabulary is one of *approach* and never of distance, of birth and rebirth, where death enters only in the picture of the "frères contraires," their hands weighed down with the heaviness of an unforgettable past— they are unable to undertake a new beginning. All the elements of this poem are equal to each other, or "ressemblants," man and bird, rock and plain, sand and snow, prism and cavern, the point of the grass blade and the texture of moss. When the divisiveness of space is overcome, size and categories have no function. The occasional startling image ("A la pointe des neiges") is swallowed up in the simple progression of the whole poem as it moves from consciousness of self to freedom and fraternity. The innocent revolution against habit and outgrown language and toward the positive integration of the natural with the human ("C'est le roc c'est la plaine / Qui se mêlent à nous") are exactly in accordance with Eluard's ideal of art, which requires that the elements and man be set at liberty and renewed in clarity. The atmosphere of purity and expansion is so intense that even the basic elements must throw off their outer covering ("l'eau et le feu se dénudent") but the sense of unique revelation is so strong that it cannot occur twice ("pour une seule saison"). Of course these last two qualities are, in another framework, the constituent qualities of the litanic form, which is at once naked (bare repetition) and forever new, each phrase starting from a fresh though single beginning: that is, what is often seen as repetition and elaboration is, if one looks at it from the other side, unique and simple.

This poem should be compared and contrasted with Tzara's *L'Homme approximatif*; although both describe pilgrimages, Eluard's poem is directed toward perfect vision and Tzara's, toward perfect language. The final purification of *L'Homme approximatif* takes place in bare and ascetic surroundings (rocks, desert, flame), and the perfection itself is spiritually difficult and physically austere ("up there all is stone"), while the movement in which Eluard participates is an ascent toward a full, harmonious, and yet facile communion of all human and natural elements, closer to Tzara's later poems of "plénitude." Both journeys depend on the human will, but Tzara's is lonelier. His solitary hero of language finally rejects the help of the shepherd who would guide him, and although he is repeatedly likened to all of us and even to those who have preferred to reject language ("comme moi comme toi comme les autres silences"), at the end, when the poet has identified himself completely with his hero, he is alone in the desert. Eluard denies any solitude for the poet ("et je ne suis pas seul"), and in the final step of the journey, the poet and his companions transcend all personal limits ("hors de nous-mêmes"). Tzara's epic, through an immense and lengthy effort of language, moves toward a final inwardness, and Eluard's, in a narrower linguistic range, toward a final expansion.

It is clear that a poetry "sans âge" can, in this context, no longer be the whispered and intimate communication of a merely personal sentiment. To reflect these universal similarities and to make moral or active statements, only a poetry of deliberate outward expansion is appropriate. Always conscious, like Aragon, of his own poetry and of the tone he wants to give it, Eluard speaks of his poems as *Le Livre ouvert* (1940), and to the act of writing he now applies the verb "Crier":

> Je me mets à crier
> Chacun parlait trop bas parlait et écrivait
> Trop bas
>
> (I begin to shout
> Everyone was speaking too softly speaking and writing
> Too softly).

The poet must create a language larger than himself, which will precede him and extend his horizons; in fact Eluard often identifies language with the path itself.

But even at the height of the optimism in *Cours naturel*, where, by a further extension, he can say of himself and his fellow poets, "Et nous menons partout" (i, 805) / (And we lead everywhere), he suddenly envisions all paths as frozen and silent and an hour stopped in a horrible immobility, denying the natural course of events as well as the power of the poet. Just to perceive the interdependence of dualities ("Et le printemps est dans l'hiver") is far less difficult than the personal experience of them the poet is forced to undergo: "Je brûle et je gèle à jamais" (i, 686) / (I burn and I freeze forever). Yet neither sensitivity nor experience is enough: the poet must also sacrifice all his pleasure in the aesthetic complexities of feeling and expression to the optimistic and sometimes blatant public language of crescendo, so that "les frissons délicats feront place à la houle." All the stress falls on the necessary simplification of poetry which miraculously (or naturally) conveys the multiplicity of vision and experience: "Ici l'action se simplifie . . ."; "Ecrire simplicité lui-même."

Pouvoir tout dire (1951) contains a summation of Eluard's fully developed poetic theory with its wholehearted faith in reality, community, and regeneration: "Plus rien ne nous fera douter de ce poème / Que j'écris aujourd'hui pour effacer hier." As all the actions of yesterday are wiped out by the *presence* of poetry, so all the distances of solitude and strangeness are effaced, and no one will ever again have to speak "une langue étrangère." But the faith in poetry is accompanied this time by a genuine modesty. All the limits outside the poet have been erased, and still the poet senses an interior limit he will never overcome: "Le tout est de tout dire et je manque de mots" (II, 363) / (All that matters is to say everything, and I lack words). The realization of the limits of language does not, however, provoke the anguish felt in Tzara's long poem; it would never serve as the emotional basis for an epic.

Profoundly different from the overwhelming, if temporary, self-confidence of 1938 which permitted Eluard to claim that the world was made to his measure, is the quiet and touching "Cinquième poème visible" of 1947, where the poet, ageless as ever, but increasingly haunted by the images of death, is thankful that he can continually give birth to a poetry which will "fit the earth." He creates bright images to balance the inevitable dark ones imposed by human circumstances and acknowledges that the earth is enough for him, even though it is no longer seen as adjusting itself to human desires. In the same way that Tzara builds his late poetry on the concepts of *plénitude* and what is *juste*, Eluard accepts the "real" limits of earth for man's accomplishments and matches his creations to its outlines. (And it is in exactly this context that he and Tzara abandon in their later poetry the surrealistic attitude which is made to no measure.) Eluard does not picture himself now as striding out from a forest, dominating the wind, or leaving his human form behind. The assurance he feels is more natural than it is exalted: "Je suis sur terre et tout est sur terre avec moi" (II, 157) / (I am on earth and everything is on earth with me).

Of all the surrealist and ex-surrealist poets, Eluard is unquestionably the clearest in his poetry and in his vision. For that reason he has been able to give, as he says himself, a

perfect form to his joy and his poetic understanding. His poems are more elemental than subtle and more lyric than profound, which is as appropriate for a poet of the people as it
is for a "frère voyant" in the community of artist and poet
visionaries.

FLAME AND DARKNESS

Poetry is, for Eluard as for Tzara, "the art of light." It is
at the same time clarity of vision, and an ordering of the
real and the imaginary into a fresh consciousness of clarity.
In an essay on the artist Jacques Villon, Eluard contrasts the
"nocturnals" of art like Caravaggio, Rembrandt, and Goya,
whose paintings show "wounded forms in an imperiled
world," with the "diurnals" like Piero della Francesca, Pous-
sin, Ingres, Seurat, and Villon, whose paintings imitate the
sun, bestowing "heat, order, and clarity" and replacing anguish with lucidity.[20] The moment of ecstasy or total equili-
brium reigns forever in the work of Villon, which celebrates
the visible world in all its radiant unity. Here light is "the
angel of geometry," the principle of rhythmic relationships,
a perfect manifestation of eternity. But Villon never turns
away from the concrete world toward pure abstraction.
Eluard points out that his paintings after 1935 are full of
harvests, of bread and wine; they represent, in their primary
structure, a simple generosity and a genuine, uncomplicated
contact with the earth which is akin to Tzara's *plénitude*.

"I am the twin of the beings I love," claims Eluard, and
in fact his own poetry is famous for the same qualities he
distinguishes in Villon's painting. All his optimistic poems,
early and late, share this atmosphere of warmth, work, order,
and clarity. They are all stamped, as are the brighter poems
of Tzara, with the images of fire and sun which are already
present in his first poems, where he expresses the desire
which remains with him all his life, that of having the sun
as a witness to his constant mobility: ("Le soleil me suit"),[21]

[20] *Jacques Villon ou l'art glorieux* (Louis Carré, 1948), p. 32.
[21] "Ah!," *Pour vivre ici*, repeated in *Les Nécessités de la vie et les
conséquences des rêves* (Au Sans Pareil, 1921).

and an inspiration to his own *vertige,* where he declares his faithfulness to the crystalline and luminous world of the poet ("Clarté des moyens employés / vitre claire").[22]

One of the short poems of the early *Les Nécessités de la vie* (1921) demonstrates the calm enumeration and awareness of totality familiar in the poetry of Reverdy and in Eluard's own later poems. The possible melancholy of its title, "Enfermé, seul," is contradicted by each of the six lines and by their harmony:

> Chanson complète,
> La table à voir, la chaise pour s'asseoir
> Et l'air à respirer.
> Se reposer,
> Idée inévitable,
> Chanson complète.

> (Complete song,
> The table to see, the chair to sit in
> And the air to breathe.
> To rest,
> Inevitable idea,
> Complete song.)

But in the same collection there is a remarkable prose poem, dedicated to Tzara, which summarizes in its brevity a strange and pathetic movement from the Dada ideals of activity, purity, and dynamic "order" through a sobering contact with reality—the initial optimism of the voyage ("aller et retour") is canceled out by images of a long passageway lined with dirty children and empty bags, and by the reddened eyes of the traveler—toward the final unhealthy images of fatigue and despair:

> L'aube tombée comme une douche. Les coins de la salle sont loin et solides. Plan blanc. . . . Façons-erreurs. Grand agir deviendra nu miel malade, mal jeu déjà sirop, tête noyée, lassitude.

[22] "Salon," *Les Animaux et leurs hommes* (Au Sans Pareil, 1920).

(Dawn fallen like a shower. The corners of the room
are distant and solid. Overall white. . . . Manners-errors.
Great activity will become naked sick honey, uncomfortable game already syrup, drowned head, lassitude.)

Thus the well-planned, necessary, precise beauty of the
gesture ends in the soft and sticky, even liquid surroundings
which threaten any future action or thought. Exhaustion
mocks the former hope of accomplishment, as the sickly
honey mocks the former solidity and order of the room "sans
mélange." This is a short, and perfect, example of the destruction of a prose poem by itself, a sort of pilgrimage in
reverse; and in this self-negation, the poem is Dada.

There could not be two more opposed attitudes than those
revealed in these examples; this striking alternation of despair
and contentment will always be characteristic of Eluard's
vision and of the poetry which it determines: "Je voulus
chanter l'ombre" / (I wanted to sing the shadow); "Et pourtant j'ai su chanter le soleil" / (And yet I have been able to
sing the sun).

An excerpt from *Défense de savoir* in a 1927 issue of *La
Révolution surréaliste* takes the place among Eluard's poems
held by the poems of despair and ennui among those of
Breton and Tzara. It makes a quiet and moving statement
on the poet's feeling of falsity and poetic impotence:

Ma présence n'est pas ici.
Je suis habillé de moi-même.
  . . .
La clarté existe sans moi.

Née de ma main sur mes yeux
Et me détournant de ma voie
L'ombre m'empêche de marcher
Sur ma couronne d'univers,
Dans le grand miroir habitable,
Miroir brisé, mouvant, inverse
Où l'habitude et la surprise
Créent l'ennui à tour de rôle.

(My presence is not here.
I am dressed in myself.
. . .
Brightness exists without me.

Born of my hand over my eyes
And turning me aside from my path
The shadow keeps me from walking
On the crown of my universe.
In the great liveable mirror,
Broken mirror, moving, inverted
Where habit and surprise
Alternately create tedium.)

When the poet loses his sense of immediacy and necessity in
the world ("La clarté existe sans moi"), the bright surface
of the mirror which reflected his genuine image is replaced by
the artificial and empty appearance of an image ("habillé
de moi-même") and the misleading obscurity for which the
poet realizes he is somehow responsible ("née de ma main").
As is the case with most surrealist poetry and theory, the
image is contemporary with and absolutely inseparable from
the poet's feeling: it is neither a prediction nor a by-product.
The image of a broken mirror in Eluard is itself the basis
of a whole poem and is never an elaboration of a prior sentiment of confusion.

But in other parts of *Défense de savoir,* the poet has sufficient strength to deny all knowledge ("carcasses of the
known"), all "illusions of memory," and all experience in
order to assert his own present power over the world:

Et je soumets le monde dans un miroir noir
. . .
Je suis au coeur du temps et je cerne l'espace. (i, 218)

(And I dominate the world in a black mirror
. . .
I am at the center of time and I surround space.)

This last line reflects once more the surrealist aspiration to a
point sublime, the center and the circumference of the uni-

verse, where even such contradictions as this are resolved.
Compare Breton's image of "The man immobile at the center
of the whirlwind," and his lines: "Je suis au centre des choses
/ Je tiens le fil." The real world is filled up ("comblé") by
the shadowy double of the poet, who conquers both the
clarity of the mirror and the laws of time and space:

> Regarde-moi
> La perspective ne joue pas pour moi
> Je tiens ma place (I, 297)
>
> (Look at me
> Perspective does not work in my case
> I remain where I am).

His prideful solitude is based on an absolute self-assurance.
But in *A toute epreuve* (1930), the poet recognizes with
sadness rather than pride "everything that separates a man
from himself / The loneliness of all beings." In the long
poem "Univers—solitude" found in this collection, the despair
is at its extreme point; the accustomed transparency of the
poet's connection with the world is interrupted, and all the
exterior light which usually accompanies it has been ex-
hausted. There is no vitality, and no communication:

> La vie s'est affaissée mes images sont sourdes
> . . .
> Je suis seul je suis seul tout seul
> Je n'ai jamais changé. (I, 297)
>
> (Life has given way my images are deaf
> . . .
> I am alone alone completely alone
> I have never changed.)

Worse even than the forbidding aspect of the outside world
and the personal solitude of the poet is the sudden annihilation of his capacity for art, which could ordinarily save him:
the most pathetic confession a poet can make is not about
himself, but about his creation—"mes images sont sourdes."
And again, in the same collection, all the simple confidence

in poetic communication returns with an unaffected faith in
the present moment:

> La simplicité même écrire
> Pour aujourd'hui la main est là.

> (Simplicity itself to write
> At least today the hand is there.)

Later, in *La Rose publique* of 1934, the poet is once more
subject to the same overwhelming despair and emptiness.
The calm garden where he used to work alone with the sun
burning his hands now becomes "an island without animals,"
disconnected from reality, inhabited only by an endless consciousness of the unreliability of individual judgment and
of one's essential uselessness to others:

> De tout ce que j'ai dit de moi que reste-t-il
> J'ai conservé de faux trésors dans mes armoires vides
> Un navire inutile joint mon enfance à mon ennui (i, 412)[23]

> (Of all I have said of myself what remains
> I have kept false treasures in my empty cupboards
> A useless ship joins my childhood to my tedium).

The image of the useless ship is an echo of the "useless
visage" Eluard describes himself as having had until the
year 1918. But here the poet loses even the appearance of
reality as his memories prove false and his language, empty.
All the constructions undertaken and all the treasures contributed by the accomplishments of personal pride are negated
by the rebirth of a vicious self-doubt.

And yet Eluard claims, in another poem from the same
collection, that even the man "filled with emptiness" must
continue to "seek the earth," even though the journey is to
be "A travers des rouilles mentales" (i, 444) / (Across
mental blights). The landscape is not all so melancholy:

> Le ciel éclatant joue dans le cirque vert
> . . .

---

[23] A contrast to Breton's "enchantment" with his own despair in
"Le Verbe être" of two years earlier.

Le verre de la vallée est plein d'un feu limpide et doux.
(I, 443)

(The blazing sky plays in the green hollow

. . .

The valley's glass is full of a fire gentle and limpid.)

The poet's vision is now of the future, of the "sure hours" of tomorrow and the day after. It is true that he is often able to call his poetry, as he does here, "Ce chant qui tient la nuit" (I, 429) / (This song containing the night), and that he sees it moving in the depths of "abolished roads"; but he is, toward the end of the poem, as sure as he was in his first poems of the poet's intimate and necessary relationship to the universe: "La lumière me soutient" (I, 444) / (The light sustains me).

Although these examples are simple, Eluard's alternations from one side of the contrary perceptions to the other are full of nuance, and they extend to all the facets of his poetry and his theory, complicating the simple surface.

REFLECTION, MULTIPLICATION, EXPANSION

For Eluard, as for all the surrealist poets, poetry is a clear but marvelous extension of vision and of comprehension, and an enlargement or crescendo of "reality." The deliberate expansion of poetic consciousness depends on a continuous series of contradictions, on the possibility of shifting from extreme to extreme, while the poet participates in all the movement and in all the *being* of which he can be aware, reflecting and *repeating* the world and refusing any interior limits: "Je ne veux pas finir en moi." He is the double of the elements surrounding him, and their being enlarges his own: "Et je respire et je me double / Du vent . . ." (II, 428). Not only is the individual consciousness identified with the consciousness of all those around him, but now he is able to move high and low, near and far, to feel himself vague and precise, "immense et plus petit"; in all directions, he is able to extend his apprehensions beyond the normal state in which such oppositions would be impossible:

Je suis la foule partout
Des profondeurs et des hauteurs. (II, 686)

(I am the crowd everywhere
Of the depths and of the heights.)

Of course, in the poems of war and of grief, it is just this *expansion* which is suddenly forbidden. Cracked or immobile mirrors replace those Eluard usually associates with motion ("miroirs mouvants"), and the passionate identification with the multitude and the exalted consciousness of multiplicity yield to a desperate solitude:

La foule de mon corps en souffre
Je m'affaiblis je me disperse. (I, 1126)

(The crowd of my body suffers from it
I am weakening I scatter.)

This is a poetry of reduction and absence, whose exact opposite is the expansive poetry of surrealist vision. Eluard's most despairing poems are haunted by the spectacle of walls closing in to shut off liberty and light, and with them, the sense of man's individual significance. He forgets and is forgotten by all, as his image, once unique "à sa propre lumière," fades away, and light succumbs to death:

Il n'y a de murs que pour moi
. . .
Entre les murs l'ombre est entière
Et je descends dans mon miroir
Comme un mort dans sa tombe ouverte. (I, 1021)

(Walls exist for me alone
. . .
Between the walls the shadow is complete
And I go down into my mirror
Like a dead man into his open tomb.)

Here a morbid self-consciousness takes precedence once more over the poet's lucid vision and ideal expansiveness ("Hors de nous-mêmes"); the poem is entitled "Mourir." A parallel poem, ironically entitled "Jouer," ends with the poet's reali-

zation that he no longer has a reflection at all. Eluard, again
like Aragon and the early Breton, is always preoccupied by
his own image and its preservation, both in his own mind
and in the sight of others. This explains his fascination with
mirrors and eyes, and his dread of walls and shadows which
contradict light and are the absolute denial of reflection and
of potential multiplicity. The preceding quotation is from his
wartime poems, where the sensation of darkness and separation are to be expected; but walls and shadows haunt all his
poetry, accompanied by various deformations of vision and
reflection.[24] The "visible poems" called *A l'intérieur de la vue*
(1948) present a further and less obvious problem: in spite
of the multitude of ideas and projects envisioned by the complexity of the poet's "yeux variés," in spite of his overwhelming desire to change everything, the human limits of perception impose a dull and perpetual symmetry. All reflections
and all responses are gradually reduced to a "mouvement
banal," and even the infinite multiplicity of a poetic imagination cannot resist a daily exposure: "J'ai tout perdu dans ce
miroir où l'on cuit le pain quotidien, où l'on reproduit dans
l'ombre mes secrets, à l'infini." (II, 156) / (I have lost everything in this mirror where the daily bread is baked, where
my secrets are reproduced in the shade, infinitely.)

Eluard's love poems present exactly the opposite vision;
in its striking innocence and essential purity, surrealist love
is the human equivalent of the image, miraculous in its unfailing capability of restoring the poet to a perfect world of
immediacy and presence. As the whole calendar of days is
seen emerging from a single dawn, so a single kiss is infinite-

---

[24] The mirror is seen as a wall when it only sends back the single
reflection. That is, before the reflection is doubled by the interrelations
of personalities and presences, its connotation of sterility and vacancy
is inescapable. But it also signifies a certain distance from the interior
spectacle, as does the window from the exterior spectacle (see Chapter 2): "But the really clever person is the one who has managed to
see his eye without the aid of a glass, the one who has let his gaze
wander over the voluptuous hollow in the back of his neck. Ah, may
the day come when we can break the mirror, that final window, when
our eyes can at last contemplate the *cerebral marvelous.*" *Les Feuilles
libres* (January-February 1924).

ly reproduced with the "faith of eternal youth" by the woman, whose endless complexities and contradictions it reveals: "Inconstante conjuguée / Captive infidèle et folle." She is at once the rain and the good weather, she appears: "Avec les plus fiers présents / Et les plus lointains absents." Again according to the notion of "one within the other," the woman loved is at once all women, and at the same time, unique: "Present a specific woman but not man or woman."[25] Eluard addresses in his *Capitale de la douleur* "celle de toujours, toute," whom he never ceases to celebrate:

> O toi qui supprimes l'oubli, l'espoir et l'ignorance,
> Qui supprimes l'absence et qui me mets au monde
> . . .
> Tu es pure, tu es encore plus pure que moi-même. (I, 197)

> (You who abolish forgetfulness, ignorance, and hope
> You who suppress absence and give me birth
> . . .
> You are pure, you are even purer than I.)

All Eluard's love poems to Gala, to Nusch, and to Dominique are infused with this sense of purity and presence. For the poet, the woman loved has a power sufficient to overcome all consciousness of distance, spatial ("l'absence") or temporal ("l'oubli"); she offers him a "perpetual childhood" of immediacy and fulfills all his "desires of light." His reliance on the individual woman is mirrored in his poetry. When Nusch dies, Eluard's poems are filled with images of black corridors and despair; when Dominique appears, the miraculous transformations, the luminous order, and the intertwining of dualities reappear in their extreme simplicity:

> O toi mon agitée et ma calme pensée
> Mon silence sonore et mon écho secret
> Mon aveugle voyante et ma vue dépassée
> Je n'ai plus eu que ta présence (II, 424)

[25] "Physique de la poésie," *Minotaure*, 6.

(You my restless and my calm thought
My resounding silence and my secret echo
My blind seer and my vision exceeded
Since then I have possessed nothing but your presence).

But the last step in shedding all traces of self-consciousness
("I am the woman") and in piercing "the wall of my mirror" has not been taken until the poet is able to love the
woman precisely for her difference from him even while he
is completely identified with her: "Connais ce qui n'est pas
à ton image" / (Know what is not in your own image).

Je t'aime pour ta sagesse qui n'est pas la mienne

. . .

Pour ce coeur immortel qui je ne détiens pas. (II, 439)

(I love you for your wisdom that is not mine

. . .

For this immortal heart that I do not possess.)

For the principle of one within the other requires that neither
the one nor the other be lost. The realization of the surrealist
marvelous depends on the continually recreated unity of two
separate things; if either is absorbed, the specifically dynamic
quality of the marvelous is denied and only a staid and stable
compound remains, ruling out any future possibility of *vertige*.

The many forms of oppositions which the surrealist poet
unceasingly perceives within himself and in his relationships
toward the exterior world are intensified and made concrete
in his relations with woman. First of all, the woman celebrated in surrealist poetry is not simply an individual who
is pictured in detail, but is at once herself and all women
("une pour toutes"). Her qualities and her actions are as
general as they are specific, as Eluard pictures her for instance in the famous prose poem "Nuits partagées" from
La Vie immédiate, where she takes off her dress "avec la
plus grande simplicité."[26] She dreams of uniting the contraries
by the unity of her own contrary qualities:

[26] And yet even this simplicity can imply its contrary: "Elle est
. . . d'une grande simplicité artificielle" (I, 379).

Par ta force et par ta faiblesse, tu croyais pouvoir concilier
les désaccords de la présence et les harmonies de l'absence

(By your strength and by your weakness, you thought you
could reconcile the disagreements of presence and the
harmonies of absence),

and for a time she manages "une union maladroite, naïve."
Yet underlying the perceptions of unity offered by both the
spirit of the *merveilleux* and of the *naïf* is a sophisticated
double:

Mais, plus bas que tout, il y avait l'ennui.

(But deeper than everything there was tedium.)

Surrealist woman is full of "calm and freshness . . . of salt
of water of sun" and at the same time, of a "violent youth
disquiet and saturated with tedium." "Nuits partagées" is in
its tone and setting remarkably appropriate to the double
but ideally unifying nature of woman, "one or many" as she
is seen by the surrealist poet, and to the alternating sentiments of surrealist love.

La lumière m'a pourtant donné de belles images des néga-
tifs de nos rencontres. Je t'ai identifiée à des êtres dont
seule la variété justifiait le nom, toujours le même, le
tien, dont je voulais les nommer, des êtres que je transformais comme je te transformais, en pleine lumière. . . .
La neige même, qui fut derrière nous l'écran douleureux
sur lequel les cristaux des serments fondaient, la neige
même était masquée. Dans les cavernes terrestres, des
plantes cristallisées cherchaient les décolletés de la sortie.

Ténèbres abyssales toutes tendues vers une confusion
éblouissante, je ne m'apercevais pas que ton nom devenait
illusoire.

(But the light has given me beautiful pictures of the negatives of our encounters. I identified you with beings whose
varicty alone justified the name that I wanted to call them
by, always the same one, yours—beings whom I transformed as I transformed you, in total light. . . . The snow

itself, which was the sorrowful screen behind us where the crystals of vows melted, the snow itself was masked. In the caves of earth, crystallized plants sought the deep fissures of the exit.

Abysmal darkness stretched toward a dazzling confusion, I did not notice that your name was becoming illusory).

The play of light and shadow and the parallel balance of reality and illusion are both pathetic and subtle, as they gradually move from positive poetic transformations toward the disintegration of fidelity and certainty, where the melting crystals of human promises contrast with, and yet equal in their reverse progression, the plants unnaturally fixed into crystalline hardness. The development is as natural as the phenomenon of melting snow, and yet it can be read as an experiment in photographic trickery with its superpositions and metamorphoses, in which the poet claims and disclaims an active role. He deliberately multiplies and transforms the woman's image, but it is the light that provides him with the pictures of their union and it is the snow that provides the melancholy and uncertain (masked) background for their vows. This is a perfect example of surrealist poetry in its successful combination of logic and illogic, obvious simplicity and implied complexity.

Love is the *irreducible* counterpart of poetry, as it suppresses all the distances included in ordinary sight and at the same time requires and favors an expansion temporal and spatial, metaphysical and actual, contradictory and unitary. As the unique woman is simultaneously many women, she reflects the image of the poet himself as a multitude of individuals, each participating entirely in the multiple and single truth to which she bears witness. Her eyes not only mirror his multiple reflection, but they give birth to an infinite series of reflections:

Multiple tes yeux divers et confondus
Font fleurir les miroirs. (i, 460)

(Multiple your eyes diverse and mingled
Make mirrors flower.)
—

Ce miroir sans limites. (ii, 58)

(This limitless mirror.)

Whereas the poet has been unable alone to "pierce the wall" of his mirror, he is now extended and illuminated in a necessarily double and paradoxical relationship: "Rien n'est simple ni singulier." (ii, 442) / (Nothing is simple or singular.) The concept of love as reflection is inextricably linked with the concept of multiplication: "Constant amour multiplié tout nu / Volume espace de l'amour / Multiplié"; "Tu multiplies mon coeur et mon corps et mes sens"; "Je t'appellerai Visuelle / Et multiplierai ton image"; "Entre en moi toi ma multitude / Puisque je suis à jamais ton miroir / Ma figurée." Even the reverse side of the multiple vision is exemplified in the love poems, where eternity has unfolded ("s'est dépliée"), so that what appeared closed has opened out into many parts.

But just as constant as the renewal of vision is the alternation of hope and despair, appropriate to the two elements of the relationship of love: each of the partners is the double for the other, in a constant clarity of reflection, and yet that reflection itself has its own double, which denies it: "Je ne suis plus le miroir." Sentiments are not simple, they are at least dual. For a surrealist, human desire is unquestionably the supreme example of dynamic extension and unceasing motion:

Désirs chemins mouvants (i, 833)

(Desires moving paths)

and still the motion itself comes *inevitably* to a sudden halt:

Mîme gêlé l'amour est immobile (i, 837)

(Love is motionless frozen pantomime).

Only the images on the surface of the poem remain in con-

stant play. The theater of language continues to function
when the human poet is the most conscious of his own
weakness.

The experiences of clear vision, multiplication, metamorphosis, and extension are submitted to the terrible tests of
darkness and invisibility, reduction and immobility. For even
the ideal universe of "ressemblances" itself has a double,
and this double is the most tragic in its implications:

> Les ressemblances ne sont pas en rapport,
> Elles se heurtent. (II, 221)

> (Similarities do not relate,
> They clash against each other.)

The surrealist poet establishes endless sets of relationships
from distant elements, in the faith that this new poetic universe will hold up against the other. But the attempt to build
a whole system on the power of analogies, on even the most
passionate conviction in the existence of a supremely strong
fil conducteur, is a risky one. The force of juxtapositions and
marvelous perceptions is not always easy to transfer outside
the realm of the poem: Lautréamont, after all, did not try to
construct a whole system on the encounter of the umbrella
and the sewing machine. It is marvelous that they should
meet on a dissection table—but momentary examples of the
marvelous do not forever guarantee either the permanence of
vision or the duration of the miracle.

Eluard is in some senses a simple poet, and certainly he
is a poet of a simple, luminous love in all its purity and its
order: "Beaux yeux *ordonnez* la lumière"; "Et des jours et
des nuits *réglés* par tes paupières"; "Et je me suis trouvé
réglé comme un aimant / *Réglé* comme une vigne"; "Le feu
mit en ordre la fête."[27] But more significantly, he is a surrealist poet, faithful until the end of his life to the play of
dualities which give to surrealism its genuine profundity and
its unlimited potentiality of expansion. In the volume of
Eluard's last love poems, there are brief, and therefore often

[27] Emphasis added.

overlooked, references to the essential alternation scattered among his famous images of pure radiance. The *vision* is not simple; it includes both the opaque and the transparent, the fresh and the aging:

De la boue et de la rosée. (II, 421)

(Mud and dew.)

—

La rosée et la rouille. (II, 686)

(The dew and the rust.)

Eluard takes as much pride in his experiences of the "ravines" as in those of the summits; the profundity of his feeling and of his expression comes exactly from the awareness of contraries, so that he can say, in these last poems: "Et nous voici plus bas et plus haut que jamais." (II, 421) / (And now we are lower and higher than ever.)

Deprived of the darker images, the range of surrealist perspective would be far more limited, incapable of the tension stretching between extremes on which its peculiar strength depends. The consciousness of possible height is magnified (or multiplied) by the other consciousness, its double in this typically surrealist vision of love.

ROBERT DESNOS

Et c'est encore toi sans fin qui te promènes
Berger des longs désirs et des songes brisés
—ARAGON, *Les Poètes*

il n'y a plus de voix sonnante
dans Paris pavé de feuilles
—TZARA, "Pour Robert Desnos"

STYLE AND THE CHANGING MOMENT

If Eluard is the most accessible of these poets, Desnos is the most difficult. He often seems to be writing on a different plane, or in a different key, from the other surrealists. Because of the peculiar quality of his tone, it is impossible to separate irony from candor, especially in the frequent interruptions he makes in order to comment on his own style. Breton describes in his *Entretiens* Desnos' extreme narcissism, his need to focus all attention on himself. In fact Desnos was expelled from the surrealist movement, according to Breton, for deviating from the collective intellectual activity toward a barren individualism or "stagnation, the kind that can result from too much self-satisfaction."[1] (The other side of the picture is that Desnos seems to have aroused a certain degree of jealousy by his success in the sleep experiments and in automatic writing, which he practiced with more

[1] *Entretiens avec André Parinaud* (Gallimard, 1952), p. 150.

facility than anyone, and this may have aggravated the feeling against him.)[2]

In any case, Desnos' chief preoccupation is always that of his own language: the early word plays of 1922 to 1923—*Rrose Sélavy, L'Aumonyme, Langage cuit*—are done with obvious enjoyment and gusto, his early novels bear constant reflections on his style[3] as do many of his essays throughout his life, and his poetry in its various periods can be seen as a series of experiments with changing form. It is understandably harder to appreciate, and in some ways less immediately interesting to look at, the work of a man who above all studies the style of his own works. Themes can be traced in an author's work, and his images can be displayed "objectively," but such objectivity is impossible with respect to a language so constantly self-referential.

Desnos is often highly derogatory toward his own writing, commenting sometimes upon his unoriginal ways of expressing things ("Banality! Banality!")[4] and at other times upon

[2] In an article called "Faillite de l'inconscient" (in *Documents*, No. 1, 1930), Desnos says: "Anyone who had seen, as I did, the leader of a group struggling for hours at a stretch over a page and scratching out his 'automatic writing,' all the while reproaching me for discouraging him by writing too quickly, would not believe that the recipe (for automatic writing) was within everyone's reach."

[3] For instance, *Deuil pour deuil* (Sagittaire, 1924), contains the following self-conscious passage:

Amour! amour! je n'emploierai plus pour te décrire les épithètes ronflantes des moteurs d'aviation. Je parlerai de toi avec banalité car le banal me présentera peut-être cette extraordinaire aventure que je prépare depuis l'âge de la parole tendre . . .

(Love! Love! I shall no longer use in describing you the snoring epithets of airplane motors. I shall speak of you with banality, for the banal will perhaps offer me this extraordinary adventure for which I have been preparing since I first started to talk . . .).

[4] Here, in *La Liberté ou l'amour* (Kra, 1927), he deliberately mocks his own beginning of a novelistic style:

(Banalité! Banalité! Le voilà donc, ce style sensuel! La voici cette prose abondante. Qu'il y a loin de la plume à la bouche. Sois donc absurde, roman où je veux prétentieusement emprisonner mes aspirations robustes à l'amour, sois insuffisant, sois pauvre, sois décevant . . .

(Banality! Banality! Just look at that sensual style! And this

his useless verbosity and looseness of style: "What noise!
What a profusion of words! . . . this text lacks rigor and
clarity of exposition!"[5] His most serious and longest reflec-

---

abundant prose. How far it is from the pen to the mouth. So be
absurd, novel where I want to make a pretentious prison for my
robust aspirations toward love, be insufficient, be poor, be decep-
tive . . .).

This severity of style is in some ways linked to the concept of *ordre*
and opposed to the logical solidity and richness of the traditional or
"materialistic" attitude toward the novel. The surrealist credo he
pronounces—"I still believe in the marvelous of love, I believe in
the reality of dreams, I believe in the heroines of night . . ."—cannot
be translated by the easy flow of a consistent, "objective" style, so
that there are constant interruptions, stammerings, and self-examina-
tions on the part of the author:

Corsaire Sanglot s'engage dans, Corsaire Sanglot commence à,
Corsaire Sanglot, Corsaire Sanglot . . .

La femme que j'aime, la femme, ah! j'allais écrire son nom. J'allais écrire "j'allais écrire son nom." . . .

Compte, Robert Desnos, compte le nombre de fois que tu as
employé les mots "merveilleux," "magnifique."

(Corsaire Sanglot gets himself involved in, Corsaire Sanglot starts
to, Corsaire Sanglot, Corsaire Sanglot . . .

The woman I love, the woman, ah! I was going to write her name.
I was going to write "I was going to write her name."

Count, Robert Desnos, count the number of times you have used
the words "marvelous," "magnificent.")

All of this puts the reader in an anomalous position, as he is forced
to watch the author watching himself. Some of it is coy, some is
precious, but it is not just a diversion for the author, any more than
is Aragon's implied examination of the problem of sincerity. Surrealist games are played seriously, and sometimes even by ex-surrealists. Desnos, who goes so far as to say he believes in the "magic
phenomenon of writing as an organic and optical manifestation of the
marvelous," and in the alchemy of the calligraphy itself as it makes
real the "mobile backdrop" of his dreams, takes his own style as a
revelation of his inmost character. In part this is a relic from the
theory of automatic writing, and in part, another sign of his self-
involvement. In any case, the self-observation is an essential element
of his work and cannot be discounted as a simple stylistic trick. For
an elaboration of this point, see Mary Ann Caws, "Techniques of
Alienation in the Early Novels of Robert Desnos," *Modern Language
Quarterly,* XXVIII, No. 4 (December 1967).
    [5] *Tihanyi—Peintures, 1908-1922, présentées par Robert Desnos*
(Editions Arts, 1936), p. 7.

tion on this subject appears in *Fortunes* (1942), where he looks back over his poems of a ten-year period in a characteristic movement of self-criticism. He speaks of his effrontery, of the "verbal fog" hiding the ambitious architecture of his poetry, and of his desire to go beyond his former conception of *la poésie* to concentrate on poems that can represent the superior level of activity he calls art ("or magic, if you like"), a combination of language and imagination.

Like the other surrealists, Desnos is inclined to express his theories of art in double terms. When he undertakes a study of eroticism, he explains its fascination for him by its "absolute" combination of the pure and the licentious, and in it he insists that everything we can write is a combination of our mind and our senses. One of the projects he mentions is to write operas, which he finds the most perfect possible mingling of drama with lyricism, and another is to study the "beautiful language" of science he abandoned twenty-five years before, so that he can eventually make poetics a "chapter" of mathematics; the new poetic language will be at once popular and precise. Desnos's poetic heroes, Villon, Nerval, and Gongora, are men who can wed the language of the people "to an indescribable atmosphere, to an acute imagery."[6] If it is of the utmost importance to maintain the sharpness and forcefulness of one's imagery against the "fuzziness" of ordinary art (as the luminous cruelty discussed before maintains order in the face of sensual facility), it is equally important not to lose contact either with the people or with the actual circumstances of the moment in which the art is created.

From the beginning to the end of his life, Desnos emphasizes the changing instant—this is the psychological background of his experiments with form, of his insistence on novelty and on the fidelity of the poet to themes which are absolutely contemporary. In a 1924 issue of *Littérature* he explains the necessity for isolating each minute from the next and for rejecting the past like a dead object; the Desnos

[6] "Réflexions sur la poésie," *Domaine public* (Gallimard, 1953), p. 403.

of two minutes ago, for instance, is already the contemporary of Charlemagne and Andromaque, and each moment starts the world over again completely: "In any fraction of time we choose to consider there takes place between our eyelashes the end of the world and its genesis. The world dates from this moment and the past is nothing more for us than a notebook, uniform and flat as a mirror where our breath makes the frost of the dream appear."[7]

The motif of *presence* which we find so frequently in Eluard is akin to Desnos' notion of the moment, a notion that implies the acceptance not just of the superficial changes of style and fashionable quirks that modify the poetic temper, but of the genuinely pressing, if temporary, concerns "so imperious that they must be expressed at any price. These themes exist at this moment and they must be expressed at this moment."[8] For Desnos, commitment to these themes, whatever they may be, is commitment to poetry itself.

Poetry is nonetheless great for being ephemeral, tied to fugitive concerns. In fact, says Desnos, "All poetry is fleeting. It passes more or less quickly, but it passes. The notion of poetry is incompatible with that of eternity."[9] So the poet, and the critic, and particularly the critic of Desnos, must accept concrete and actual conditions in the face of all the temptations to the easier timeless perspective of the abstract.

THE SPECIFIC AND THE FLEETING:
AN "AESTHETICS OF UNDERSTANDING"

Desnos attaches as much importance to the concrete as he does to the moment, the notions being to some extent interdependent. Like Tzara and Aragon he considers the concrete a necessary determinant of the poetic attitude, even in his earliest statements on art, such as this one (from the 1924 issue of *Littérature* just quoted): "I condemn to irremediable

[7] "André Breton ou face à l'infini," *Littérature*, No. 13 (June 1924). This theme is a constant in Eluard's poetry, where the "past is only what we make of it," where everything that man creates "disappears with the man he was yesterday."

[8] "Réflexions sur la poésie."

[9] "Enquête sur la poésie indispensable," *G.L.M.* (March 1939).

downfall those who . . . believe in even a momentary in-
tangibility of form and of matter." In two articles written
in 1930 for *Documents* Desnos attacks the abstract and cold
immobility of *beauty* on which "all mediocre literary satisfaction depends" in order to champion the warm and changing
nature of life in its most concrete sense:

> What we have is life with its procession of strange mani-
> festations, of miracles, of profound glances, of insults, of
> warm embraces! It is not beauty that we love, she leaves
> us as cold as herself.[10]

> To put things in a concrete form! this elementary goal of
> all art, of all expression, of all human activity, is not within
> the reach of everyone. . . .[11]

There is no tolerance for the mystique of inexplicable beauty.
Starting with Lautréamont's statement: "Nothing is incomprehensible," Desnos announces the coming of an "aesthetics
of understanding." Here ideas will be reduced to their most
concrete or easily grasped components and divested of their
abstract facade. One of the chief differences between Breton
and Desnos is apparent in their statements on this point:
while Breton speaks of "la clé des champs" or the key to the
fields, Desnos describes Góngora as a poet "who would take
away with him the fields themselves and not the key to
them." While Breton speaks of "le point sublime" as the
unattainable but definite image of the surrealistic resolution
of dualities, Desnos pushes further toward a concrete *dépassement* of surrealism as we know it: "It seems to me that
beyond surrealism there is something very mysterious to be
reckoned with, that beyond automatism there is the intentional, that beyond poetry there is the poem, that beyond
poetry received there is poetry imposed, that beyond free
poetry there is the free poet."[12] And whereas for Breton

[10] "Pygmalion et le Sphinx," *Documents*, No. 1 (1930).
[11] "La Ligne générale," *Documents*, No. 4 (1930).
[12] "Réflexions sur la poésie," p. 404. In his "Notes sur le roman"
(Manuscript, Bibliothèque nationale, n.a.f. 14063, p. 63), Desnos
maintains, in this same pattern, that there is no *free novel*, but that
there can be a *free novelist*.

poetic creation is above all, like some "found objects," a
witness to the power of the marvelous, for Tzara and Desnos
the creation is an object marvelous in its own right. Breton
never denies the value of the poem, but its value is inseparable
from all the miraculous surrealist discoveries it represents.

Like the objections to surrealism formulated by Tzara,
Aragon, and Eluard in their later and more "political"
period, the objections of Desnos to Breton's surrealism are
founded on its narrowness and its unreality. In 1930, to
signal his break with Breton, Desnos writes a *Troisième manifeste du surréalisme* in which, along with the other attacks
on Breton (for example, that he creates nothing, "which
seems to me the height of literature") he criticizes him chiefly
for orienting surrealist theory in such a manner as to en-
danger free and realistic thinking, opening the way for
religion:

> I who have some right to speak of surrealism, I declare
> that the surreal only exists for the non-surrealists.
>
> For the surrealists, there is only one reality unique, entire,
> open to all.
>
> To believe in the surreal is to repave the road of God. . . .
> And I here proclaim André Breton tonsured by my hand,
> deposed in his literary monastery, his secular chapel.[13]

This attack is interesting not so much for its revelation of
Desnos' change of attitude toward Breton, of which he himself says "What does that prove?" but of his new insistence
on *reality* as the all-inclusive principle.

But it is also obvious that Desnos considers himself still a
surrealist in the genuine meaning of that word as he defines
it, a believer in one unique reality. And in fact he continues to write on art in a "traditional" surrealist style. For
instance, insofar as it renders on canvas the temporary states
of the world the painting of Labisse "is destined to be a
painting of desire rather than a painting of possession"[14]

[13] *Troisième manifeste du surréalisme*, in Nadeau, *Documents surréalistes*, p. 161.
[14] *Félix Labisse* (Sequana, 1945), p. 12.

(compare Breton's "Leave the prey for the shadow"). And he then expresses as eloquently as Breton the surrealists' love for the real world: "its marvelous reality, this reality included in every valid notion of surrealism."[15]

In his commentaries on the Hungarian painter Tihanyi, Desnos explains that even paintings which are technically "abstract" are as "concrete" as they are meaningful, since they are directly tied to the mentality of the artist and can be fully interpreted, or at least comprehended. The primitive youthfulness and the uncomplicated pleasures ("drinking, eating, sleeping, loving") represented in Tihanyi's work testify to the purity of a people who have been able to guard themselves from the influence "of Byzantium and Rome, their crafted metals, their precious materials, their jewels."[16] Simplicity will remain one of the highest virtues for all the surrealists and ex-surrealists, and preciosity one of the most corrupting evils. It is important for the observer of art, as well as for the artist, to maintain a simple clarity of style, especially in trying to express the essential humanity of painting and the commonplace similarities that link men to each other. The conclusion of these commentaries closely resembles the conclusion of many of the later essays of Eluard, Aragon, and Tzara in its image of the sun rising "as it will rise for all men in the near future,"[17] but it resembles also, though with significant and obvious differences, the conclusion of Breton's *Les Vases communicants*: "From then on the poetic work will be carried on in broad daylight. There will be no more attacks against a few men who will eventually become all men. . . . They will already be outside, mingling with the others in the sunlight and will not have any more guilty or intimate a gaze than the others for truth when she comes to shake her hair streaming with light at their dark window."[18] One might say that, for Breton, the possibility of poetry in broad daylight is the condition of all liberty; the "communicating vessels" are the figurative double

[15] *Ibid.*, p. 17.   [16] *Tihanyi—Peintures*, p. 7.
[17] *Ibid.*, p. 10.
[18] André Breton, *Les Vases communicants*, p. 199.

of men in poetic communication (*la télépoésie* of the second Manifesto), while for Desnos and the others, the sun represents a different sort of liberty, more political than poetic. But from another point of view it can be argued that Breton's concept of liberty includes, as he claims it does, material liberty to the same extent that the politically oriented concept technically includes spiritual liberty, this view reflecting once more the theory of interdependence familiar to surrealism.

THE POETRY OF POLARITY

Like Breton, Desnos consciously accentuates the principle of polarities and their identification in his poetry and also in his theoretical writings. We have already seen how his last statement on poetry defines it as a combination of commonplace language and mysterious atmosphere. By far the majority of his statements on all subjects are phrased in the same pattern, where the delirious is united with the lucid, the senses with the intellect, and so on. In fact even the distinction Desnos makes in 1924 between beings capable of imagination and those incapable of it is based on the ability or the lack of ability to understand the union of two obviously opposite things. The surrealists, of course, are perfect representatives of the former group, while unimaginative minds are characteristic of those who can neither make the essential identification between dream and matter nor grasp "the law of the constant relationship between the known and the unknown, health and sickness, the finite and the infinite . . . who are given to considering only one of these terms."[19] Desnos' article "La Muraille de chêne" in the first issue of *La Révolution surréaliste* allies the opposing concepts of love and death, in what might be considered an example of the

[19] "André Breton ou face à l'infini." In her article "Le Merveilleux surréaliste de Robert Desnos," *The French Review* (November 1966), Tatiana Greene underlines several more subtle dualities in the early works of Desnos, such as the frequent "glissement" of the future toward the past, the "double postulation" of the name Corsaire Sanglot toward the crime committed (the Corsair) and the suffering undergone (the sob), and most important, the exaltation of a love "qu'il souhaite inaccessible."

romantic inheritance in surrealism combined with the Dadaist ideal of *ordre*, joyous and unsentimental: "I cannot imagine love without an admixture of the taste of death, free however of all sentimentality and all sadness. Marvelous satisfactions of sight and touch, perfection of pleasures, only by your intervention can my thought communicate with death. The transitory character of love is also that of death. If I pronounce a eulogy of one, I start with the other. . . ."

Less unusual but more important is his obsession with the relationships of dream and reality, of which Desnos makes a more prolonged and serious examination than any other surrealist. At times he treats the subject lightly, as in his *Siramour*, the love story of a mermaid and a seahorse. He ironically comments that it takes place: "let's not forget it, on a real plain, on a real riverbank, under a real sky. And it is a question of a real battle and a real mermaid, while a real sea ebbs and flows."[20] The repetition of the "real" is at once exaggerated and effective. But generally Desnos treats the theme in a more subtle way. In his introduction to the "Journal d'une apparition" (1926) he explains his interest in the problem: "For me it is less a question of having accepted as real certain facts normally considered illusory than of placing dream and reality on the same level without caring whether it is all false or all true."[21] But in *Les Trois solitaires*,[22] a prose poem on the domain of sleep described as "a territory outside of time and space," Desnos speaks of the marvels and the terrors of dream, of the threat it poses to human love: "I remember beings for whom the shadows of night were without thorns, and the dark roads without ruts or patches. For them, a new mythology presented only favorable aspects. . . . And yet the orchard of dream never produced any but decayed foliage, nor any but worm-eaten fruits, and the very love which gave birth to the dreams was always killed by them. If you love and if you want to love, do not dream."

[20] *Domaine public*, p. 200.   [21] *Ibid.*, p. 347.
[22] *Les Trois solitaires: oeuvres posthumes, nouvelles et poèmes inédits de Robert Desnos* (Les Treize Epis, 1947).

The collection *A la mystérieuse*, published in 1926, contains four poems that focus on this point. The first, "O douleurs de l'amour" shows the poet with his eyes closed on *imaginary* tears and his hands stretched out toward nothingness. He is still dreaming in a way characteristic of his 1920 poems and still making the link he made in 1924 between love and death:

> J'ai rêvé cette nuit de paysages insensés et d'aventures dangereuses aussi bien du point de vue de la mort que du point de vue de la vie qui sont aussi le point de vue de l'amour.

> (I dreamed last night of absurd landscapes and of adventures dangerous both from the point of view of death and from that of life, which are also the point of view of love.)

But the poem continues in a completely new way, less startling in its outline than in its details:

> O douleurs de l'amour, anges exigeants, voilà que je vous imagine à l'image même de mon amour, que je vous confonds avec lui
>
> O douleurs de l'amour, vous que je crée et habille, vous vous confondez avec mon amour dont je ne connais que les vêtements et aussi les yeux, la voix, le visage, les mains, les cheveux, les dents, les yeux

> (Oh pangs of love, exigent angels, I now picture you in the very image of my love, confusing you with my love
>
> Oh pangs of love, you whom I create and clothe, you blend with my love of whom I know only her clothing and also her eyes, her voice, her face, her hands, her hair, her teeth, her eyes).

Here the plural and immaterial "douleurs d'amour" which remain after the poet's dream become evident in the daylight as they merge with an extended sensual description of the woman's clothing. This is natural enough, since the pangs of love are usually considered to result from an encounter and not to foreshadow it. But Desnos first expresses a mock astonishment at the confusion in his mind and then confesses the unreality of these "angels" whom he has to invent continually. Even within this obvious structure there is polarity of form—for instance, the confusion is initiated once by the poet ("voilà . . . que je vous confonds") and once by the pangs of love he has created ("vous vous confondez"); and there is a switch in the opposite direction from the love as a product of dream but having its own reality ("Au réveil vous étiez présentes, ô douleurs de l'amour") to the emphasis on the poet's own action: "vous que je crée et habille." Though there are no descriptive adjectives attached to his knowledge of the real woman, so that this bareness contrasts with the wealth of the previous spectacle, the form of the sentence "dont je ne connais que . . . et aussi . . ." is mocking, as is the catalogue that follows. It does not matter whether Desnos is teasing us or himself: the end of the poem is ambiguous to the point of discomfort.

The next poem, and the most famous, is addressed to the actress Yvonne George.[22a] The poet's concern is that the dream may not fit the reality:

> J'ai tant rêvé de toi que tu perds ta réalité
> . . .
>
> J'ai tant rêvé de toi que mes bras habitués en
> étreignant ton ombre à se croiser sur ma poitrine
> ne se plieraient pas au contour de ton corps,
> peut-être.

[22a] The so-called "dernier poème à Youki," cited by Berger, Buchole, et al., is simply a retranslation into French of the rough and truncated translation into Czech of this poem, made at the time of Desnos' death for his obituary in a Czech newspaper. "J'ai rêvé tellement de toi / J'ai tellement marché, tellement parlé, / Tellement aimé ton ombre, / Qu'il ne me reste plus rien de toi. / Il me reste d'être l'ombre parmi les ombres / D'être cent fois plus ombre que l'ombre / D'être l'ombre qui viendra et reviendra / Dans ta vie ensoleillée." Adolf Kroupa, in his "La légende du dernier poème de Desnos," *Les Lettres françaises*, 9-15 June 1960, speaks of the tragic "préssentiment" felt in this poem. But because Desnos, like Breton, insisted on the continuity of his love, it is not unjustifiable to consider the poem addressed to Youki, as it was to Yvonne. (I am indebted to Mme Marie-Claire Dumas for her clarification of this point.)

Et que, devant l'apparence réelle de ce qui me
hante et me gouverne depuis des jours et des
années, je deviendrais une ombre sans doute.

(I have dreamed of you so much that you become unreal
. . .

I have dreamed of you so much that my arms accustomed, in embracing your shadow, to meet on my chest
would perhaps not fit the contour of your body.

And so much that faced with the real appearance of that
which has haunted and ruled me for days and years, I
would doubtless become myself a shadow.)

The woman loved becomes unreal for the poet by the very
intensity of his dreaming. And confronted by her real appearance, he himself might become a shadow. The initial
doubt about the possible reconciliation of dream and reality
("peut-être") is intensified to the level of an assertion ("sans
doute"). "O balances sentimentales": the interjection is the
exact center of the poem and reflects the two parts of reality
and dream, shadow and sun, poet and woman loved. But in
the concluding lines, as the first half of the opening theme
is restated ("J'ai tant rêvé de toi") without an accompanying
threat to the woman's reality, the dream takes on an ambiguous value:

J'ai tant rêvé de toi, tant marché, parlé, couché avec ton
fantôme qu'il ne me reste plus peut-être, et pourtant, qu'à
être fantôme parmi les fantômes et plus ombre cent fois
que l'ombre qui se promène et se promènera allègrement
sur le cadran solaire de ta vie.

(I have dreamed so much of you, have so walked,
talked, slept with your phantom that nothing is left to me
perhaps, and yet, but to be a phantom among phantoms
and a hundred times more shadow than the shadow which
walks and will walk gaily on the sundial of your life.)

Negative in appearance, this poetic statement tends nevertheless toward the positive—although the poet's shadow is not the one moving "allègrement" over the sundial (with all the undertones of frivolity contained in the "allègrement," his is a deeper and more *real* shadow. The inner union is only reflected in the exterior reality, its image. Furthermore, Desnos, with his characteristic subtlety, has balanced the more obvious exterior images with the quiet assertions of language: if the "peut-être" here echoes the first and dubious "peut-être," it is immediately followed by a courageous assertion: "et pourtant." From the purely linguistic point of view, the "and yet" is the counterpart of the earlier echo, "doubtless," but the feeling can be seen as reversed. I shall probably be only a shadow—and yet far more shadow than ordinary shadows. The marvelous of the dream is the surest guarantee of the marvelous unity beyond the actual fact of separation.

The poem is deeply convincing in its transition from the irreality of the dream to the super-reality of the sunlit life in which the dream will always be contained by implication. Breton's prose descriptions of this marvelous phenomenon, in which he stresses the image of the *vases communicants*, are just as convincing; they are, in fact, the basis of surrealist theory. But this example moves far beyond any prose statement that could be made even by a writer of Breton's stature: it can only be compared with Breton's greatest poems. Even if one could forget the tragic circumstances surrounding the death of Desnos, even if one ignored the terrible prediction within the poem—the exact opposite of Breton's "Nuit du tournesol," although it uses the same oppositions of terms (nuit / soleil, ombre / ensoleillé)—one could not deny that in its splendid concision and perfect motion from shadow to the union of shadows, to their contrast with the sunlight and to the final inner union of shadow and sun, this is one of the most moving poems ever composed. Even if all the depth of tragedy and implied tragedy is removed from the element of shadow and all the possibilities of happiness from the element of sun, so that the horrible personal irony of the shadow implied forever in the sun disappears, the poem itself refuses a purely surface or intellectual reading. This refusal of separation within the work is the most difficult aim of surrealist poetry.

The third poem in the series, "Les Espaces du sommeil," alternates a description of the dream world where the seven marvels are seen "naturally," with the refrain "Il y a toi," in a sort of balance equating the presence and the value of the woman with that of the dream and the marvelous in a typical surrealist union of love and poetry. She is at once the unknown and the known, the guarantee for his illusions and the refusal of them, because she will only appear when the poet's eyes are *closed* to dream as well as reality. Associated by its litanical form and by its series of images of the *merveilleux* with many other famous surrealist works, "Les Espaces du sommeil" is the most intricate of all these poems which deal with the problem of dream and reality. The self-consciousness seen in Desnos' other works shows up even here: separating a list of perfectly ordinary images (trains, boats, a clock, a slammed door) from a list of more singular ones—a cock's crow from two thousand years ago, the scream of a peacock in a park on fire, and sinister handshakes in a pallid light—is a lament which reminds us of Aragon:

Mais encore moi qui me poursuis ou sans cesse me dépasse.

(But still I who pursue myself or constantly transcend myself.)

And after the description of the elusiveness of the woman there comes an odd statement, particularly touching in its incompleteness:

Toi qu'en dépit d'une rhétorique facile où le flot meurt sur les plages, où la corneille vole dans des usines en ruines, où le bois pourrit en craquant sous un soleil de plomb.

(You who in spite of a facile rhetoric where the tide dies on the beaches, where the crow flies in the ruined factories, where the wood rots cracking under a leaden sun.)

Here Desnos may be denigrating his own ease with words and imagery, proved in the "hypnotic sleeps," as he contrasts all the last part of the sentence in its lyricism of style and vision with the simple word "Toi," devoid of rhetoric and more difficult to seize than the "marvelous" itself. In the next line, Desnos speaks of the woman as the basis for his dreams and the impulse for his "mind full of metamorphoses." His poetry and his visions depend on her and yet she is forever elusive, as she is forever present, both in reality and in the dream. Most tragic of all, her presence in the daytime, announced casually at the end of the poem, seems a sudden mockery of all the nighttime marvels, and of the poem itself. The second half appears to be missing, and the first half, no matter what marvels it contained, is now trivial. Why bother to describe all the wonders of the world and all the attempts of the poet to overtake the woman he loves within the *space* of his dream if she is also present, and still surrounded with the charm of the unattainable, in the ordinary daylight? All the dreaming and all the description of the *merveilleux* are in some way negated by her daytime presence, as they were before complicated by her deliberate elusiveness as she insisted on being sensed there ("deviner") without actually appearing ("paraître"). And after all those complications, she is finally perceived in a perfectly simple manner, like the end of any ordinary catalogue:

Dans la nuit il y a toi.
Dans le jour aussi.

(In the night you are there.
In the day too.)

The ending, insofar as it implies a possible meeting, might have appeared to be the exact reverse of the "Tu rêves" at the end of Aragon's poem, since the latter seems to imply a separation between the dreamer and the poet—had we not known that Desnos is speaking to a heroine always absent in spite of her illusion of presence:

Toi qui restes insaisissable dans la réalité et le rêve

(You who remain elusive in reality and in dream).

So that this poem, one of the most positive in appearance, unites the marvelous and the real, knowledge and the illusion, in an extreme complexity and psychological *déchirement*, whether willed or involuntary.

In all three poems, the dream or the sentimental creations of the poet are more real than the object of the love—a reader given to psychological interpretations might define this as a result of Desnos' self-involvement (or as Breton would say, his narcissism). There is in the same collection a very short poem, "A la faveur de la nuit," which makes the point even more clearly. Here, the fact that the poet calls upon the illusion not to reveal itself as an illusion to him, demonstrates that he is perfectly aware of its nature:

> Cette ombre à la fenêtre c'est toi, ce n'est pas une autre, c'est toi.
> N'ouvre pas cette fenêtre derrière les rideaux de laquelle tu bouges.
> Fermes les yeux
> . . .
> La fenêtre s'ouvre: ce n'est pas toi.
> Je le savais bien.
>
> (That shadow at the window is you, it is no one else, it is you.
> Don't open that window where you are moving behind the curtains.
> Close your eyes
> . . .
> The window opens: it is not you.
> I knew it all along.)

Desnos concentrates on many other sorts of polarity as well —the most interesting poems of this early period before 1930 are structured around contrasts and oppositions, concrete and abstract. The poem "Si tu savais," again from *A la mystérieuse*, is also based on multiple dualities—on the complex and contrary concepts of desire and distance, of knowledge and ignorance, submission and freedom, reality and illusion, actual absence and emotional presence:

Loin de moi et cependant présente à ton insu,
Loin de moi et plus silencieuse encore parce que je
   t'imagine sans cesse,
Loin de moi, mon joli mirage et mon rêve éternel, tu ne
   peux pas savoir.
Si tu savais.
. . .

Loin de moi, ô mon présent présent tourment . . .
Si tu savais.
Loin de moi, volontaire et matériel mirage.
Loin de moi c'est une île qui se détourne au passage des
   navires.
Loin de moi un calme troupeau de boeufs se trompe de
   chemin, s'arrête obstinément au bord d'un profond préci-
   pice, loin de moi, ô cruelle.
. . .

Si tu savais comme le monde m'est soumis.
Et toi, belle insoumise aussi, comme tu es ma prisonnière.
O toi, loin-de-moi à qui je suis soumis.
Si tu savais.

(Far from me and still present without your knowing it,
Far from me and more silent still because I imagine you
   always,
Far from me, my pretty mirage and my eternal dream, you
   cannot know.
If you knew.
. . .

Far from me, oh my present present torment . . .
If you knew.
Far from me, willed and tangible mirage.
Far from me an island turns away as the boats go by.
Far from me, a calm herd of oxen mistakes the path, stops
   stubbornly beside a steep cliff, far from me, oh cruel one.
. . .

If you knew how the world submits to me.
And you, beautiful unsubmissive one, how you are my
   prisoner.

You, far from me, to whom I submit.
If you knew.)

The main contrast between absence and presence is placed
in a context of unreality by the references to dreams and
mirages (complicated in one instance by the adjective "matériel," a contrast of the same sort as the simultaneous distance and presence of the loved one). She cannot know,
but if she knew—the unfinished statement once more produces the inexplicably sad undertone characteristic of the love
poems of Desnos, an undertone accentuated by the litanic
form ("Loin de moi . . . loin de moi. . . . Si tu savais. . . . Si
tu savais") and by the inner repetition "présent présent."
She is the prisoner of the poet's imagination, of the mirage
that he voluntarily pictures, but he is subject to the same
mirage in its silence and unrelenting implication of cruelty.
As in Breton's image of the girl mysteriously threatened by
the branches that might scratch her and the precarious position of the rocking chair on the bridge, there is here an unexplained menace in his picture of oxen near a precipice.
Surrealist poetry frequently refers to a mysterious physical
danger outside the poet's own world which intensifies the
feeling of *distance* that must be surmounted but can rarely
be overcome, even within the marvelous and unifying presence of the poem. Breton's sinister images were foreshadowed
by the unnatural diagonal slant of the curtain and of the
jasmine pickers, and Desnos leads up to this image by the
unnatural action of the island turning aside. The play of
contradictory concepts and images here is like the earliest
word play the surrealists enjoyed, only lifted to a higher
and far more complicated level. For its emotional thrust
this poem depends, as do the greatest surrealist poems, on an
atmosphere of conscious ambiguity.

    Les Ténèbres (1927) represents an intensification of de-
liberate poetic ambivalence. Frequently, brief oppositions of
images are suddenly combined with unaccustomed or ambiguous actions to create an atmosphere of the marvelous
without the prolonged and overrich elaboration that can oc-

casionally give an impression of preciosity in less successful writing:

> Le schiste éclairera-t-il la nuit blanche du liège?
> Nous nous perdrons dans le corridor de minuit avec la
>   calme horreur du sanglot qui meurt
> . . .
> Accourez girafes
> Je vous convie à un grand festin[23]
> Tel que la lumière des verres sera pareille à l'aurore
>   boréale
> Les ongles des femmes seront des cygnes étranglés
> Pas très loin d'ici une herbe sèche sur le bord du chemin.[24]

> (Will the schist brighten the white night of cork?
> We shall lose ourselves in the midnight corridor with the
>   calm horror of the dying sob
> . . .
> Come quickly giraffes
> I invite you to a feast so magnificent
> That the light from the glassware will rival the aurora
>   borealis
> The womens' nails will be strangled swans
> Not very far from here a plant shrivels at the side of the
>   path.)

While the unnatural whiteness of the women's nails contrasts with the natural whiteness of the swan and the natural phenomenon of the aurora borealis, they are all related to the image of the "nuit blanche." The more routine "lumière des verres" echoes the "éclairera-t-il?" and the violence of the strangulation (unnatural) and the understated but natural

---

[23] To fit the pattern of doubling and oppositions like those Desnos elaborates between love and death, one could quote as the double of this line, a line from his book on eroticism (*De l'érotisme considéré dans ses manifestations écrites et du point de vue de l'esprit moderne* (Editions Cercle d'art, 1953): "O femmes aimées! vous que j'ai connues, vous que je connais, toi blonde flamboyante, toi brune et couverte de fourrures sacrées, toi encore . . . je vous convie toutes à mon enterrement. . . ."

[24] "Au petit jour," *Les Ténèbres* (in *Domaine public*).

death in the last two lines ("une herbe sèche") echoes the horror of the dark corridor and the figurative death of the sobbing. Since the idea of a "grand festin" is as bizarre in this context as the giraffes and lizards the poet invites for company, this short poem (ten lines in all) is extremely unsettling. Desnos' earliest poems, as we have already seen, frequently hint at a certain unspecified menace in an otherwise almost ordinary landscape, like many of the poems of Breton and Eluard—for instance the following excerpt from "Passé le pont":

> Taisez-vous ah taisez-vous laissez dormir l'eau froide au
> bas de son sommeil
> Laissez les poissons s'enfoncer vers les étoiles
> Le vent du canapé géant sur lequel reposent les murmures
> Le vent sinistre des métamorphoses se lève
> Mort aux dents mort à la voile blanche mort à la cime
> éternelle
> Laissez-la dormir vous dis-je laissez-la dormir ou bien
> j'affirme que des abîmes se creuseront

> (Be still ah be still let the cold water lie at the bottom
> of its sleep
> Let the fish plunge down to the stars
> The wind from the giant canopy where the murmurs rest
> The sinister wind of metamorphoses rises
> Death to the teeth to the white sail death to the eternal
> summit
> Let it sleep I say let it sleep or else I declare that abysses
> will deepen).

In many cases, Desnos' poems have the same kind of lyrical flow as do Breton's and contain the same distinctive repetitions of ideas and words, the combination of these elements assuring uninterrupted communication between apparently contradictory concepts and images. The repetitious poetic litany produces a deliberately reassuring tone of certainty and even of facility in the smoothly articulated passages of Desnos just discussed. These poems are not facile, but neither are they impenetrable: obscurity, according to

Desnos, cannot be a quality of the poem-object, since all aesthetic objects are necessarily comprehensible. The following example, again litanic in structure, is built on a series of obviously contrasting images:

> Salut de bon matin à la fleur du charbon la vierge au grand
> coeur qui m'endormira ce soir
> Salut de bon matin aux yeux de cristal aux yeux de lavande
> aux yeux de gypse aux yeux de calme plat aux yeux
> de tempête
> Salut de bon matin salut
> La flamme est dans mon coeur et le soleil dans le verre
> Mais jamais plus hélas ne pourrons-nous dire encore
> Salut de bon matin tous! crocodiles yeux de cristal orties
> vierge fleur du charbon vierge au grand coeur.[25]

> (Early morning greetings to the flower of coal the good-
> hearted virgin who will put me to sleep tonight
> Early morning greetings to the crystal eyes to the lavender
> eyes to the gypsum eyes to the dead calm eyes to the
> tempest eyes
> Greetings early morning greetings
> The flame is in my heart and the sun in the glass
> But never again alas will we be able to say
> Early morning greetings everyone! crocodiles crystal eyes
> thistles virgin flower of coal good-hearted virgin.)

The oppositions here are more complex than a simple one-to-one relationship. Though the flowers are directly opposed to the thistles, they are also allied by connotation with glass and crystal; the latter are, like gypsum and the virgin, the opposites of coal, but so are the flame and the sun. Yet the fire can be thought of as produced by the coal, like a useful flower. The calm and the early morning itself share the peaceful atmosphere of the glass and the crystal as the sun and the flame indicate the possible brilliance of both. The violence of the tempest and the unhappiness of the sobbing contrast with all the calm elements and with all the shining

---

[25] "Vieille clameur," *ibid.*

or possibly shining ones; on the other hand, the dead calm
is in opposition to the loveliness of the flame, and the darkness of the coal is instinctively allied in the romantic imagination with the storm and the melancholy as a kind of irrational night opposed to the clear rationality of day. If one
were to make a simplified sketch of the relationships, it would
look more or less like this chart:

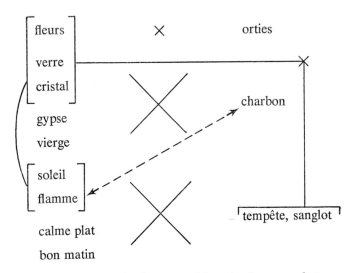

There are a series of other oppositions in the poem between
mother-of-pearl, marble, an edelweiss flower, diamonds, and
white fur and clouds on one hand with shadows and sleep
on the other. The "jamais plus hélas" echoes the desolation of
the bare stalk which is the first image in the poem, and casts
over the whole poem a retrospective melancholy and an aura
of loneliness, since it follows directly upon an atmosphere of
comradeship: "Salut de bon matin quand l'ivresse est com-
mune" (Early morning greetings when the drunkenness is
shared).

All of Desnos' poems examined so far show the same qualities as those of *A la mystérieuse*. Beyond the surface play
of images in their complexities of contrast and union, a great
depth of feeling is implied, a complete background of emo-

tion. Whereas the poems of Eluard and the late poems of
Aragon and Tzara manifest the feeling on the surface, those
of Breton and Desnos are a constant *appel* beyond that surface.

The most remarkable poem in this series, "Jamais d'autre
que toi," is a desperate picture of loneliness that begins as a
simple love poem; this particular paradox is a pathetic and
frequent form of the surrealist duality. A perfect union of
the delirious and the lucid, of "poetic" images ("seul comme
le verre") and "realistic" ones ("ton ombre s'agrandit"), the
poem is at once eloquent and unrhetorical:

> Jamais d'autre que toi en dépit des étoiles et des solitudes
> En dépit des mutilations d'arbre à la tombée de la nuit
> Jamais d'autre que toi ne poursuivra son chemin qui est
> le mien
> . . .
> Jamais jamais d'autre que toi
> Et moi seul seul seul comme le lierre fané des jardins de
> banlieue seul comme le verre
> Et toi jamais d'autre que toi.

> (Never anyone but you in spite of stars and solitudes
> In spite of mutilated trees at nightfall
> Never anyone but you will pursue her path which is mine
> . . .
> Never never anyone but you
> And I alone alone alone like withered ivy in suburban
> gardens alone like glass
> And you never anyone but you.)

The images are so fitted to the poem that they do not stand
out from it as they might in a lesser poem; and the poetic
devices—such as the expansion from the single and apparently positive "jamais" to the forceful reiteration "jamais jamais"
which renders still more tragic the triple "seul seul seul"—
cannot be considered precious in this restrained but intense
setting. Desnos' poems of this period represent surrealist poetry at its highest point.

SIMPLICITY AND ENIGMA

After 1930 and Desnos' separation from the surrealist group, his essays on art and poetry are full of the themes we find in the late Tzara, Eluard, and Aragon: simplicity, youth, joy, totality, responsibility, activity, and so on, these themes having in spite of their unsurrealistic application the implied connection with surrealist theory that we have seen in each case.

All five poets considered here write on Picasso, who, more than any other painter, exemplifies all the qualities they aspire to in their work, both as surrealists and as postsurrealists. In one of his essays on the artist, Desnos explains that Picasso is at the crossroads of all contradictions, and that his work exemplifies the unity, the completeness and the vitality only imperfectly reflected in the work of other artists: "It seems that among so many fragmentary universes, his universe is total and that every man can, according to his luck and his material, lose himself or find himself there. This universe of Picasso's is, more than anything else, life. Never has the human species uttered against death a more triumphant and more resounding cry."[26] Picasso is at once responsible and free, he speaks to the intelligence and to the senses. His canvasses in their strict *attention* and *exigence* (a minute focusing of the more general concept of *ordre*) prevent any diversion or distraction on the part of the spectator by involving him in an attentive complicity. The epitome of "active vision," they realize all the diverse possibilities of the universe, whose time and space they contain and are contained by in a supreme example of the now familiar theory of "one within the other." In another article on Picasso, Desnos suggests that the observer put himself in the place of the painter, that he try to see the veracity of the world as Picasso sees it. Only through art, which is the supreme method of knowledge, can the super-reality of the world be experienced; and it is a reality so strong "that it contradicts, that it shows up as false all

[26] *Introduction à Picasso, Peintures, 1939-46* (Editions du Chêne, 1946).

that education, habit, and a certain cowardice of our senses have accustomed us to take for reality."[27] Here again we are aware of the stylistic delight Desnos takes in opposing things to each other, falsity or so-called reality to the real that contradicts it, revelation to cowardice and habit. Picasso re-creates reality in uninhibited happiness, "at once physical and poetic," a happiness that according to Desnos contains the notions of lucidity and exaltation, desire and satisfaction.

Around 1936 Desnos' poetry has a new simplicity of form, and celebrates life and happiness in the same manner as Eluard's "Chanson complète" or his *Poésie ininterrompue I*, and the paintings of Tihanyi and Picasso. The following example (one of the "inédits" in the Seghers edition of Desnos), concerns the relation between the poet and the outside world rather than the contrast of dream and reality:

Tu prends la première rue à droite
Tu suis le quai
Tu passes le pont
Tu frappes à la porte de la maison.

Le soleil rayonne
La rivière coule
A une fenêtre frémit un pot de géranium
Une voiture passe sur l'autre rive.

Tu te retournes sur le gai paysage
Sans t'apercevoir que la porte s'est ouverte derrière toi
L'hôtesse se tient sur le seuil
La maison est pleine d'ombre.

Mais sur la table on aperçoit le reflet
Le reflet du jour sur un fruit et une bouteille
Sur une assiette de faïence et sur un meuble
Et tu restes là sur le seuil entre le
Monde plein de semblables à toi-même
Et la solitude bourdonnante
Du monde entier.

[27] "Les sources de la création: Le Buffet du Catalan," *Les Problèmes de la peinture*, Gaston Diehl, ed. (Confluences, 1945), p. 158.

(You take the first street to the right
You follow the wharf
You cross the bridge
You knock at the door of the house.

The sun shines
The river runs by
At a window a pot of geraniums trembles
A car passes on the opposite bank.

You turn back to the cheerful scene
Unaware that the door has opened behind you
The hostess stands on the threshold
The house is full of shadow.

But on the table there is the reflection
The reflection of the daylight on a piece of fruit and a bottle
On a china plate and a piece of furniture
And you stand there on the threshold between the
World full of people like yourself
And the humming solitude
Of the whole world.)

In Desnos' simplest poems, such as this one, there is no trace of self-consciousness, and the intellect and the senses respond together, as he said they should. The contrasts we expect are here, but expressed in a very modest tone ("soleil / ombre," "solitude / semblables," outside and in). This poetry is absolutely free of any rhetorical "self-satisfaction," being turned as much away from the poet as toward him. It is in this elementary framework and with this simplicity of statement that he writes the more outgoing love poems ("Moi qui suis Robert Desnos, pour t'aimer") and the poems of fraternity and humanism ("Hommes de sale caractère / Hommes de mes deux mains"), which predominate in the war years:

Que ma voix vous parvienne donc
Chaude et joyeuse et résolue[28]

(So let my voice come to you
Warm and joyous and firm).

[28] "Le Veilleur du Pont au Change," collection "Europe," (Editions de Minuit, 1942). Appeared under the name Valentin Guillois.

Almost all the good resistance poetry is written in this exalted, repetitious and hymn-like manner. The familiar image
of the sun rising and the salutation "Bonjour!" like the
"Salut!" both he and Tzara use so often, continue to mark
the poetry of the political ex-surrealists.

The volume *Etat de veille* (1943), contains several poems of the utterly simple kind just quoted, written in a purposely traditional but popular form:

Couchons-nous sur le pavé
Par le soleil chauffé, par le soleil lavé[29]

(Let's lie down on the pavement
Heated by the sun, washed by the sun)

Je n'aime plus la rue Saint-Martin
Depuis qu'André Plattard l'a quittée[30]

(I don't like Saint-Martin street any more
Since André Plattard has left it).

But the poem "Demain" in the same collection has the sonnet form Desnos was to use in his last years, and it makes an
absolute contrast of style and content to the poems of simplicity and warmth:

Agé de cent mille ans, j'aurais encore la force
De t'attendre, ô demain pressenti par l'espoir.
Le temps, vieillard souffrant de multiple entorses,
Peut gémir: Le matin est neuf, neuf est le soir.

Or, du fond de la nuit, nous témoignons encore
De la splendeur du jour et de tous ses présents.
Si nous ne dormons pas c'est pour guetter l'aurore
Qui prouvera qu'enfin nous vivons au présent.

(A thousand years old I would still have the strength
To wait for you, oh tomorrow foreseen by hope.
A sick and bruised old man, time may moan:
The morning is new, new is the night.

Yet, from the depths of night, we bear witness still
To the day's splendor and to all its presents.

[29] "Couplet du trottoir d'été."
[30] "Couplets de la rue Saint-Martin."

> Sleepless we wait and watch for the dawn
> To prove that at last we live in the present.)

Here the oppositions of images are for the most part temporal; they remain within the traditional range of time contrasts ("demain / présent," "matin / soir," "nuit / jour"). The form of the poem is unsurprising in each of its details— in its inversions ("le matin est neuf, neuf est le soir"), its comparisons (time as an old man) and its transfers (from the age initially assumed by the poet to the age of time, in spite of the contrast of strength and weakness); in its devices (the breathless moan of the old man translated into jerkiness of rhythm—"Peut gémir: Le matin") and its echoes ("neuf-neuf," "pressenti-présents-présent"). This poetry seems to be the exact opposite of the almost hypnotic litanical and lyrical form of surrealist poetry that envelops the reader's senses. The appeal here is more to the intellect and to logic than to the senses; deliberately crafted, the poem represents neither hidden subtlety nor apparent simplicity.

Calixto and *Contrée*, also written in 1942-43 but not published until 1962, show in general the logical and traditional form of Desnos' "neoclassic" poetry, relieved by occasional bursts of surrealist vision such as Calixto's image splitting the sky open like an eye: ("Par ton image, Calixto, comme un oeil le ciel est fendu"), reminiscent of a celebrated shot in the surrealist film *Le Chien andalou*. But the concepts on which these poems are based and the form of the poetry itself, are far more delicate and intricate than those in the poem discussed above.[31] The great distance between Desnos and the other surrealist or ex-surrealist poets (and between these

---

[31] A letter from Desnos to Eluard (of October 8, 1942) published in the Album Eluard (p. 261) speaks of the sonnets in *Contrée*: "I grope along, but the images, the words, the rhymes assert themselves like the notches of a key. Everything must be useful and indispensable for the poem to stand, for everything to be in it, and nothing more, for it to be complete. I wonder why they take on so easily the form of a sonnet. I think more and more that automatic writing and speech are only the elementary stages of poetic initiation, which break down the doors. But behind these doors there will be others with safety locks which will not give way unless you look for, and find, their secret. Inspiration becomes a more subtle intoxication."

poems and all his earlier ones), can be measured most accurately by comparing with the other poems some of his late poetry which focuses on exactly the images of light and dark on which much of the discussion in this book has been based.[32]

One of the most beautiful and puzzling poems in the last collection exemplifies the "pathetic sense" Desnos himself sees in the paintings of André Masson.[33] It is a poem of re-

[32] The following examples need no commentary or translation. The light / dark terms are italicized, and the terms closely associated with them:

Mais, tout à l'heure encore, un *arc-en-ciel* de *nuit*
Enjambait la vallée et la *lune* vers lui
Roulait. Le *jour* parut et tout ne fut que *brume*
Mérite-t-il vraiment le nom de *jour*, ce *jour*
Dont s'encrasse la ville et la vie et l'amour?
Oui, car la *flamme* enfin, dans le *brouillard* s'*allume*
("L'Equinoxe," *Contrée*.)

Tu es née, à *minuit*, du baiser de deux sources,
Alceste, et l'univers ne t'offre que *reflets*,
Lueurs, lampe allumée au lointain, *feux follets*
Et dans le ciel les sept *flambeaux* de la Grande Ourse.

Il fait *noir* et, partant au signal de la course,
Tu ne soupçonnes pas que la *nuit* se soumet
Et se dissout quand le *soleil*, sur les sommets,
Par le chant des oiseaux répand *l'or* de sa bourse.

Je sais que reviendront *l'aurore* et *le matin*.
. . .

Mais saurai-je à ta soeur qui doit naître en *plein jour*,
Nymphe Alceste, annoncer, dès *midi*, le retour
Du *crépuscule*, de la *nuit* et du silence?
("La Nymphe Alceste," *Contrée*.)

La *nuit* est tombée en des *gouffres* connus
Où le *jour* la suivra d'une chute docile
Car il dresse déjà sur les monts son corps *nu*.

Il se baigne à la source, il franchit la vallée,
Il pénêtre la mer de son *reflet* puissant. . . .
("Le Bain avec Andromède," in *Choix de poèmes*,
L'Honneur des poètes, 1946.)

[33] *André Masson* (Rouen, n.p., 1940). Desnos is fond of pointing out "le pathétique" of a painter's work; in the case of Tihanyi, he sees it in the natural and irreconcilable conflict between the artist and the creations, whereas for André Masson it shows up rather in the atmosphere surrounding the subjects. Masson's *Combat d'animaux* is an extraordinary theatrical spectacle of cruelty: though the artist

gret and age, where light is seen as the paralysis of logic, and
the illogical tempestuous past, as a dream from which the
poet has unwillingly awakened. Together with its denial of
youth, the poem "Le Paysage" finally denies flexibility and desire, vitality and imagination, as all the images become sta-
tionary and *real*:

> J'avais rêvé d'aimer. J'aime encore mais l'amour
> Ce n'est plus ce bouquet de lilas et de roses
> Chargeant de leurs parfums la forêt où repose
> Une flamme à l'issue de sentiers sans détour.

> J'avais rêvé d'aimer. J'aime encore mais l'amour
> Ce n'est plus cet orage où l'éclair superpose
> Ses bûchers aux châteaux, déroute, décompose,
> Illumine en fuyant l'adieu du carrefour.

> C'est le silex en feu sous mon pas dans la nuit,
> Le mot qu'aucun lexique au monde n'a traduit
> L'écume sur la mer, dans le ciel ce nuage.

> A vieillir tout devient rigide et lumineux,
> Des boulevards sans noms et des cordes sans noeuds.
> Je me sens me roidir avec le paysage.

> (I had dreamed of loving. I love still but love
> Is no longer that bouquet of lilacs and roses
> Drenching with perfumes the forest where lies
> A flame at the end of unswerving paths.

> I had dreamed of loving. I love still but love
> Is no longer that storm where the lightning
> Builds bonfires on castles, confuses, unsettles,
> Illuminates fleeing the crossroad farewell.

---

traces no anthropomorphic relationship, any man observing this
spectacle feels the "tearing" in his own flesh. The colors in this am-
bience of "unimaginable genesis" shriek with "cries of love, cries of
pain, cries of rage," which reminds us of Breton's essays on Max
Ernst in whose atmosphere of eternal genesis the painted objects
"shriek" to find themselves brought together in such contradictory
ways. It is natural that writers of great energy should choose to comment on painters of similar energy.

It's the flint afire under my step in the night,
The word that is in no dictionary
The foam on the sea, in the sky this cloud.
As one grows old things become bright and hard,
Nameless boulevards and knotless cords.
I feel myself growing rigid with the landscape.)

It is clear that Desnos is making a definite distinction between the world of his past dreaming and his present world,
a distinction underlined by the first use of the pluperfect and
its repetition; but he seems in many ways closer in spirit
to the love that "is no longer" than to the present one. Both
are really described in the present tense, and the sheer quantity of space devoted to the past love is greater. Far more
important, Desnos obviously regrets all that love can no
longer be for him: the heavy perfume, the flame, and the
certainty of the first stanza as well as the stormy passion of
the second, strong enough to overturn ordinary laws of nature and to confuse even in its illumination. The lines spilling
over one another and the images of determination (unswerv-
ing paths, crossroad farewell), of rapidity (lightning, fleeing), of joy (bouquet, bonfire), and of nobility (castles) suggest a forcefulness which will be diminished in the third
stanza.

Now the flame, the bonfire, and the lightning are reduced
to the flint under the feet (directly contrasting with the bon-
fires above the castles), and the step in the night is the
equivalent of the flame-marked path, but on a more modest
level. In place of the storm and confusion, there are indefinite and evanescent images: a word as yet untranslated,
foam, and cloud. Here there is no suggestion of movement
or strength, and the step itself seems arrested. The fourth
stanza explains the change that the poet has gradually undergone; the unsettling passion of youth has finally given way to
a fixity which is evident and without mystery (knotless cords)
and in which the former illumination with its implied action
has become only a static brightness, paralleled by the unmoving form of the verses in what is almost a series of stills.

By contrast, it was precisely in one of his essays on the cinema that Desnos had claimed to be interested only in "mobile constellations." He had also said that the role of the artist should be to make everything concrete ("Rendre concret!"); in view of the surrealist fascination with the concrete, with specific words and place names, the nameless boulevards here, like the untranslated word, bear further witness to his loss. Anonymity and a vague calm are part of the rigidity that eventually replaces the motion and unsettling mystery essential to surrealist vision. As Desnos identifies himself unwillingly with the fixed landscape, the paths of his youth turn at last into broad boulevards, from which the flame and the perfume are forever gone.

If this poetry combines the delirious with the lucid, it is only in order to have one deny the other. If this is the static result of the optimistic belief in "one reality, unique and entire," as Desnos describes his vision of surrealism, it is a pity; a greater contrast to surrealist flexibility and the surrealist marvelous could not be imagined. And if this is an accurate picture of the landscape "beyond surrealism," it is not an encouraging one: we are far from the joyous freedom Desnos sensed in Picasso.

We do not know what kind of poetry Desnos would have gone on to write had he lived, since he felt that every moment had its own poetry, differing entirely from that of the preceding one in a constant movement of *dépassement* or transcendence:

> Nausée de souvenirs, regrets des soleils veufs
> Résurgence de source, écho d'un chant de brume,
> Vous n'êtes que scories et vous n'êtes qu'écume.
> Je voudrais naître chaque jour sous un ciel neuf.[34]

> (Nausea of memories, regrets of widowed suns
> Resurgence of a spring, echo of a song of mist,
> You are only dross and only foam.
> I would like to be born each day under a new sky.)

[34] "La Ville," *Contrée*.

To encompass the themes of the moment in the form of the moment—that Desnos should suddenly adopt a traditional form of poetry is on the surface no more important than that Eluard, or Aragon, or Tzara should do the same, no more serious than what Desnos calls "changes of fashion . . . changes of fads." But the fact that he is always so attentive to his own style makes his case unlike that of the others, who choose, for political reasons, easier forms to appeal to greater numbers. Desnos is not taking a deliberate step toward the easily understood; he is rather proving the truth of his earlier declaration that the Robert Desnos of two minutes ago is already contemporary with Charlemagne. This is, after all, the surrealist notion of freedom from limitation, of *disponibilité*: "All poetry is fugitive."

And yet, if we were to follow his advice on the subject of Picasso twenty years later, we would be forced to lay more stress on his unity than on his multiplicity, and to admit that Desnos, too, carries all his work with him at all times. Such a dilemma would delight the poet who was above all proud of discovering how to write "endings of poems that remain suspended (and not unfinished)."[35]

[35] "Postface de *Fortunes*," *Domaine public*, p. 330.

CONCLUSION

A la date voulue tout arrivera en transparence . . .
—DESNOS, *Les Ténèbres*

Les Vases communicants lays down clearly and definitively the theoretical basis for the surrealist endeavor of linking. There, in an unassuming footnote,[1] Breton explains that the highest task poetry can set for itself is the comparison of two distant objects so as to show their concrete unity and to confer upon each a strength lacking in its former isolated situation: the breaking down of their formal opposition is an essential step toward the realization of their full meaning. As long as the *exterior* laws of distance and disproportion go unchallenged, man is not making a surrealist use of his imagination. Surrealism is based on a permanent movement of unification, in which the distance between the perceiver and the perceived, reality and the imagined, the abstract and the concrete, thought and the illogical image is drastically reduced and even, under ideal conditions, suppressed altogether. And yet in all the writers connected with surrealism there remains a vivid consciousness of the concept of opposition and an instinctive tendency to stress the alternation

---

[1] *Les Vases communicants* (Editions des Cahiers Libres, 1932), p. 114. Breton pushes Reverdy's concept of the image as the meeting of two widely separated elements beyond the simple aesthetic realm toward conclusions of a far more general nature.

between extreme limits, as if in order to create the momentum essential for the constant extension and expansion of surrealist poetry.

Each of these poets underlines different groups of contradictions, stresses different qualities in his theories and his poetry, is haunted by different paradoxes. As Breton's development of surrealist theory represents the alternation of extremes in its purest aspect, his love poetry represents their resolution in a miraculous union at once simple in statement and complex in vision. Aragon, interested first in problems of freedom and then in those of language, involves the reader and possibly also himself in the problem of disentangling pose from sincerity. (It is ironic, and perfectly appropriate to the perspective adopted here, that the poet of "realism" should engage us in the dilemma of separating reality from artificiality.) In Tzara and in Eluard the poetic image is at its most powerful, as it varies from light to dark. Tzara occupies himself with the fluctuation itself, and with the nature of a poetic language capable of infinite variations of light and obscurity, progression and immobility. Eluard plainly identifies light with the clear reflection of his own image, and with the multiple transformations and identifications made possible by his vision of poetry and of love, dark signifying for him the absence of both and the denial of his own reflection. For all these poets, the principle of simplicity is strong enough to determine a final poetic unity of opposites, which in no way diminishes their separate strength, but rather contributes to it.

Underlying all the complex superstructure of objects, their representations and our perception of them, is the fundamental polarity surrealism tries to overcome, that of the dream and the real. Desnos, whose early fascination with that polarity is immediately translated into what may be perhaps the deepest and most moving surrealist poems of all, finally passes "beyond surrealism" toward an intentional rigidity of style that freezes the complexities of thought into a static form, where there is no room for oppositions or alternating movements: "I feel myself growing rigid with the landscape." It is not a question of free poetry, he says, but of a poet free to renew himself every minute. The most elusive of all the surrealist and ex-surrealist poets, and the only one who seems to stand outside his writing, he leaves the hardest internal path for the reader to follow.

This study opens and closes with the problems of language and of understanding. Aragon emphasizes the limitation of the word, the difficulty of our following him in his passage from surrealism to realism, and the futility of any attempt to pursue another human being in his creative imagination. But when Breton expounds surrealist theory, he does so in the knowledge that the enthusiastic will understand the properly complex and yet simple surrealist language; when Tzara proclaims the beliefs and nonbeliefs of Dada he makes us understand that the language of Dada is not meant to be understood, is not limited to communication, but left free in a purposely self-destructive vocabulary of clarity and obscurity. Eluard, in every aspect of his theoretical and creative language a speaker of effortless clarity, a creator of luminous relationships and a luminous vocabulary, is a poet always conscious of darkness, separation, and silence, a poet of expansion and multiplicity always haunted by their opposites and willing to absorb them into the totality of his work. Yet it is Desnos, the most complex of the surrealist poets, who brings us back to the problem of understanding in its most extreme form, a form which interrupts the *play* of the readers and the poetry: "Do you have change for my coin? No one can ever have the change for my coin."[2]

Intellectual understanding presupposes a separation between the reader as subject and the text as object, a separation refused by Breton's statement: "Nothing is an object for us; everything is a subject."[3] Surrealist understanding requires a total involvement of the reader so that he shares the space and the duration of the text and participates in its expansion. Here, in the "place where all contraries are resolved," it is not

[2] Robert Desnos, *Deuil pour deuil* (Gallimard, 1962), p. 128. The text is from 1924; his notion of an "aesthetics of understanding" is developed later.

[3] André Breton, *Le Surréalisme et la peinture* (Gallimard, 1928), p. 59.

a question of reducing the difficulties by translating the surrealist coin into any nonsurrealist equivalent. To do so would be to move further from the surrealist presence instead of nearer to it. "Besides, it is not my wish—you understand me, multitude—that the surrealist text, any more than the dream, lapse into the category of fixed forms."[4]

[4] Louis Aragon, *Traité du style* (Gallimard, 1928), p. 193.

PRINCIPAL WORKS CONSULTED AND SOME ADDITIONAL WORKS OF POSSIBLE INTEREST

PRINCIPAL WORKS CONSULTED

LOUIS ARAGON

I. THEORY

Une Vague de rêves (privately printed). Paris, 1924.

Traité du style. Paris, Gallimard, 1928.

La Peinture au défi. Paris, Corti, 1930.

Matisse—Dessins, thèmes et variations, précédé de "Matisse-en-France." Paris, Fabiani, 1943.

Deux voix françaises—Péguy, Peri. Paris, Editions de Minuit, 1945.

L'Enseigne de Gersaint. Neuchâtel, Ides et Calendes, 1946.

Apologie du luxe. Geneva, Skira, 1946.

L'Homme communiste. Paris, Gallimard, 1946.

Preface to *Dessins de Fougeron*. Paris, Les Treize Epis, 1947.

La Culture et les hommes. Paris, Editions sociales, 1947.

Chronique du bel canto. Geneva, Skira, 1947.

Preface to Eluard, *Poèmes politiques*. Paris, Gallimard, 1948.

"Au jardin de Matisse," *Henri Matisse*. Paris, Maison de la Pensée Française, 1950.

Picasso—Sculptures, dessins. Paris, Maison de la Pensée Française, 1952.

Picasso, deux périodes, 1900-14, 1950-54. Paris, Maison de la Pensée Française, 1954.

L'Exemple de Courbet. Paris, Editions Cercle d'Art, 1952.

Avez-vous lu Victor Hugo? Paris, Pauvert, 1952.

Hugo, poète réaliste. Paris, Editions sociales, 1952.

A la lumière de Stendhal. Paris, Denoël, 1954.

Entretiens sur le musée de Dresde (with Jean Cocteau). Paris, Editions Cercle d'art, 1957.

J'abats mon jeu. Paris, Les Editeurs Français Réunis, 1959.

Preface to *L'Anthologie de la poésie occitane 1900-1960*.

(Andrée Paule Lafont, ed.). Paris, Les Editeurs Français Réunis, 1962.
Preface to Roger Garaudy, *D'un réalisme sans rivages*. Paris, Plon, 1963.
Entretiens avec Francis Crémieux. Paris, Gallimard, 1964.
Les Collages. Paris. Hermann (coll. Miroirs d'art), 1965.
Shakespeare. Paris, Editions Cercle d'art, 1965.

II. POETRY

Le Mouvement perpétuel. Paris, Gallimard, 1926.
Persécuté-Persécuteur. Paris, Editions surréalistes, 1931.
Le Crève-Coeur. London, Editions Horizon—La France libre, 1942.
Les Yeux d'Elsa. New York, Editions de la Maison Française, 1942.
Le Musée Grévin. Paris, Editions de Minuit, 1943.
Les Yeux et la mémoire. Paris, Gallimard, 1954.
Le Roman inachevé. Paris, Gallimard, 1956.
Le Nouveau Crève-Coeur. Paris, Gallimard, 1958.
Elsa. Paris, Gallimard, 1959.
Poèmes. Paris, Club du Meilleur Livre, 1960.
Les Poètes. Paris, Gallimard, 1960.
Il ne m'est Paris que d'Elsa. Paris, Laffont, 1964.
Le Voyage de Hollande et autres poèmes. Paris, Seghers, 1964.

III. OTHER

Le Paysan de Paris. Paris, Gallimard, 1926; 1966 (Livre de poche).
Les Voyageurs de l'impériale. Paris, Gallimard, 1947.
Le Fou d'Elsa. Paris, Gallimard, 1963.
La Mise à mort. Paris, Gallimard, 1965.
Blanche ou l'oubli. Paris, Gallimard, 1967.

ANDRE BRETON

I. THEORY

Les Pas perdus. Paris, Gallimard, 1924.
Les Vases communicants. Paris, Editions des Cahiers Libres, 1932; Gallimard, 1955.
Point du jour. Paris, Gallimard, 1934.
L'Amour fou. Paris, Gallimard, 1937.

Trajectoire du rêve, texts assembled by Breton, Paris, Cahiers G.L.M., 1938.

Anthologie de l'humour noir. Paris, Editions du Sagittaire, 1940.

Arcane 17. New York, Brentano's. 1945.

Préliminaires sur Matta (exposition chez René Drouin). Paris, 1947.

La Lampe dans l'horloge. Paris, Editions Robert Marin, 1948.

Les Statues magiques de Maria. Paris, Drouin, 1948.

Entretiens avec André Parinaud. Paris, Gallimard, 1952.

La Clé des champs. Paris, Editions du Sagittaire, 1953.

Toyen (with Péret). Paris, Editions Sokolova, 1953.

Commentary for the *Exposition internationale du surréalisme, 1959-60*. Paris, Cordier.

Manifestes du surréalisme. Paris, Pauvert, 1962.

Le Surréalisme et la peinture. Paris, Gallimard, 1928; Brentano's, 1945; Gallimard, 1965 (this edition includes all prefaces, essays, articles on art).

II. POETRY

L'Air de l'eau. Paris, Editions des Cahiers d'art, 1934.

Poèmes. Paris, Gallimard, 1948.

Le Revolver à cheveux blancs. Paris, Editions des Cahiers Libres, 1932.

Signe ascendant. Paris, Gallimard (Collection Poésie), 1968. (Includes *Des épingles tremblantes, Constellations, Le la.*)

III. OTHER

Les Champs magnétiques. Paris, Au Sans Pareil, 1920; Gallimard, 1968.

Nadja. Paris, Gallimard, 1928; 1963.

TRISTAN TZARA

I. THEORY

Preface to Louis Marcoussis, *Planches de salut*. Paris, Jeanne Bûcher, 1931.

Answer to *Journal des poètes*. Paris, December 22, 1932 (pamphlet).

"Max Ernst and his reversible images" (1934), in Max Ernst, *Beyond Painting*. New York, Wittenborn, Schultz, 1948.

Preface to Henri Rousseau, *Une Visite à l'exposition de 1889.*
Geneva, Cailler, 1947.
Le Surréalisme et l'après-guerre. Paris, Nagel, 1947.
Introduction to Arthur Rimbaud, *Oeuvres complètes.* Lausanne, Editions du Grand-Chêne, 1948.
Picasso et les chemins de la connaissance. Geneva, Skira, 1948.
Introduction to Tristan Corbière, *Les Amours jaunes.* Paris, Le Club Français des Livres, 1950.
Preface to *Poèmes de Nazim Hikmet.* Paris, Les Editeurs Français Réunis, 1951.
Introduction and notes to Guillaume Apollinaire, *Alcools.* Paris, Club du Meilleur Livre, 1953.
L'Egypte face à face. Lausanne, Editions Clairefontaine, 1954.
Hommage à Attila Jozsef par les poètes français. Paris, Seghers, 1955.
Preface to Ilarie Voronca, *Poème choisis.* Paris, Seghers, 1956.
Preface to *Exposition de Philippe Bonnet.* Paris, Berggruen, 1956.
Propos sur Bracelli. Paris, Brieux, 1963.
Sept manifestes Dada, suivis de lampisteries. Paris, Pauvert, 1963.

II. POETRY

De nos oiseaux. Paris, Kra, 1923.
L'Arbre des voyageurs. Paris, Editions de la Montagne, 1930. (Includes *L'Arbre des voyageurs, A perte de vue, Le Feu défendu.*)
L'Homme approximatif. Paris, Editions Fourcade, 1931.
Où boivent les loups. Paris, Editions des Cahiers Libres, 1932.
L'Antitête. Paris, Editions des Cahiers Libres, 1933. (Includes *Monsieur AA l'antiphilosophe, Minuits pour géants, Le Désespéranto.*)
La Main passe. Paris, Guy Lévis Mano, 1935.
Sur le champ. Paris, Seghers, 1935.
Grains et issues. Paris, Denoël et Steele, 1935.
Ramures. Paris, G.L.M., 1936.
Vigies. Paris, G.L.M., 1937.
Ça va. Cahors, Centre des Intellectuels, 1939.
Midis gagnés. Paris, Denoël, 1939. (Includes *Abrégé de la nuit, La Main passe, Mutations radieuses, Midis gagnés.*)
Le Signe de vie. Paris, Bordas, 1946.

Vingt-cinq et un poèmes. Paris, Fontaine, 1946.
Terre sur terre. Geneva, Editions Trois Collines, 1946.
Entretemps. Paris, Le Calligraphe, 1946.
Morceaux choisis. Paris, Bordas, 1947.
Phases. Paris, Seghers, 1949.
Sans coup férir. Paris, Aubier, 1949.
La Première main, Alès, Pierre Albert Birot, 1952.
La Face intérieure. Paris, Seghers, 1953.
Le Temps naissant, Alès, p.a.b., 1953.
Miennes. Paris, Caractères, 1955.
La Bonne heure. Paris, Jacquet, 1955.
A Haute flamme. Paris, Jacquet, 1955.
Le Fruit permis. Paris, Caractères, 1956.
Frère bois, Alès, p.a.b., 1957.
Juste présent. Paris, La Rose des vents, 1961.
De la coupe aux lèvres (choix de poèmes 1939-61). Rome, Edizioni Rapporti Europei, 1961.
Premiers poèmes, suivis de cinq poèmes oubliés. (Claude Sernet, ed.). Paris, Seghers, 1965.

III. OTHER

La Fuite. Paris, Gallimard, 1941.

PAUL ELUARD

I. THEORY

Eluard-Dausse collection of documents for the journal *Le Surréalisme au service de la révolution.* Museum of Modern Art, New York.

Preface to E.L.T. Mesens, *Alphabet sourd aveugle.* Brussels, Nicolas Flamel, 1933.

Avenir de la poésie. Paris, G.L.M., 1937.

"Au Pays des hommes," *André Masson.* Rouen (no publisher), 1940.

Poésie involontaire et poésie intentionnelle. Paris, Poésie, 1942.

Preface to Dominguez, *Exposition à la Galerie Louis Carré.* Paris, 1943.

A Pablo Picasso. Geneva, Editions Trois Collines, 1944.

Preface to Rousseau le Douanier, *Exposition au Musée d'Art Moderne.* Paris, 1944.

Picasso à Antibes. Paris, Drouin, 1948.

Jacques Villon ou l'art glorieux. Paris, Louis Carré, 1948.

Preface to Catalog No. 15 for Pierre Bérès, Inc., New York, 1948.

Preface to Albert Flocon, *Perspectives* (gravures). Paris, Maeght, 1949.

La Poésie du passé. Paris, Seghers, 1951.

Anthologie des écrits sur l'art. Paris, Editions Cercle d'art, 1952.

Les Sentiers et routes de la poésie. Lyon, Les Ecrivains Réunis, 1952.

Lettres de jeunesse. Paris, Seghers, 1962.

II. POETRY

Capitale de la douleur. Paris, Gallimard, 1926.

L'Amour la poésie. Paris, Gallimard, 1929.

A toute épreuve (with *La Vie intérieure*). Paris, Gallimard, 1930.

Les Yeux fertiles. Paris, G.L.M., 1936.

Thorns of Thunder. (George Reavey, ed.). London, Europa Press and Stanley Nott, 1936. (Translations by Samuel Beckett, David Gascoyne, Eugène Jolas, George Reavey, etc.)

Médieuses. Paris, Gallimard, 1939.

Dignes de vivre. Porrentruy, Chez les Editeurs des Portes de France, 1947.

Corps mémorable [pseud. Brun]. Paris, Seghers, 1947.

Premiers poèmes (1913-1921). Lausanne, Mermod, 1948.

Poèmes politiques. (Préface d'Aragon). Paris, Gallimard, 1948.

Une Leçon de morale. Paris, Gallimard, 1949.

Poèmes. Paris, Gallimard, 1951.

Les Derniers poèmes d'amour. Paris, Seghers, 1963.

III. OTHER

Eluard, Paul. *Oeuvres.* Paris, Editions de la Pléiade, 1968.

ROBERT DESNOS

I. THEORY

Tihanyi—Peintures 1908-1922, présentées par Robert Desnos, Paris, Editions Arts, 1936.

Preface to L. G. Damas, *Pigments*. Paris, G.L.M., 1937.

Troisième manifeste du surréalisme. (Included in Maurice Nadeau, *Histoire du surréalisme.* Paris, Seuil, 1945; Vol. II contains a collection of *Documents surréalistes.*)

"Combat d'animaux," in *André Masson.* Rouen (no publisher), 1940.

Félix Labisse. Paris. Sequana, 1945.

Les Problèmes de la peinture. (Gaston Diehl, ed.). Paris, Confluences, 1945.

Introduction à Picasso, Peintures 1939-46. Paris, Editions du Grand-Chêne, 1946.

De l'érotisme considéré dans ses manifestations écrites et du point de vue de l'esprit moderne. Paris, Editions Cercle d'art, 1953.

II. Poetry

The Night of Loveless Nights. Anvers (no publisher), 1930. (In Eluard-Dausse Collection, Museum of Modern Art, New York.)

Choix de poèmes, L'Honneur des poètes. Paris, Editions de Minuit, 1946.

Nouvelles inedites. Paris, Les Treize Epis, 1947.

Oeuvres posthumes. Paris, Les Treize Epis, 1947.

Les Trois solitaires. Paris, Les Treize Epis, 1947.

Domaine public. Paris, Gallimard, 1953. (Includes *Corps et Biens, Fortunes*, and others.)

Mines de rien. Paris, Broder, 1957.

Calixto, suivi de Contrée. Paris, Gallimard, 1962.

III. Other

La Liberté ou l'amour, suivi de Deuil pour deuil. Paris, Gallimard, 1962. (First editions: *Deuil pour deuil*, Paris, Sagittaire, 1924; *La Liberté ou l'amour*, Paris, Kra, 1927).

Le Vin est tiré. Paris, Gallimard, 1943.

Desnos, Youki. *Les Confidences de Youki.* Paris, Arthème Fayard, 1957.

JOURNALS

L'Archibras.
Bief.
Bifur.

La Brèche.

Cahiers Dada surréalisme.

Cahiers d'art.

Dada.

Documents.

Etudes cinématographiques. (Nos. 38-39 on surrealism.)

Europe. (Nov.-Dec. 1968, special issue on surrealism.)

Les Feuilles libres.

Inquisitions. (Journal of the group "d'Etudes pour la phéno-ménologie humaine," only number.)

Littérature.

Médium.

Minotaure.

L'Oeil.

Le Point.

Proverbe.

La Revue européenne.

La Révolution surréaliste.

Sic.

Le Surréalisme au service de la révolution.

Le Surréalisme, même.

Variétés.

VVV.

XXᵉ siècle.

Special issues of *Artforum, L'Esprit Createur, Yale French Studies.*

MISCELLANEOUS GENERAL WORKS

Belaval, Yvon. *Poèmes d'aujourd'hui.* Paris, Gallimard, 1964.

Bellmer, Hans. *Petite anatomie de l'inconscient physique.* Paris, Le Terrain Vague, 1957.

Cazaux, Jean. *Surréalisme et psychologie.* Paris, Corti, 1938.

Champigny, Robert. *Le Genre poétique: essai.* Monte Carlo, Editions Regain, 1963.

Eliot, T. S. *To Criticize the Critic.* New York, Farrar, Straus, and Giroux, 1965.

Entretiens sur le surréalisme. (Décades du Centre Culturel International de Cerisy-la-Salle.) Paris, Mouton, 1968.

Jouffroy, Alain. *Saint-Pol-Roux.* Paris, Mercure de France, 1966.

Surréalisme: sources, histoire, affinités. Paris, Galerie Charpentier, 1964.

Surrealismo e simbolismo. Padua, CEDAM, 1965.

SOME ADDITIONAL WORKS OF POSSIBLE INTEREST

ANTHOLOGIES

An Anthology of French Surrealist Poetry. (J. H. Matthews, ed.). Minneapolis, University of Minnesota Press, 1966.

L'Art de la peinture. (J. Charpier, ed.). Paris, Seghers, 1966.

The Dada Painters and Poets. (Robert Motherwell, ed.). New York, Wittenborn, Schultz, 1951.

La Poésie surréaliste. (J. L. Bédouin, ed.). Paris, Seghers, 1964.

SHORT PARTIAL LIST OF CRITICAL WORKS

1. On Surrealism

Alquié, Ferdinand. *Philosophie du surréalisme.* Paris, Flammarion, 1955.

Balakian, Anna. *Literary Origins of Surrealism.* New York, King's Crown Press, 1947.

———. *Surrealism: the Road to the Absolute.* New York, Noonday Press, 1959.

Baron, Jacques. *L'An 1 du Surréalisme, suivi de L'An dernier.* Paris, Denoël, 1969.

Benayoun, Robert. *Erotique du surréalisme.* Paris, Pauvert, 1964.

Crastre, Victor. *Le Drame du surréalisme.* Paris, Editions du Temps, 1963.

Fowlie, Wallace. *Age of Surrealism.* Bloomington, University of Indiana Press, 1960.

Gershman, Herbert. *The Surrealist Revolution in France* with *A Bibliography of the Surrealist Revolution in France.* Ann Arbor, University of Michigan Press, 1968.

Jean, Marcel. *Histoire de la peinture surréaliste.* Paris, Seuil, 1959.

Matthews, J. H. *An Introduction to Surrealism.* University Park, Pennsylvania State University Press, 1965.

———. *Surrealism and the Novel.* Ann Arbor, University of Michigan Press, 1966.

Monnerot, Jules. *La Poésie moderne et le sacré.* Paris, Gallimard, 1945.

Nadeau, Maurice. *Histoire du surréalisme.* Paris, Seuil, 1954.

Passeron, René. *Histoire de la peinture surréaliste.* Paris, Flammarion, 1968.

Pierre, José. *Le Surréalisme.* (In *Histoire générale de la peinture.*) Paris, Editions Rencontre, 1967.

Read, Herbert. *Surrealism.* London, Faber and Faber, 1936.

Rubin, William S. *Dada, Surrealism, and Their Heritage.* New York, Museum of Modern Art, 1968.

Schuster, Jean. *Archives 57/68: batailles pour le surréalisme.* Paris, Losfeld, 1969.

2. On Dada

Cahiers Dada surrealisme.

Hausmann, Raoul. *Courrier Dada.* Paris, Le Terrain Vague, 1958.

Hugnet, Georges. "L'Esprit Dada dans la peinture," *Cahiers d'art 7,* No. 1.

――――. *L'Aventure Dada.* Paris, Galerie de l'Institut, 1957.

Richter, Hans. *Dada: art et anti-art.* Brussels, Editions de la Connaissance, 1965.

Sanouillet, Michel. *Dada à Paris.* Paris, Pauvert, 1965.

Verkauf, Willy. *Dada: Monograph of a Movement.* New York, Wittenborn, 1958.

Waldberg, Patrick. *Chemins du surréalisme.* New York, McGraw-Hill, 1965.

3. On Aragon

Garaudy, Roger. *L'Itinéraire d'Aragon.* Paris, Gallimard, 1961.

Gavillet, André. *La Littérature au défi. Aragon surréaliste.* Neuchâtel, A la Baconnière, 1957.

Gindine, Yvette. *Aragon prosateur surréaliste.* Geneva, Droz, 1966.

Juin, Hubert. *Aragon.* Paris, Gallimard, 1960.

Raillard, Georges. *Aragon.* Paris, Editions Universitaires, 1964.

Sur, Jean. *Aragon: Le Réalisme de l'amour.* Paris, Editions du Centurion, 1966.

4. On Breton

Balakian, Anna. *André Breton,* Oxford University Press, forthcoming.

Browder, Clifford. *André Breton, Arbiter of Surrealism,* Geneva, Droz, 1966.

Carrouges, Michel. *André Breton et les données fondamentales du surréalisme.* Paris, Gallimard, 1950.

Caws, Mary Ann. *Surrealism and the Literary Imagination: A Study of Breton and Bachelard.* The Hague, Mouton, 1966.

――――. *André Breton.* New York, Twayne, 1970.

Eigeldinger, Marc. *André Breton, essais et témoignages.* Neuchâtel, A la Baconnière, 1950.

Massot, Pierre de. *André Breton, le septembriseur.* Paris, Losfeld, 1967.

Matthews, J. H. *Breton.* New York, Columbia University Press, 1966.

Mauriac, Claude. *André Breton: essai.* Paris, Editions de Flore, 1949.

Poirier, Louis [Julien Gracq]. *André Breton: quelques aspects de l'écrivain.* Paris, Corti, 1948.

La Nouvelle revue française. April 1967. (Special issue: "André Breton et le surréalisme.")

5. *On Eluard*

Decaunes, Luc. *Paul Eluard.* Paris, Editions Subervie, 1964.

Eglin, Heinrich. *Liebe und Inspiration im Werke von Paul Eluard.* Bern and Munich, Francke, 1965.

Jean, Raymond. *Eluard par lui-même.* Paris, Seuil, 1967.

Onimus, Jean. *Les Images de Paul Eluard.* Aix, Annales de la faculté des lettres et sciences de l'université d'Aix, 1963.

Perche, Louis. *Paul Eluard.* Paris, Editions Universitaires, 1964.

Valette, Robert. *Le Poète et son ombre: livre d'identité.* Paris, Seghers, 1963; Paris, Tchou, 1967.

Issue of *Europe.* 1952.

6. *On Desnos*

Buchole, Rosa. *L'Evolution poétique de Robert Desnos.* Brussels, Palais des Académies, 1956.

Simoun. Nos. 22-23 (1956), Oran, Algeria.

7. *On Each of These Poets*

Editions *Poètes d'aujourd'hui,* Paris, Seghers.

INDEX